DEAD & GODLESS
DONALD J. AMODEO

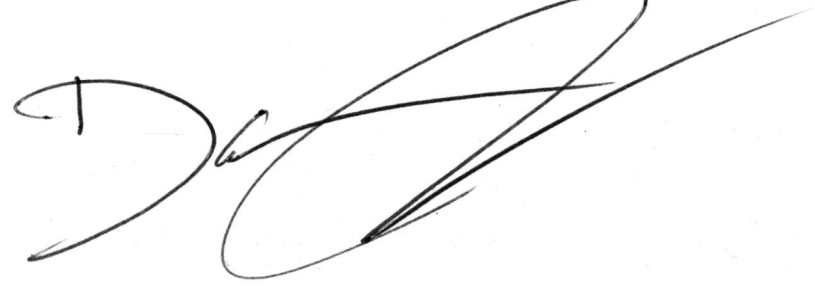

Dead & Godless
Donald J. Amodeo
DeadAndGodless.com

Edited by Penny Fletcher (PennyFletcher.com),
with contributions by Christine Amodeo and
Steven Kospender.

All referenced brands and artistic works are the
property of their respective owners.

Cover design by Renu Sharma
TheDarkRayne.com

ISBN 978-0-9910366-0-8

1

THE REAPER RIDES THE J LINE

A deep freeze iced the gears of time, entombing the city in day-long twilight. Corwin drank it in and threw out his chest. His breath steamed with satisfaction.

"There's nothing like the smell of the subway in winter! Garbage, piss and a fresh coat of bleach—I love public transportation!"

"Great, then you won't mind us making an extra stop," Mary said cheerily, her auburn hair bouncing as she descended the stairway beside him. "I need to drop a few things off at my mom's place."

"Hasn't she had the place blessed to ward off people like me?"

"She doesn't hate you, Corwin." Mary's smile was unwavering. "Quite the opposite. She prays every night for the conversion of your stubborn atheist soul."

"Wonderful."

"I know you're just dying to argue with her, but I do appreciate your discretion."

"A wise man chooses his battles," said Corwin in a stoic tone.

Mary cast him a warm glance. Her mother was one of the few people with whom Corwin resisted the urge to debate all things metaphysical (or superstitious, as he preferred to say).

"Visiting doesn't make you feel too uncomfortable, I hope?"

"Not at all! The fact that your mother's house has more crucifixes than the Vatican makes me feel right at home."

Corwin's boots clomped onto off-white tiles at the foot of the stairs. They were taking the J line and had made good time. The next train was yet several minutes away. In this cold, at least he didn't have to worry about the ice cream melting. He lugged two overstuffed bags of groceries, snowflakes dusting his shoulders and flaxen hair.

"What's all the commotion?" inquired Mary.

Following her gaze, Corwin noticed an odd sight ahead. The usually scattered crowds had congregated around a single spot near the edge of the platform. A hum of anxious voices joined the rustling of coats as they pressed in for a closer look.

"Somebody should do something," muttered a short, round-faced woman.

Corwin peered over her head and spied the cause of the scene. A homeless man lay sprawled on the tracks, his grubby fingers still gripping the neck of a liquor bottle in a paper bag. He might have been asleep, knocked out or already dead for all Corwin could tell, but whatever the case, the man wasn't moving.

"Check this out!" exclaimed a teenage girl, holding her phone aloft to record the event.

"Do you think the train will hit him?" asked one of her giggling friends.

"If it does, this video is totally getting a million hits!"

"What the hell is wrong with you?" snapped Mary.

Without waiting for a reply, she pushed forward and crouched towards the ledge.

"Hold it," said Corwin with a firm grasp on her sleeve. She shot him a look of iron resolve, but he wasn't letting go. "Are you really planning to drag that guy up here?"

"Somebody has to."

"He's probably twice your weight!"

Staring into her eyes, Corwin sighed, fully aware that it would take more than the laws of physics to keep Mary off those tracks.

"Listen, there's no need for both of us to climb down," he reasoned. "I'll do the dragging. You wait here and help pull him up."

The J line's platform was one-sided, with the rear wall of the station rising opposite the ledge and sporting some freshly-inked graffiti. Before Mary or his own better judgment could object, he plopped the groceries down beside her and leapt onto the tracks.

What have I gotten myself into this time?

The tracks suddenly felt a lot lower than they had looked from atop the platform. Corwin glanced back to make sure Mary wasn't following and his gaze briefly wandered the crowd. A young woman clutched her purse, its leather studded with a silver ichthys—the Greek symbol for fish that Christians had repurposed, now the latest in Jesus fashion.

3

Off to her right, a rabbi stroked his beard pensively, looking on from under the wide brim of his derby hat.

That's right, just leave it to the godless heathen, thought Corwin with smug irony. But then again, he couldn't really blame them. They were the sane ones. It was he who was defying all good sense, risking his neck for the sake of some homeless drunk whose greatest contribution to society was warming a park bench.

Corwin leaned over the man and grimaced from the stench. He reeked of alcohol and old socks, and looked no better, with bits of food lodged in his dark, scraggly beard.

"Hey buddy, wake up!"

He jostled him by the shoulder. No response. From the shadowy depths of the tunnel, a low, rhythmic rumble arose. A light pierced the gloom.

"Come on!"

With a hard pat on the cheek, Corwin elicited a weary groan from the man. He was starting to awaken, but not fast enough. *I haven't got time for this.* Hooking his hands under the man's armpits, he struggled to heave him towards the platform. To Corwin's relief, a tall fellow in glasses and a trench coat set down his briefcase to offer assistance.

"You take one arm, I'll take the other," he said, rushing onto the tracks.

Corwin wasn't about to argue. With each passing second, the metallic roar grew louder. Was it possible that the train would brake in time? Surely somebody had to have called 911. That is, unless everyone in the crowd was under the assumption that someone else had already called. The Bystander Effect. Corwin had heard of it before, though he never expected to be a living example.

4

"Give us a hand!" yelled his partner as they neared the ledge.

Summoning the wherewithal to stand, the homeless man planted his feet, but his balance failed him. Luckily Mary reached down and grabbed one of his hands. Corwin pushed from behind, and soon others in the crowd were helping to haul him up. The tall businessman vaulted onto the platform.

"Thanks for the help," Corwin called after him.

"You can pay me back later."

"Hurry!" urged Mary.

Corwin didn't dare look towards the train. He boosted the vagabond with one last shove and clasped Mary's outstretched hand. Safety was only a short climb away. Then a heavy boot struck him square in the chest.

While clambering onto the platform, the drunk's knee had slipped, his clumsy kick finding its mark at just the wrong moment. Corwin felt Mary's fingers slip from his grasp. He was falling. A steel rail greeted the back of his skull with a sharp *thunk*.

Blacking out for an instant, a surge of adrenaline was the only thing that kept him conscious. He vaguely heard Mary screaming over the ringing in his ears.

"Corwin, get up! Corwin!"

As he turned his head, the world blurred into slow motion, yet one thing was crystal clear. In that split second, he saw every dent, every scratch in the paint, every glimmer of light reflected in the glass. The look of horror on the conductor's face was burned into his mind. Corwin had never seen anything as vividly as he saw the front of that train speeding towards him.

A chill draft pulled at his cashmere coat. He felt his heart beating, the cool touch of the steel tracks, and then Corwin felt nothing at all.

Sparks flew from the rails and the brakes squealed in protest as the J scraped to an emergency stop. Mary collapsed to her knees, her eyes wide with a vacant stare. She couldn't cry out, couldn't speak. The breath had been robbed from her lungs. It all seemed so unreal.

"Get yer hands offa me!" slurred the drunk beside her.

With a violent twist, he shook free from the grip of those who had helped to pull him out of harm's way. The stunned commuters parted before him. Bleary eyed, he glared into the crowd, completely oblivious to what had just taken place. No one spoke a word to explain, not that he would have listened. Only hushed voices and quiet sobs filled the station.

Spitting curses, the man stomped off for the stairs.

"Don't nobody in this town know how to mind their own damn business?"

2

LEGAL REPRESENTATION

Corwin was dead. And yet he still *was*. Like a man half dreaming and half awake, he gazed down upon the station with a peculiar sense of detachment. His body, or what remained of it, was hidden from view beneath the train cars, a spatter of blood on the headlights the only sign of his untimely passing. He imagined himself as an unrecognizable smear staining the tracks. The thought didn't bother him.

From above, the shuffling crowd was all heads and shoulders, but Mary's green sweater was impossible to miss. She knelt beside the edge of the platform with her head in her hands. A pang of guilt struck him. She was everything good about this rotten world, and now he was leaving her. How could he have been so careless? He yearned to swoop down, wipe the tears from her eyes and whisper a promise that he would always be there. A kind lie, one that would forever go untold. An irresistible force was pulling him away from her, away from all that he knew, and there was no use fighting it. It was time to go.

Corwin belatedly realized that reaching out and touching anything was beyond his power, for he had nothing to reach out with. Thinking of sight, he saw. Thinking of sound, he heard. But Corwin had no eyes or ears. Lighter than air and even less tangible, he was a consciousness without a body.

This can't be real.

An exhilarating sense of freedom filled him, but also a creeping dread. This weightless, borderless realm of the spirit was an exciting place to visit, but he was *at home* in a body, and the prospect of not returning to one made him feel lost, incomplete.

The ceiling of the subway station sank through him like a cement cloud. Soon snowy streets were receding below. An endless procession of cars and pedestrians hurried about the business of life. Cyclists tempted fate, weaving in and out of traffic while travelers waved down taxis and beggars tried to wring the last drops of sympathy from a city that was running dry. Broad windows climbed a high-rise office building where room after room of workers hunched towards computer screens, their fingers rattling keys. They didn't look particularly happy.

At least that's over with.

He ascended higher, past the tallest rooftops and loftiest spires, until all the city spread forth beneath him, a concrete expanse that faded to white hills and misty waters on the horizon. Here, so close to their birthplace, the snowflakes whirred with youthful vitality. They danced in the wind's embrace, seesawing and gusting, obscuring the land behind a wondrous veil that grew thicker as he rose.

A dense sheet of clouds swallowed him and the busy world slipped away. Corwin was somewhere new, somewhere dark.

"Hello?" he called out into the solemn shadows.

The sound of his own voice affirmed what he knew instinctively, that his vocal cords were back where they belonged. He blinked, felt solid ground under his feet.

"Is anyone there?"

Corwin's words bounced off walls high and far. It was his only clue as to the size of the place, for the darkness was so complete that he could scarcely tell whether his eyes were open or closed. A profound silence descended as the last echo died. Extending his arms, he quested a few tentative steps.

Straight ahead, a brilliant light blossomed, its gleam giving shape to a long corridor ribbed with soaring gothic arches.

"Really? A light at the end of a tunnel?" remarked Corwin incredulously. "You'd think that they could come up with something different for a guy who just got hit by a subway train."

Having nowhere else to go, he set off towards the beckoning light, admitting that he was indeed curious about its source. Radiantly aglow with shimmers of blue and gold, it at first gave the impression of being a doorway, but upon drawing near, Corwin found himself staring through the panes of a tall, arched window.

The shining land on the other side took his breath away. Across a diamond sea, the walls of an idyllic city rose from a shoreline. Pearlescent towers and the boughs of huge, verdant trees peeked over the parapets, converging towards a column of solid light that lanced from the center of the city into the heavens. Waterfalls cascaded off the rocky cliffs of islands that floated amidst the clouds, and innumerable stars beamed brightly through the crisp blue of the midday sky.

Corwin pressed his palms to the glass, straining his eyes to take it all in, but the land was so very far away. He could only glimpse its splendor from where he stood in the passage.

To his left the hallway bent and he noticed two more windows, identical in size and shape, but offering altogether different views.

"Somebody must have slipped some LSD into my coffee this morning."

The first revealed a wooded valley where mossy fountains rilled under the shade of poplars and cypress trees. In the middle was a meadow, upon which a great carpet had been spread. Threads of gold and lavender wove patterns through the deep red tapestry. Atop it, a king's feast was laid out, fixed with succulent meats and glazed pastries that made Corwin's mouth water just looking at them. Piles of treasure were heaped, sparkling jewels and doubloons and stacks of dollar bills. Beautiful young men and women lounged in faceless masks, a few strips of silk their only clothing. Wisps of smoke wafted from hookahs and wine glistened in crystal carafes. And there were also more abstract prizes, plaques of honor and ticking timepieces and mirrors.

But for all the pleasures that the tapestry promised, no one was indulging. A middle-aged man stood off to the side, emptying his pockets. He tossed silver coins one-by-one onto the carpet, and it seemed that parting with each pained him greatly. However, his expression eased as his pockets lightened. Others strolled amidst the trees and fountains, free but not quite at peace. Corwin could sense a distinct loneliness in the air, the longing of separated lovers, desperately hoping to reunite.

Approaching the last window, he gazed out across the dunes of a searing desert. Lines of emaciated figures marched, their sallow skin stretched taut against their bones. They were shackled at the ankles and joined with long chains. Flames leapt from the blistering sand wherever their bare feet stepped, and their backs were bent with the weight of ponderous slabs of rock. Corwin watched as one man set down his boulder, only to pile another atop it before heaving them both onto his bony shoulders. The whip of a hulking guard with the head of a goat lashed his back, and wearily he resumed his march.

An obsidian tower loomed beyond the desert. Like the tip of a spear, its monolithic walls tapered sharply, stabbing at the cloudless sky. Farther still, a column of light arose, not unlike the one that he had seen through the first window. But while that column had been a beacon of life, here its blaze scorched the land, bringing only misery and death. It occurred to Corwin that this whole world was a twisted reflection of that one, the glittering sea replaced by a barren sea of sand, the twinkling stars swapped for the dust rings of shattered moons.

From the tower a sonorous bell tolled. The damned paused in their march and a cold hand closed around Corwin's heart. The bell was tolling for him, claiming him. He covered his ears.

"Get out of my head!"

With a determined effort he wrenched himself away from the joyless window. Silence returned at once, calming his nerves as he pressed on.

He didn't have far to go before the hallway came to an end, and there stood a white door. It was cracked, a sliver of warm light spilling out into the passage. Corwin clutched the knob and ventured cautiously within. The room that met his eyes had all the trappings of a posh corner office, minus the view. No windows disturbed the walls. The carpet was burgundy, the hardwood furniture polished to a shine. Fine art and framed certificates hung proudly, alongside glass shelves where bottled ships and samurai swords and all manner of curious trinkets perched.

Before Corwin could study any of them too closely, something gave him pause. He wasn't alone. At the sound of a carefree voice, he spun to his right.

"Corwin Francis Holiday, I presume," spoke a man seated behind an executive desk. "Well, not that it's much of a presumption. Considering that my secretary hasn't made a single mistake in the last eight hundred years, I'm quite certain that you're Corwin."

"I, that is, yes," stammered Corwin, eyeing the man suspiciously. He was positive that no one had been there a moment ago.

The gray-eyed stranger twirled a pen in one hand, his relaxed demeanor testifying that, unlike his guest, he apparently found nothing about the present situation to be out of the ordinary. A wave of dirty blonde hair contrasted with his dark eyebrows and the stubble that shaded his chin. He was maybe in his mid-thirties. He wore a charcoal suit, perfectly tailored, with a matching tie and a white collared shirt.

"Please, have a seat," he said, indicating a chair that sat opposite the desk. "Make yourself comfortable."

Not taking his eyes off the man, Corwin lowered himself awkwardly into the chair. The stranger drew a tin cigarette case from his breast pocket and flipped it open.

"Care for a smoke?"

"I don't smoke," replied Corwin.

"No, of course you don't, or at least you never have, but if you ever wanted to try, well, now's the time! I mean, you're already dead. What's the harm?"

"I'll pass," Corwin insisted.

"Suit yourself."

Putting the cigarette to his lips, he snapped his fingers and a tiny flame sparked to life, hovering above one fingertip. A spiced aroma filled the air as he puffed contentedly and sank a little deeper into his seat.

Corwin was still at a loss.

"And you would be . . ."

"Attorney Ransom J. Garrett, at your service."

With another snap, a beveled glass nameplate instantly appeared on the desk, denoting its owner in bold text, with the words "Attorney at Law" centered just underneath. He reached over and Corwin absently shook his hand.

"I'll be representing you," continued Ransom.

"Representing me?" echoed Corwin with a quizzical look.

"In the trial, naturally. I believe your kind call it a Final Judgment."

For a long second Corwin's jaw hung open. Then something clicked in his mind. Realization dawned and he burst into a chuckle.

This time it was Ransom who looked confused.

"This is finally starting to make sense!" declared Corwin. "Everything that I'm experiencing right now, it's all a dream, a very vivid dream!" He plucked a bronze paperweight off the desk, tossed it and caught it with a swipe of his hand. "It truly is astonishing to think that the human mind is capable of such a convincing illusion!"

"That train must have hit you pretty hard," remarked Ransom.

"Indeed," Corwin assured him. "Why, I'm probably as good as dead, but it's been shown that just before a man dies, there's one last surge of brain activity."

"And that's what you think this is?"

"What else could it be?" He fixed Ransom with a knowing stare. "You said 'your kind' earlier, which is to say that you're not a human, but an—"

"An angel," Ransom offered.

"Yes, an angel! Don't you see it?"

Ransom was scratching his head.

"I might not be a Christian, but I was born into a Christian culture. Heck, I even went to Catholic school for a few years. Heaven, Hell, Purgatory, angels . . . It's only natural that such images would linger in the back of my mind.

"Had I been born somewhere else, maybe things would be different," Corwin went on. "Instead of an angel, you might have been one of my ancestors, or Buddha, or my animal spirit guide."

Propping one elbow on his desk, Ransom buried his face in his palm and massaged his aching temples.

"I think we could both use a drink," he decided, promptly rising and heading for the liquor cabinet.

Fetching a stout crystal flask, he produced two rocks glasses and set them on the bar, then bent down to open a wood panel door that blended with the rest of the cabinetry. Inside was a small freezer, from which he drew a pail of ice and tongs.

"What can I get you? Bourbon? Scotch? Gin?" With each word, Ransom flicked the side of the flask, the shade of the liquid within changing from amber to gold to clear.

"No thanks," Corwin replied. "If this is to be my last dream, I believe I'd like to stay sober for it."

"I sure wouldn't," muttered Ransom, ice cubes tinking as he tipped back his glass.

He replaced the stopper and brought the flask with him as he returned to his tufted chair behind the desk.

"Don't you think this is a rather long dream for someone whose skull is no longer in one piece?"

"It would seem that way," Corwin admitted. "I can only guess that some part of my brain is still functioning. In any case, it's not as though I can really trust my perception of time here. Most dreams last only a few minutes, yet they often feel much longer. Who knows how much time has passed on the outside?"

"Well it's good to know that you've got this all figured out." Ransom poured himself another double shot. "Still, it's a shame that you have to spend your last dream stuck with me."

"It's not exactly surprising," said Corwin. "I suppose you've always been there, a distant fear or hope in the supernatural, suppressed by my more rational thoughts. As they say: 'For the believer there will always be doubt, and for the skeptic, always—'"

"Possibility," chimed Ransom.

"See! Even the way that you finish my sentences!"

The attorney scribbled a reminder on his notepad.

"Don't finish sentences," he mumbled.

The office's front door swung open and in strode a young woman wearing designer glasses, her chestnut hair in a bun. A red skirt and suit jacket hugged the curves of her figure. Despite the sudden entrance, Corwin was too absorbed in his own thoughts to pay any heed.

"You, this place, it's all a creation of my subconscious mind," he mused, speaking as much to himself as to Ransom.

"The Corwin file, sir," said the woman.

She bent over the desk to deposit a stack of neatly organized documents.

"Thanks Elsie," Ransom replied.

He regarded the file, flipping briefly through its hundred or so pages while ignoring his client's rambling. It took only a glimpse for the angel to memorize the contents therein.

Corwin's gaze followed the secretary as she strutted away.

"She's *definitely* a part of my subconscious."

With a coy smile and eyes that said "good luck," Elsie vanished behind the door.

"Now then," Ransom tapped the paper stack back into shape, "how might I impress upon you the reality of your present predicament?"

Rising, he began to pace leisurely around the perimeter of his desk.

"As I understand it, a human being will snap out of a dream in the event of certain sensations," Ransom snapped his fingers, "such as the sensation of falling."

Corwin squinted, broad daylight assaulting his eyes. When his vision adjusted, he saw that his chair was no longer in the attorney's office, but teetering precariously atop the edge of a canyon. The Grand Canyon. Orange and brown strata striped the cliff sides. His feet dangled over thin air, five hundred feet of jagged rocks descending steeply to where the Colorado River snaked below.

"Um, Mr. Ransom? I have this thing about heights," started Corwin, clutching his seat with a white-knuckled grip, but Ransom's shoe was already planted on the rear of his chair.

The attorney's lips curled into a wicked grin.

"Oh, I wouldn't worry. Maybe this is one of those flying dreams!"

Before his client could say another word, he kicked out, sending both the chair and its occupant sailing into the gorge. Corwin's stomach lurched. He flailed his arms, the fall twisting and turning him about so that the riverbed and the open sky traded places in a mad whirl. A desperate scream echoed off the canyon walls. Yet even as the wind roared in his ears, Ransom's words rang out clearly.

"Of course, falling isn't the only way to wake up. I've heard that the threat of sudden, intense pain or death can have a similar effect."

Wait, I can't die. I'm already dead!

But the rational voice in the back of Corwin's mind didn't matter. What mattered was the rocky bank of the Colorado speeding rapidly towards him. He clenched his teeth and shut tight his eyes.

The bone-crunching thud made even Ransom wince a little.

Twitching like some half-dead insect, Corwin noticed three things. First, that he was still alive. Second, that a throbbing pain pulsed through every inch of his body. And third, that the ground beneath him was not sand and stones, but a plush carpet. With a miserable groan he pried one eye open.

Surrounding him once again was the familiar décor of Ransom's office. The angel reclined behind his desk, savoring a long drag on a cigarette. Forcing his sore limbs into motion, Corwin laboriously climbed back into his chair, which by all appearances had weathered the fall without so much as a scratch. He patted the dirt from his rumpled coat and stared flatly at his attorney.

"I think I'll take that drink now."

3

SHADES OF CHANGE

A soothing fire seared in Corwin's throat as he sipped the bourbon, the heat sinking like a coal to the pit of his stomach and then radiating out to his finger tips.

"Maple. A zesty note of citrus. And a hint of vanilla on the finish." He cocked an eyebrow. "Don't tell me, is this Angel's Envy?"

"A man who knows his bourbon!" commended Ransom. "The Force is strong with this one."

The angel swished the red-gold liquor in his glass.

"Do you still believe yourself to be dreaming?"

"I'm not sure," said Corwin. "If right now I'm undergoing surgery in the emergency room, that fall might have been a wave of pain coursing through my unconscious mind, this bourbon a dose of anesthesia."

Ransom stroked the bristles on his chin thoughtfully.

"Perhaps a higher cliff . . ."

DONALD J. AMODEO

"No!" Corwin hastily interjected. "No more cliffs!" He raised his hands in supplication. "Look, I get it. You want me to accept that this is my afterlife. I don't know that I can believe that just yet, but seeing as I'm stuck here, let's say I'm willing to assume that there's a chance—a remote, absurd possibility that what you say is true."

"In other words, you're willing to play along." Taking a brief measure of his client, Ransom nodded with a hard-eyed grin. "I can work with that.

"Discerning dreams from reality can be a messy business," he continued. "I don't suppose you can prove that your previous life wasn't a dream?"

Corwin didn't have to think long.

"No, I don't suppose I can."

"All knowledge begins not with facts, but with an assumption: the assumption that your senses aren't lying to you; that reality is, for the most part, as it appears."

"That's funny to hear, coming from an angel. Doesn't religion rest upon the notion that reality is more than it appears?"

"That there is more to reality than you can know by your senses, yes," answered Ransom, "but not that your senses are wrong. Like a gravitational pull evidencing a hidden black hole, the seen gives clue to the unseen."

"Well I won't deny that religion is rather like a black hole," Corwin said dryly.

He cracked his neck and pumped one arm, rotating his shoulder. The pain from the fall still lingered in his joints.

"If I'm already dead, how come it hurts so much? Shouldn't I be haunting your office as a disembodied spirit about now?"

"That's no way to spend your afterlife," replied Ransom. "To be human is to be body and soul. Granted, your current vessel is only temporary."

"It's a pretty good replica," noted Corwin as he glanced at his reflection in one of the glass cabinet doors. "You even got the missing button on my coat."

"Death is a jarring experience. Having a familiar body tends to make things go smoother. Just don't start thinking that you're invincible. That body is more resilient than your old one, but it can still bruise and bleed. Feelings of pain or pleasure are no less real here than in the mortal world."

"So I've noticed. Is there another afterlife waiting if by chance I manage to get myself killed in this one?"

"Death can be a mercy, a release from pain. You will find no such release in this place. There are fates worse than death here."

"Sounds heavenly," moaned Corwin. "So what now? As far as my 'final judgment' is concerned, why not get it over with? If the lord almighty is as just and merciful as they say, I don't see what I've got to be worried about."

"You're clearly not lacking for confidence." Ransom's gaze sharpened. "Are you so sure that your case is airtight?"

"I should hope so, unless your god is a tyrant! Last I checked, I did just die saving somebody's life."

"An admirable final act," agreed Ransom, "one which secured you my invaluable services, but I'm afraid your situation is a bit more complex than that."

"Why? Because I'm an atheist?"

"You weren't just any atheist, Corwin. You were zealous and outspoken, a veritable Saint Paul of atheism. Wherever you went, you employed that intellect of yours to the purpose of convincing men to abandon their faith."

"And what of it?" challenged Corwin. "Sure, I encouraged people to embrace reason rather than superstition, to look to science rather than an invisible old man in the sky for answers, and what was the result? Have my words ever driven anyone to strap on a bomb? Did I ever once cause harm to those who happened to disagree? No. Unlike so many of your *peace-loving* believers, I've never resorted to violence to advance my ideals."

"It's true enough that you haven't spilled any blood," Ransom conceded, "but the prosecution isn't going to build its case upon charges of battery.

"Suppose for a moment that such a thing as the soul exists. Unlike mortal vessels, souls endure forever, but they can be lost, cut off from all love and happiness if they choose to reject its source. Should it be shown that your actions were instrumental in the loss of even one person's eternal soul, do you not think that that would weigh heavily against you?"

Corwin had never seen a soul, never heard one. He considered it altogether illogical to believe in something for which there was no material evidence, but that wasn't to say that he didn't understand the concept. Of all religion's crazy doctrines, the idea that some part of him might transcend the physical and live on was perhaps the most alluring.

"This trial is not nearly as open-and-shut as you would like it to be," said Ransom. "The prosecution adamantly believes that your soul is rightly the property of Hell, and they'll stop at nothing to see you burn. You're going to need my help."

"Your *help* strikes me as more dangerous than the trial," Corwin replied as he rubbed the back of his neck, the memory of getting kicked off a cliff still fresh in his mind. "And as for my part in this? What would I be expected to do?"

"Only to cooperate." Ransom cracked his wolfish smile. "The first rule of order here is to know thyself. We're going to see just how godless you really are."

That Corwin had little choice in the matter hadn't eluded him, but more than that, he had always relished a good battle of ideas. Perhaps this bizarre dying dream was what he had truly wished for all along.

"I hope you don't expect me to make it too easy for you."

"I expect you to fight me every step of the way. But do not attempt to lie." The attorney's tone darkened. "We angels are not easily lied to, nor are we forgiving of those who try."

Corwin, however, had no intention of deceit. Fully convinced that truth and reason were on his side, he doubted very much that any of the angel's tests would prove insurmountable.

"Lies are a coward's defense. I won't have need of them."

"Excellent." With a clap, Ransom folded his hands. "Then let's get started."

He made as if to get up, but then stopped halfway.

"One more thing!"

Rifling through his pockets, Ransom's fingers finally came upon what he was looking for, withdrawing a cross affixed to a slender chain. The golden necklace glinted in the light, its sharp contours simple and elegant. He slid it reverently across the desk.

"You had best put this on."

Corwin eyed the cross skeptically.

"I've heard of dressing for court, but isn't this a bit much? Will your omniscient god be fooled into thinking that I'm a good Christian if I just look the part?"

"Trust me," said Ransom. "It may come in handy."

"You know I don't believe in your good luck charms."

"Believe what you will. You can think of it as a fashion statement for all I care. But for now, I strongly suggest you shut up and do as your defense attorney asks."

With no small amount of disdain, Corwin gave in and looped the gold chain around his neck, the cross dangling below his collar.

"Remember this," Ransom said gravely, "if ever you are separated from me and find yourself in a desperate situation, hold onto that cross."

The warning stirred dark thoughts in Corwin's head. Just what kind of "desperate situation" might his attorney fear? Before he could dwell upon it too deeply, Ransom sprang to his feet.

"Well then, no point in wasting any more time."

He struck off for the office's front door, motioning for his client to follow.

"Where are we going?" asked Corwin.

"To a place you once knew."

Ransom clasped the doorknob, the bolt sliding with a click as he gave it a twist. It was the same door through which his secretary had come and gone, and Corwin half expected to glimpse the marble halls of a heavenly law firm on the other side, but instead a wall of white light flooded his vision, engulfing both of them in a flash.

A springy carpet of grass cushioned the soles of his boots. The bright light resolved into an afternoon sky, cobalt blue and dotted with cotton clouds. In the center of the park, a brass gentleman struck a scholarly pose amidst the maple trees. He was flanked by Georgian buildings that harkened to an age when architects strove to capture invisible truths in stone. The leaves had begun to turn, painting the fields with splashes of crimson and gold.

Everywhere students were roaming about. Some hurried to their classes while others meandered in the park, conversing with friends or simply taking in the pleasantly brisk day.

"Recognize anything?" inquired Ransom as they strolled beneath a shaded walkway that bordered the park, its ceiling upheld by a row of austere pillars to their right.

"My old university," breathed Corwin.

"An institution where young minds are molded, not always for the better."

Corwin smirked at the jab. "You don't sound too fond of education."

"On the contrary," replied Ransom. "The pursuit of God has long gone together with the pursuit of knowledge about his handiwork, but the most important lessons—those of how to live rightly—are seldom taught in your universities anymore."

"I don't know about that," said Corwin. "They do encourage ethics of a sort. It's called Political Correctness."

"Ah yes, an ethical code in which the greatest sin is causing offense. Do you ascribe to it?"

"No thanks. Being considerate is well and good, but I think people ought to grow some thicker skin. In my experience, you can't take a stand for anything without offending somebody."

Ransom seemed satisfied with the answer and they continued down the path. As a steady flow of students filed past, Corwin couldn't help but notice that something was odd. No one had spared him or his sveltely-clad companion so much as a glance.

"Can they see us?"

"No. We are merely shades in this time and place," explained Ransom.

"Interesting." Corwin snatched a textbook off the nearby balustrade, beside which two men stood chatting. "Does that mean I'm like a poltergeist right now?" he asked as he sent the book bobbing and swaying before them, adding a ghostly moan for good measure.

With a beleaguered sigh, Ransom shook his head.

"When a shade touches something, it creates a sort of copy, one that exists on our plane, but not theirs."

His hopes deflated, Corwin tossed the textbook over his shoulder, leaving the students to carry on in their discussion, blissfully unaware. A second look confirmed that, indeed, the original book had reappeared right in the same place. Armed with this revelation, a new plot sprang to mind as he spotted a comely blond, the threads of her yellow sweater show-casing an impressive degree of elasticity.

"Can I make a copy of her?"

"It only works for things without souls," Ransom stiffly replied.

A wave of Corwin's arm proved as much. His hand passed right through the girl's waist as though she were nothing more than a hologram.

The strangeness of being a shade was disconcerting, yet intriguing. Corwin felt like a scientist having happened upon a new discovery, his mind awhirl with questions. If touching things created copies, was there a limit to how many copies he could make? Or was it a choice? Could he walk through walls if he felt so inclined? What if he were to meet other shades? Did dead people make a habit of roaming the earth like creepy, voyeuristic tourists?

As the possibilities played out in his head, his roving gaze strayed to the windows, where the park's florid reflection shone in the glass. There were joggers and picnickers and benches home to studying students. It was a scene that could have belonged to any sunny afternoon. Almost.

One man stood apart. Wearing a dark suit and a fedora, he leaned against a maple with *The Times* spread open before him, but he wasn't reading the news. His black stare was leveled towards the windows, towards Corwin.

Not towards me, Corwin realized. *At me.*

In the reflection their eyes met. Slowly the stranger lowered his newspaper, a mirthless smile on his lips, and Corwin's blood turned to ice. He swung his gaze away from the windows, into the park, finding only dead leaves. There was no one beneath the maple tree.

4

DARK WINDS RISING

Braxton Hall's entrance was a set of glass and aluminum double doors that bespoke modern sensibilities informing the Georgian bricks. Following on the heels of a troop of students, Corwin and Ransom stepped inside and shortly took a turn, ascending a broad stairway to the second story. The angel halted at a classroom's rear door.

"Sounds like class is already in session."

Like a pair of tardy students, they slipped in quietly and found a place against the far wall. It was a modestly-sized room with windows to one side and seven rows of desks, mostly filled. A man whose abundantly gray hair clashed with his tanned, only slightly lined face leaned behind a podium in a plaid dress shirt. He spun the words of his lecture with a preacher's passion.

"Professor Valentine!" exclaimed Corwin. "Now there was a man who had a knack for teaching! His course on existentialism introduced me to philosophy. But that's strange . . ." He gave the man a hard stare. "He looks as though he hasn't aged a day."

"Has he?" questioned Ransom. "Don't assume that the same chains of time that bind mortal men apply to me."

"Sorry! I didn't realize that my lawyer was the *Ghost of Christmas Past.*"

Corwin reflected that the mild weather and turning of the leaves had been rather out of place for the season.

The professor relaxed against his podium, a copy of Albert Camus' *The Stranger* in hand. He was reading an excerpt.

> . . . It was as if I had waited all this time for this moment and for the first light of this dawn to be vindicated. Nothing, nothing mattered, and I knew why. So did he. Throughout the whole absurd life I'd lived, a dark wind had been rising toward me from somewhere deep in my future, across years that were still to come, and as it passed, this wind leveled whatever was offered to me at the time, in years no more real than the ones I was living.

Snapping the book shut, he lifted his gaze to regard the class.

"A dark wind rising from my future," uttered Valentine. "Camus describes death as a dark wind, an irresistible force that lays low all the acts of our lives. But it's also a source of meaning, a commonality that binds us. We all die, and so we are all brothers.

"But is death enough? Is the reaper's inevitable march enough to provide a source of meaning in our lives? Nietzsche didn't think so.

"The existentialists and the nihilists agree in their rejection of an afterlife, but not in the implications. Nietzsche believed that the absoluteness of death rendered life meaningless, while Sartre and Camus believed that man could create his own meaning."

"But isn't it true that Camus never considered himself an existentialist?" objected a woman with black-rimmed glasses.

"Camus didn't much care for labels," answered the professor. "But in his quest for meaning despite life's absurdity, his thoughts largely echo those of men such as Sartre."

"Doesn't Nietzsche's own concept of the superman contradict the principles of nihilism?" inquired a flaxen-haired boy in a hooded sweatshirt.

"Good catch, Corwin! Nietzsche's model man was one who thinks for himself and lives by his own rules. And yet, if everything is as meaningless as nihilism suggests, what does it matter whether you live by your own rules or someone else's? Is it not all the same in the end?"

The sight of his younger self gave Corwin a peculiar sense of déjà vu, and for the first time since the train's lethal impact, he genuinely felt as if he were in a dream. Was that dark wind of which Camus spoke already swirling about him? At any moment, might this dream shatter and banish him not to the waking world, but to nothingness?

Professor Valentine's lecture drew to a close and soon students were emptying out into the halls. Outside the windows, the sun was setting. A violet curtain shrouded the heavens, save where the horizon blushed coral in the west. Pivoting a desk, Ransom sat atop it and threw one leg up on the chair.

"Why take me here?" asked Corwin. "If a philosophical debate is in order, I feel that I may require more bourbon."

"Before you attended this university," said Ransom, "you already had your doubts about God and Christianity, but here something changed. Those doubts solidified into a worldview, turning you from an agnostic into a hardened atheist. Do you recall what spurred that change?"

"I guess it was the first time that I'd applied critical thinking to religion. Once you stop trying to justify the fairy tales, all that's left are contradictions and wishful thinking."

"Yes, yes." Ransom waved a hand dismissively. "That's all very enlightening, but it's not really what I wanted to know. What changed you wasn't anything that you realized about religion. It was something you realized about yourself."

The angel's words struck a chord and Corwin understood at once what he meant. It wasn't any clever argument or decisive piece of evidence that had swayed him. To question a creed was easy, and the merit of such arguments could be endlessly debated by those who felt compelled to do so, but to look in the mirror and question one's innermost self . . . that took a bit more resolve.

"I came to see that I'd been accepting beliefs, or at least entertaining them, simply because they were comforting. They were what I had always been told, and easier than seeking my own answers. At first it was scary letting go of religion's promises, walking the tightrope of life without a spiritual safety net, but if I was to be honest with myself, it was a step that I had to take."

"Good!" Ransom clapped him on the shoulder. "That's more like it!"

Corwin blinked hard, unsure whether the angel staring back at him was still playing for the same team.

"Humans are creatures of passion," said Ransom. "Whether finding faith or rejecting it, the decision is often more a matter of the heart than of the head. Take the atheist who scorns God on account of the foolishness that men do in his name, or the believer who clings to faith because the harshness of life without the hope of Heaven is too much for his fragile spirit to bear."

"People believe what they want to believe," affirmed Corwin.

"When perceived truth differs from the truth one desires, a person must choose. You chose the right master, Corwin. In your self-reflection, you stumbled upon a simple and profound, yet seldom followed principle."

"And that would be?"

"That the only good reason to believe something is if it's true."

A decade earlier, Corwin had arrived at the same conclusion while pouring through volumes of philosophy, asking the fearful questions that he had avoided all his life.

"But the truth I found led me to reject your god."

Ransom stood, and as he did so the world darkened until only the faint orange disk of the sun remained. A shadowy cross divided it, and then it was no longer the sun, but a four-paned ocular window. Hazy light streamed into a stuffy room stacked with boxes, chests and forgotten furniture. Corwin had to stoop, checking his head as he ducked under the beams of the low, vaulted ceiling. From the rear of the attic, a staircase creaked with footsteps. An elderly man's spectacles peeked over the floorboards.

"A man finds an old, dusty painting in the attic," said Ransom, his character living out the story in time. "He rubs one corner and uncovers a feathered wing. You're like that man, thinking you've found the portrait of a bird, but the wing belongs to Saint Michael."

A thick gloom washed over them and Corwin saw that he was back in the classroom, twilight's first stars poking through the dusky sky.

"If I was wrong, then life is surely a cruel trick, a puzzle meant to deceive," he argued. "Let the lord drag me into his courtroom and I'll tell him the same thing that Bertrand Russell once said: 'Not enough evidence, God! Not enough evidence!'"

"You chose to limit 'evidence' to that which fits neatly into units of measurement. Even there you might have found clues, but it is not my intention to belittle your convictions. That fear of which you spoke, it is a trial faced by every truth seeker who challenges his own preconceptions."

"Even angels?" Corwin couldn't resist asking.

Ransom laughed. "The Father's existence was never in question to my kind. Our test was not one of faith, but of pride."

"Yet somehow you managed to pass," Corwin said slyly. "Whatever did god demand that was so humiliating any-way?"

"That's nothing that pertains to your case."

"It's *my* soul on the line. Indulge me."

Ransom strolled to the windows, a faraway look in his eyes.

"Long before the dawn of this universe, there existed an age when we angels were the Father's only children. Ours was a realm of thought and song and symmetry. Then came man. By all estimation, your race was vastly inferior to us, yet even so, the Father doted on you, favoring the lowest of humans with no less love than that which he bestowed upon the wisest and mightiest of the seraphim. Confounded by his ways, some began to distrust, but another test would prove greater still, for the Father not only cherished you. He became one of you.

"When one beholds God in all his glory, worship comes as naturally as the sense of awe that stirs within when staring up at the stars or at a majestic mountain range. We recognize our smallness and are filled with humility and wonder. But what if the Father should humble himself? When it was foreknown that he would become man, the thought was too much for some of my brothers to stand. Lucifer, whose power and beauty was first among us, decided that rather than bend the knee to a God made flesh, he would rebel. And so was fought the Betrayer's War."

"Do all angels think so little of us?" inquired Corwin, more surprised than offended.

"Your race's history doesn't exactly inspire confidence. Most humans sin so often and so readily that you appear to comprehend your world no better than booklice devouring a novel comprehend the words written on its pages."

"Well it's comforting to know that racism isn't a uniquely human vice."

"How eagerly would you bend the knee and pledge your eternal loyalty to a God who took the form of an insect? A rodent? A wafer of bread?"

Ransom left the question hanging in the air. Turning away from the windows, he lit up another cigarette.

"You still doubt that this place is real."

"I am a skeptic, after all."

"A skeptic!" scoffed Ransom. "Everyone's a skeptic. Religious people are skeptics too. They're skeptical of atheism."

"A materialist then, or an empiricist," elaborated Corwin. "My personal philosophy has no need of anything so insubstantial as faith."

"No need of faith?"

"You know what I mean! I have faith that the sun will rise, that gravity will keep me from floating away, that my car will start when I turn the key in the ignition. But my faith is rooted in the world's physical laws, not in any supernatural, metaphysical delusions."

"I see," said Ransom. "Tell me, what is religion's place in your mind?"

Corwin considered his words carefully.

"Religion is a crutch. Man desires something outside himself to lean on, to afford a sense of security, but this I did not need. I could walk on my own."

A heavy silence passed between them and the humorless mask of Ransom's face left Corwin wondering if perhaps he had roused his attorney's ire.

"That sounds about right," Ransom said at last.

"You're agreeing with me?" blurted Corwin in disbelief.

The angel shrugged.

"Your overdramatic choice of words has more sting than substance, but the assertion that man yearns for something outside himself on which to lean—I don't disagree with that. Where our difference lies is in what that longing means."

"I suspect our differences run a bit deeper."

"But surely even you must admit that religion is a natural inclination of man?"

"That seems obvious enough," conceded Corwin. "Why are we here? What happens when we die? Everyone likes to imagine that there's some grand meaning behind it all. Burial rites are as old as humanity, and it's not hard to see why."

"As I recall from your file, you even wrote an essay about it."

"I made a frequent habit of putting my thoughts to paper. Sometimes we see ideas clearer when we write them down."

"Fortunately it makes my job easier as well," said Ransom. "In your essay, aptly titled 'Why People Cling to Religion,' you identify three main causes of religious thought. Why don't we start by revisiting them?"

"It's been years!" protested Corwin. "I'm sure I made plenty of salient points, but I doubt how well I can remember them now."

"Over time the human brain grows forgetful, but when you came here we took the liberty of installing a few upgrades."

"Upgrades?"

"Picture your brain as a computer, your soul as the operator. If you try looking back, I think you'll find your memory to be most adequate."

It was more than adequate. As Corwin searched his mind, the past vividly unfolded, immersing him in a sensory flood. He saw himself typing his college essay, the words crisp on his laptop screen. He thought back further, to his tenth birthday. His dad had taken him to see the Yankees play. The stadium roiled like a boiling kettle and cheers erupted at the crack of a bat. Lost in a forest of jerseys, he smelled hotdogs and soft-baked pretzels and nacho cheese. Years later he was stuffing suitcases and cramming them into his car. His mother watched through the window blinds as he drove away, never looking back, never saying goodbye.

Another time and place, and Corwin was standing in the rain, getting drenched without a care as a girl in a Volkswagen Beetle asked him for directions. The cold downpour couldn't begin to dull the warmth of her hazel eyes.

"Ikea? That's a big store to miss."

"I know," she laughed. "Can you tell that I'm new in town?"

"I can tell that I'd love to take you out for dinner."

Mary gave him a smile, but not her number.

"Just head south on Columbia," he said. "It'll be on your right."

"Thanks, uh . . ."

"Corwin," he offered. "I didn't catch your name."

"It's Mary. Nice to meet you, Corwin."

As her car pulled away, Corwin rushed back under the awning where his lanky friend Josh had been waiting, sipping coffee from a paper cup and watching the scene with some amusement. Corwin didn't stay long.

"Hey, where are you going?" called Josh.

"I just remembered that I'm urgently in need of a new end table!"

He caught up with her halfway through the labyrinthine furniture store, near where weary shoppers went to rest and recharge like families at Disney World, sating their hunger with hot plates of Swedish meatballs and chicken tenders.

She was staring holes through a collection of colorful throw rugs.

"I like the green one, myself," said Corwin. "It really brings out your eyes."

Mary turned, her look playfully accusing.

"I'd say it's a small world, but it's not *that* small."

"Do you like brownies—I mean the super gooey, fudgy kind—because I happen to know of this one place . . ."

Swept up in the memory, Corwin lost all track of time. A wistful smile crept onto his face. In many ways, Mary was his polar opposite. Upbeat and stubbornly traditional, she was prone to letting her emotions guide her, a trait that sometimes infuriated Corwin when he tried to talk matters of faith or lack thereof. Reckless as a wildfire, she was the kindest, most interesting and most beautiful person that he had ever met, and he missed her deeply.

"Ahem," Ransom cleared his throat, dragging his client back to the present. "Your three causes?"

"Yes, well, they're three hopes really," said Corwin, regaining his composure, "and they address the question of why ordinary people pursue religious faith, not the deceitful use of religion by certain kings or clergy."

"Misuse, I would say, but go on."

"First, people turn to religion because they hope for knowledge. Second, people turn to religion because they hope for purpose. And third, people turn to religion because they hope for justice."

"Knowledge, purpose and justice," repeated Ransom. "That should give us plenty to start with."

A driving wind, black as pitch, howled outside the glass, rattling the windows and smothering the stars. The room's halogen lights flickered nervously.

"Now let's go," said the angel. "This place won't be safe for long."

5

THE LONGEST NIGHT

Beyond the classroom, the building loomed dark and deserted. Walls of stone muffled the wind and clapped with the echoes of their footsteps upon the glossy tiles.

"What do you mean 'this place won't be safe'?" asked Corwin as he hurried after the dim beacon that was his attorney's cigarette. "What's going on?"

"Never mind that," Ransom replied without slowing. "I'm more interested in why your essay omitted the fear of death. Many atheists are happy to blame religion on man's mortality and call it a day."

"It's not that they're wrong, but endless life could also mean Hell. People want more than that. They want the things that make life worthwhile, things like peace, fulfillment and happiness."

"And do you think that you would have been happier, had you believed in God?"

"No, I don't," answered Corwin, who had never held much regard for the sort of atheists who said things like "I wish I could believe" when confronted by apologists. "Ignorance isn't bliss."

He tensed visibly, his memory dredging up a vision long buried.

"So are you going to tell me what happened?" prodded Kevin Holiday. "Did Danny give you trouble again?"

The evening had darkened, but sitting in the car with his father, there was no hiding the puffy red welt that had formed beneath Corwin's left eye. He still wore his cleats and uniform, his jersey damp with sweat from practice.

"He couldn't get the ball past me all day," boasted Corwin. "You should have seen how red his face got! In the bathroom after practice, he said he was going to teach me a lesson. I put my guard up like you told me. He still got one punch in, but I nailed him pretty hard in the nose!"

"I'm gonna have to have a talk with that coach," said Kevin.

"No, Dad! You can't! I can handle this."

"You boys are supposed to be a team. If Coach Mason can't keep you from each other's throats, I'm pulling you out of there."

"Danny isn't so bad. After I hit him, he told me that I punch really good. He hopes that we're on the same team next practice."

Kevin suppressed a chuckle. *Can't stop boys from being boys,* he figured. *Beating each other up one day, best friends the next.*

"Well I'll let it go for now, but good luck explaining that bruise to your mom."

Corwin's spirit sank like the Titanic. Dad might understand, but stopping his mother from making a fuss would be a battle of a whole different order.

"You hungry?" his father asked.

"Starving!"

"How does a bacon cheeseburger sound?"

"And a hot fudge sundae?"

"You drive a hard bargain, Mister."

Kevin turned towards the nearest McDonald's and cranked up the air conditioner. Though the hour wasn't late, the streets here were already asleep. He stopped at a needless red light, no passing traffic to be seen.

From between two buildings a woman dashed, tawny hair flying out behind her. Seeing their car, she ran out onto the road.

"Help!" she shouted, waving her hands hysterically.

Kevin lowered the windows as she pounded on the passenger-side door.

"You've got to help me!"

"Calm down," urged Kevin. "Tell me what's wrong."

"Someone's chasing me! Please, just get me out of here!"

Peering past her, back towards the alley, Corwin's father searched for some sign of her assailant, but if he was out there, he wasn't showing himself. The night was still, the shadows silent. Kevin popped the locks.

"Climb in the back. We'll take you someplace safe and you can call the cops."

"I don't think so," rumbled a harsh voice.

Kevin's gaze snapped to his left, finding the barrel of a revolver pointed straight at him. Poised outside his window was a man with chrome teeth and a headscarf.

"Get out of the car!"

"Alright," said Kevin. "Just take it easy."

A thousand thoughts and fears raced through his mind as he unbuckled his seatbelt, looked at his son and opened the door. The woman had dropped the act and Corwin was shocked silent.

"Don't worry, Corwin. It's going to be okay."

Jittering impatiently, the thug thrust his gun closer.

"Get the fuck out!" he hollered. "Now!"

His accomplice grabbed Corwin's hair and dragged him from the car. She held him at a distance with one arm wrapped around his neck.

"Just let the boy go!" pleaded Kevin as he stood, his hands raised.

In response, the carjacker pistol-whipped him across the jaw.

"Dad!" cried Corwin.

"Give me your wallet!" the thug demanded. "And your phone!"

With blood's coppery taste on his lips, Kevin reached into his pocket. *Got to keep it together.* The barrel came level with his forehead, the gun's owner glaring.

"I don't think I like the way that you're looking at me."

A frightful rage seized Corwin. Tucking his chin, he bit the woman's arm. Her grip flew loose with a scream.

"You little shit!"

As Corwin sprinted towards his father, the anxious carjacker panicked. His revolver swung in the boy's direction—a sight Kevin couldn't abide.

"Corwin, no!"

Even with Corwin's enhanced memory, the next moment was hard to picture. There was a shout, a twisting blur of bodies, and a gunshot.

"Carlos, what the fuck are you doing!?" yelled the woman.

Pale-faced, the thug withdrew a step, eyes flitting, hunting for witnesses that he hoped not to find. His accomplice was already fleeing the scene. Abandoning all thought of the car or the wallet, he turned and ran.

Corwin's father lay on his side, a scarlet blotch forming around the place where he clutched his stomach. Corwin flung himself down beside him.

"Dad! Dad!"

Several windows in the surrounding buildings brightened. Soon Corwin heard the sirens, saw the red and blue flashing of emergency lights.

"If anything else comes to you, just give us a call," said the officer, an Asian woman whose face was easy to trust. "Every little detail helps."

The police departed, giving Corwin and his mother some time alone. His father had been rushed down the hall to the ER. All they could do now was pray. But was God really listening? Maybe his mother knew. Maybe that's what she was doing as she stared mutely into her lap, her body and mind drawn inwards like a turtle retreating behind its shell.

Corwin slid one of his hands towards her and she took it without a word or a glance. It crossed his mind that he ought perhaps to say something, but he didn't know what. The past hour of questioning had left him mentally exhausted.

On the hospital waiting room's TV, two talking heads bloviated over the latest piece of controversial legislation. Corwin didn't understand the politics, but he understood the hurling of blame, and his mind began to play a cruel game of if-onlys.

If only I hadn't wanted to stop for dinner . . . If only I hadn't broken free from that woman's grasp . . . Dad's life might not be in danger right now.

A doctor with dark circles under his eyes stepped into the room.

"Mrs. Holiday?"

Eager for news, Corwin and his mother quickly stood to join him.

"Is Kevin going to be alright?" asked Samantha.

"Fortunately the bullet missed your husband's stomach. We were able to remove it and stop the bleeding. His condition is stable."

The doctor's words were encouraging, but his expression severe.

What is he not saying? wondered Corwin.

"Thank God!" Samantha squeezed her son's shoulder. "When can we see him?"

"He's still under anesthesia, but you'll be able to talk to him soon. Before that, there's something else you need to know."

Corwin's mother picked up on the note of apprehension in his voice.

"Was there some problem?"

"When we went in, the bullet wasn't the only thing that we found." The doctor paused for a breath and his weary eyes softened. "Mrs. Holiday, I'm sorry to have to tell you this, but your husband has pancreatic cancer."

6

WHEN SCIENCE IS SILENT

"My dad was a good man, a good father," said Corwin. "The cancer took everything from him. It tore at him from the inside, until even the simplest tasks were so painful that he couldn't get out of bed. He couldn't eat without vomiting. His skin lost its color and he became so thin that you'd think he was a prisoner at Auschwitz. What did he ever do to deserve a death like that?

"It hurts to think that he's gone and not in some better place, but when I do think back, at least I don't have to tell myself that it was all part of some vain deity's twisted plan."

"So instead of a heartless God, you chose a heartless universe," surmised Ransom. "And that made you happy?"

"I never said I was happy."

"It is well that you didn't." The angel took one last drag and flicked his cigarette, its twirling filter burning down to a solitary ember before meeting the floor. "No sane man comes to the conclusion that there is no Heaven and is happy about it."

"Though he might take some consolation in the thought of no Hell," Corwin retorted.

He glanced back at the classroom's lonely glow. The hallway stretched farther than it had any right to. More than once, he felt as though unseen eyes were watching him. A chill prickled the back of his neck and a scratch sounded from the shadows. His gaze swung to the windowed door of Room 213. Something flitted past the desks, or perhaps it was nothing, a sputtering cough of his dying mind.

"Care to tell me where we're headed?"

"We've got a long journey ahead, and it begins where your essay begins: with knowledge."

"As long as knowledge takes us someplace else," Corwin said anxiously. "There's just something about an abandoned school . . ."

"Schools, like temples, are places of culture and ritual," spoke Ransom. "In these halls, the young undergo rites of passage. And just as sound may leave an echo, or light an afterimage, the spirit, too, can linger in its way."

"Next you're going to tell me that ghosts are real."

"Heights, hospitals, abandoned buildings . . . For a materialist, you certainly have a lot of phobias. Why should mere bricks and mortar invoke any feeling in you at all?"

"Even I have an imagination!" protested Corwin. "Nobody thinks empirically all the time."

"Sadly, there are those pitiable souls who, looking at the world, see only math and never magic. Such an existence sounds dreadfully dull."

"Not so dull as living under the medieval edicts of an anal-retentive god."

Accepting the barb with a grin, Ransom let the matter drop.

"You say that man hopes for knowledge. What kind of knowledge?"

"Knowledge about our world, about the universe."

"You mean the physical universe?"

"I know of no other universe," attested Corwin. "Man seeks to understand why the sun rises and sets, why lightning strikes, why droughts or floods ruin the harvest. When primitive peoples desired such knowledge, but lacked the scientific means to grasp it, they turned to religion. God conveniently fills in the gaps."

"Fair enough, but must it be either-or?" pressed Ransom. "Can not both gravity and God's will account for why a tree falls in the forest?"

"Believers like to say that, but they're quick to forget should the tree happen to fall on their house. And the point is that god isn't necessary. We can explain the universe without him. With each step forward that science takes, religion's absurd claims are forced to retreat further."

"As is proper. Barring the miraculous, to clash with proven science is a sure sign of false religious thought."

"But can't you see the writing on the wall? The gaps that your god fills grow ever smaller and more insignificant."

"You misunderstand. The Father is not a God of the gaps. He is not some invisible actor in nature, but rather the reason why nature exists at all—why there is something rather than nothing."

"The ultimate retreat!" declared Corwin. "But if god is beyond nature, then he cannot be observed or studied. He is unknowable, and therefore irrelevant."

"You speak as if science is man's only means to gain understanding."

"All true understanding is scientific understanding."

"I wonder," mused Ransom, his thoughts drifting off.

At the gloomy hallway's end, Corwin squinted to make out an oddly-fashioned door. Instead of a doorknob, an iron wheel protruded from its center. The angel gave it a firm twist. Metal squeaked, the wheel locking soundly into position with a clunk. As Ransom pried the heavy door open, pale light poured into the corridor. He motioned to Corwin.

"After you."

The passage on the other side was scarcely wide enough to fit one man abreast, and so they proceeded in single file. Steel walls were interrupted by hatch-like doors with cables and pipes hugging the ceiling. Corwin felt a subtle sway in the floor and heard Ransom's voice over his shoulder.

"Our destination is straight ahead."

"Where are we?"

"A nuclear submarine in the North Pacific. You could say we're surrounded by twenty-thousand tons of science."

A crewman approached from one of the side passages. Seeing Corwin and Ransom, he halted and snapped a salute.

"Captain," came the man's greeting.

It was only then that Corwin noticed the stripes on his sleeve. His cashmere coat had been replaced with a beige suit jacket. For a confusing moment he stood slack-jawed, but a nudge from Ransom prodded him onward.

"Me? I'm the captain?" he asked in a panicked whisper.

"Sounds like a lot of responsibility."

"But this isn't reality!"

"It may not be your reality, but that doesn't mean that this world isn't real."

Corwin regarded his attorney, who was now his first mate, with a puzzled look.

"We can discuss reality later," said Ransom. "Right now, it seems that your presence is urgently required in the control room."

The narrow passage let out into a chamber with a low ceiling and instrument panels crowding the walls. A half-dozen officers manned their stations, one of them with a low-frequency radio in hand.

"Captain, it's Admiral Harrison."

Corwin stepped around the periscope that plunged through the center of the room and hesitantly took the brick-shaped radio piece.

"Hello?"

"The President has authorized the strike," informed a gravelly voice on the other end of the line. "You should be receiving the launch codes now. Proceed immediately with operation Overkill."

"Wait, what?"

"You have your orders, Captain."

With a click, the admiral was gone. A bewildered Corwin stood staring into space, radio static droning in his ear. As the terminal beside him spat out a string of letters and digits, his first mate sprang to action.

"Launch codes confirmed. Condition red!"

The control room dimmed, illuminated only by the crimson glow of the emergency lights. Every officer stood poised and alert.

"Establishing target coordinates. Captain, your key," called Ransom.

In the angel's hand glinted a titanium key. Corwin reached instinctively into his side pocket and his fingers closed on the cool, hard edge of its partner. Among the switches and dials on the panel in front of him was the slit of a lock.

"On the count of three!"

"Remind me why I'm doing this?"

"One, two . . ."

It doesn't matter. None of this is real, thought Corwin, but no matter how much he tried to rationalize it, everything about the situation felt disturbingly wrong. *An angel wouldn't start a nuclear war, right?*

"Three!"

The captain and his first mate twisted their keys in unison. Above a bright red button shielded by glass, the word "armed" blazed ominously. Ransom leaned over and flipped up the guard.

"It's all yours, Captain."

"Hold on a second!" Corwin's finger trembled over the fateful button. "I don't understand. At least tell me the circumstances!"

"What difference does it make? Just press the button!"

"It makes all the difference in the world!" insisted Corwin. "I don't even know who we're firing at! Are we the defender or the aggressor? How many people are going to die if I push that button?"

"Perhaps ten. Perhaps ten million. One number is as good as the next," Ransom said dispassionately.

"This is insane! I must know the situation!"

"And if I told you, would you understand which course of action to take?"

"Surely an informed decision is better than a blind one!"

"But I thought that all true understanding is scientific understanding. Explain to me why firing a nuclear missile is just or unjust. Explain it with *science!*"

"I, but that is," Corwin choked on his words. Could he quantify the value of human life? Taking a labored breath, he struggled to think clearly. "It's in our genes, a feeling evolved from herd instinct."

"You're dancing around the subject, Captain!" growled Ransom. "I didn't ask you to explain *why you feel* a sense of justice. I asked you to validate that feeling scientifically. Show me the equation that proves why the jumble of atoms you call a living human being is *better* than the jumble of atoms you call a corpse."

"I can't!" stammered Corwin. "There is no such equation!"

"Then the answer cannot be known scientifically. The question must be irrelevant!"

"I won't do this! I won't play your game!"

His voice shaking, Corwin snapped shut the guard and took a fearful step away from the button.

"Our orders come straight from the top. To disobey is treason!" In a flash, Ransom drew his sidearm, pressing its cold barrel to the side of Corwin's head. "I'm afraid I'm going to have to relieve you of command, Captain."

"Whoa!" Corwin threw up his hands. "I thought we were past the whole persuasion-by-physical-abuse stage in our relationship!"

"Let me make this easier for you. In a short time, this world's sun will explode in a supernova, extinguishing all human life. Why not push the button?"

"Because . . . Because I . . ." Corwin's mind groped for an answer, finding nothing.

"If I pull this trigger, science can tell me the velocity of the bullet, the heat in the chamber, the trajectory of the blood that splatters on the wall. But science can't tell me if I *should* pull the trigger or not. Answering that question requires something more."

"Whatever, just put the gun away!"

The astonished crew looked on, no one daring to utter a word. Beads of sweat rolled down Corwin's face. With a slow and deliberate motion, Ransom holstered his weapon.

"As long as we understand each other."

Corwin exhaled with relief.

"I think we've spent enough time here," said the angel.

That was one sentiment that Corwin undoubtedly agreed with. As if the whole ordeal were long forgotten, the submarine's officers summarily returned to their duties, paying little heed while the captain and first mate exited the control room.

"Is it true that these people are doomed?" asked Corwin when they were back inside the narrow passage.

"All mortals are doomed," replied Ransom. "Eventually the last star will burn out and the last atom come undone. No universe can sustain organic life forever."

"You're a real ray of sunshine," Corwin said sarcastically. "Were you honestly going to shoot me?"

"It's not as though the bullet would have killed you."

"But I bet it would've hurt like hell."

Ransom didn't deny it.

"So I'd have a horribly painful, gaping hole through my skull and yet still be alive." Picturing the scenario, Corwin arched his lips in a thoughtful frown. "That makes me both terrified and strangely curious."

Steam hissed from a pipe suspended along one of the adjoining passages as a diligent crewman worked the joint with a wrench.

"There's more of mechanism than meaning to science," said Ransom. "Science is the wrench in your hand. It is a means to an end."

"And you can use a wrench to tighten a bolt or to crack someone over the head," Corwin added. "I know that science is morally neutral, but there's no getting around the fact that a lot of supposedly good religion is bad science."

"As you said, man hopes for knowledge. Much knowledge that primitive religions laid claim to was rightly the domain of science. Much, but not all. I needed to show you that the scope of human understanding is not limited to the empirical. You already believed that, of course, but your intellect had yet to catch up with your heart."

Corwin was about to argue that his heart knew little more than how to pump blood when a sudden dizziness came over him. Stumbling, he tipped forward, his arms braced against either side of the cramped passageway. A dark haze clouded his vision and his mind swam with vague sounds and silhouettes. Corwin's consciousness started to slip away, and then he heard a voice. From across an infinite void, a woman was calling his name.

"Corwin!" Mary's voice was distant but unmistakable. "Corwin, wake up!"

7

AN ABSURD HOPE

"Corwin!"

The touch of Ransom's steady hand on his shoulder jolted the world back into focus. Like a boxer recovering from a knockout blow, Corwin slowly straightened up, shaking off the daze. The angel eyed him with a penetrating stare.

"Are you alright?"

"Just a little dizzy. I'm sure it's nothing," said Corwin, though neither he nor Ransom seemed entirely convinced of the latter.

"There's a chance that your soul isn't fully attuned to your new vessel yet. Maybe you should rest."

"I'll be fine," Corwin promised.

The suspicion was still evident on Ransom's face as he led on, but he made no attempt to press the subject further. Returning to the hatch door, he again turned the iron wheel, the portal groaning on its hinges.

"Watch your step," he warned. "The ground here is uneven."

Enveloped by darkness, Corwin could barely discern his own feet, much less the precarious terrain beneath them. The hatch had deposited the two travelers in the dank depths of a cave. It was cool and quiet, save for the soft murmur of a stream that cut its way along the middle of the path, always to their right.

"I don't see how you could argue with my second hope," remarked Corwin, his voice reverberating off the shadowy walls. "Everyone longs for a purpose, a deeper meaning behind this life. Religion is born from such hopes."

"But you claim that religion is a false hope?"

"God is an invention of man, wishful thinking, nothing more."

"And why is it that man should be so obsessed with finding a purpose?"

"That's just how we evolved," Corwin explained. "An accident of higher brain functions."

"You sound rather distrustful of your own nature," observed Ransom. "Might not this most innate of human desires—the desire for meaning—be a clue to be grasped, rather than an illusion to be dispelled?"

"That's all very poetic, but desiring a thing does not make it so. I desired a million dollars. All I got for my Christmas bonus was a gift certificate to Cracker Barrel."

"But wealth does exist," reasoned the angel. "If you had a fundamental desire for something that didn't, then that would make you most unusual."

"I always dreamed of being captain of the starship *Enterprise*."

"Fundamental desire," Ransom emphasized. "I speak not of elaborate fantasies."

"And here I thought you were trying to defend religion!"

With a hopeless smirk, Ransom forged on, his sure gait carrying him easily over the rocks. Corwin's vision had adjusted, but it was all he could do to keep an eye on the back of his carefree attorney. Warily he negotiated the trail, listening for where the stream burbled at the bottom of tiny waterfalls, giving clue of a descent.

Before long the path leveled out. Sunlight broke though the mouth of the cave ahead, sparkling on the water and glimmering off the staggered, sharp-edged facets of the crystalline floor. It rendered a view strikingly different from what Corwin had expected. The cave's every surface was of rose-tinted quartz, as was the outside world.

They strode forth and were greeted by an alien sky. Beyond the scudding clouds, the rings of a gas giant sliced towards the horizon and a swollen sun burned balefully. The land fell away towards a jade sea, its endless waves broken only by leaning crystal spires in the far-off distance. Hexagonal pillars jutted here and there from the earth, sometimes in stepped bunches, and upon these reposed humanlike beings whose skin was translucent, their bodies pulsing with an inner light. The men and women alike were bald, naked and faceless, mannequins of living glass.

Unlike the hard edges of the crystal landscape, most of its inhabitants were smoothly sculpted. Only those perched atop the highest pillars bore skin that mimicked the sharp angles of the quartz. These sat motionless, the light within them having died. Corwin presumed them to be corpses, though the younger creatures scarcely moved either, their silent gaze transfixed upon the sea.

As Ransom approached, a female calmly turned her head to regard him. She sat upon the taller of a twin-pillar cluster.

"Otherworlder, you cast a deep shadow," she spoke telepathically, the glow of her mind waxing with each word. "Does no light pass through you?"

"I am but a mirror," replied Ransom. "I reflect a light that is not my own."

His eyes blazed white-hot for an instant, the flash so intense that his figure darkened like a star in eclipse.

"A light so brilliant cannot harbor wickedness," judged the woman. "What brings you to our island? Have you come on account of the trial?"

"That depends which trial you're talking about. Is something amiss in your fading land?"

"It is as you say. This land fades. None still live who remember the days when our sun was young, and we that remain but await the coming of the New Sun. We do not fear the night, for our souls shine all the brighter, but though we want for nothing, the resplendent light of day is our greatest joy. So it was for all, until the fog bewitched the one who stands accused."

"The fog?" questioned Ransom.

"I dare not speak of it. I can tell you only that the accused suffers from nightmares that plague him even by day. He looks to things that are not, and knows no peace."

"And where is this trial being held?"

Lifting a slender arm, the woman pointed down the shoreline to her right.

"Follow the red moon. Where the earth spurns the ocean and rises to claim the sky, there you will find the Elder Council."

The dying sun hung high in the heavens as Corwin and Ransom struck off along the coast, keeping the ruddy face of the planet's smallest moon ever before them. They journeyed past stands of jagged trees, white-stemmed and amber-leafed, their branches laden with gemstone fruits. Corwin nearly jumped from shock when a nearby boulder stirred without warning, revealing crab-like legs tucked underneath.

"This world is stranger by far than the last," he said, a spirit of adventure quelling his fears. "Would you have me believe that this is a real place or just a product of your imagination?"

"What makes you think that it can't be both?" replied Ransom. "My imagination is quite a bit more powerful than yours."

"So you can shape reality? Create worlds by imagining them?"

Ransom chuckled. "It doesn't work precisely like that. We're more like assistants, sketching a rough image. The Father alone knows the position of every whirling electron. What needs to be understood is that there are degrees to reality."

"How can reality have degrees?" complained Corwin. "Things are either real or they're not."

"Even in your own world, that's not the case. Some entities posses a higher order of reality than others, just as a mouse is more real than a stone, and you more real than a mouse."

Corwin wrinkled his brow. "That might make sense to you, but I'm not seeing it."

"What would you rather be," posed Ransom, "a mouse or a stone?"

"A mouse, I guess. I'd prefer having a tiny brain to having none at all, and at least I could scurry about. Existence as a stone would feel rather like . . ."

"Like not existing at all," concluded the angel. "The more something resembles the Father, the more real it is, for the closer it is to the source of all reality."

"But if god isn't real, then your whole metaphysical order falls apart."

"An understatement, to be sure. Without God, reality is but another idea in the mind of man." He looked to Corwin with a wry smile. "That is to say, not something I'd put much stock in."

They crested a hill of jutting quartz steps and gazed up at what could only be their destination. Past the shallow dip of a valley, the elevation climbed steadily, soaring and tapering to a point that leaned out over the sea like the head of an overturned steam iron. A half-circle of crystal columns crowned the outer rim of its peak—the venerable seats of the Elder Council.

Seeking the most direct route, Ransom chose a ledge that snaked along the perilous face of the escarpment.

"Now would not be a good time to have another one of your dizzy spells," he yelled over the gusty wind.

"I'll try to keep that in mind."

Corwin glanced down to his left and immediately regretted it. Three hundred feet below, foaming waves crashed against the foot of the lofty cliff. He shrank back, his side glued to the rock face.

"You just *had* to take this shortcut," grumbled Corwin.

"Everything worth doing in life is a little scary," Ransom replied.

"But not everything that's scary is worth doing!"

The ledge grew dreadfully narrow in places, now and again forcing them to clamber on their hands and knees up steep inclines. The edges of the rose-colored quartz dug into Corwin's palms, but he wasn't about to let go. At last he pulled himself over the lip of the cliff's summit, his tension easing at the wonderful sight of level ground.

Nine elders stared down solemnly from atop the curved colonnade that bordered the area, weighing the crimes of the solitary figure who stood below.

"We have heard the evidence. Do you deny the charges against you?" asked the Speaker of the Council.

"I do not," the accused blinked in answer.

"Then you know what has to be done. The fog must be dispelled. We cannot allow it to corrupt the minds of our young. Cast yourself into the sea and pass unto the great darkness with honor."

Bowing his head, the accused accepted his sentence with a sullen step towards the precipice.

"Just a moment!" interrupted Ransom. "Before he leaps to his doom, might I ask that one a few questions?"

The Speaker's gaze fell upon the two outsiders suspiciously.

"What is your business here, otherworlders?"

"Dealing with foggy minds is a talent of mine," answered Ransom. "Perhaps I could offer a better solution."

A flicker of voiceless words flashed between the elders as they debated the brash angel's proposal.

"Very well," decided the Speaker. "Ask what you will, but know that his fate rests with the Council."

Ransom strode up to the condemned man and looked deep into his glassy, guilt-ridden visage, his body language telling all without the need of a face.

"You don't look so dangerous, merely confused," said Ransom. "I may be able to remedy that, but you must tell me of this fog. What phantoms haunt your dreams?"

The telepathic being shifted his weight uneasily.

"I know not the words for these visions that torture me so," he lamented, lifting his listless head skyward. "I see dark flesh seared by flames. It cracks and spits, its juices dribbling. Beside it rest mounds of carved cloud, steaming and golden-crusted. There are gemfruits, but unlike any I've ever seen, for these are round and soft, ripe as the sun. Ruby nectars glisten like great dew drops in the shardleaves. And as I gaze upon these things, a hollowness groans within me, gnawing at my insides."

Ransom tilted his head. "What a curious affliction."

"He's hungry!" Corwin declared.

"Ah, but why should he be? He is a star child, and like the stars themselves, his kind needs no sustenance. No living thing in this universe does, you see. They live until the fires within them grow cold, never knowing food or drink."

Corwin balked at the notion. If the organisms of this plane had no biological use for food, then they would never have evolved a hunger for it. That there lived one among them who did was absurd.

"Then one who dreams such dreams should not exist," he stated flatly.

"Then man should not exist!" Ransom shot back, "If there is no true meaning behind your lives, then you are no different from this haunted star child. The longing for a higher purpose is deeply rooted. To not seek it is the most unnatural thing in the world. If it is an illusion, a fabrication, then your existence is absurd, just as a hungry man is absurd in a reality without food."

He turned again to the accused.

"Have you never seen these things before, never heard or felt them?"

"Not in all my life," responded the man. "They are but visions, a cruel curse of the fog. Surely, such things cannot be."

"They are more than visions," Ransom proclaimed. "What neither you nor my client has bothered to consider is this: that an innate desire evidences the object of that desire."

It was a principle that Corwin was familiar with, one that had confounded several of the most famous atheist thinkers, leading men such as Sartre and Camus to declare that life was ultimately absurd. In the angel's worldview, man's desires corresponded to reality, but Corwin's man was a creature conflicted, his spirit forever at odds with the cold, hard facts of the world.

Ransom laid a hand on the troubled star child. He faced the Council and his steely eyes flared brighter than the sun.

"This one need not die! Exile him to the forest. I will take care of the rest."

At the sight of the angel's blazing eyes, the Speaker nearly tumbled from his perch. His sworn duty was to safeguard his people, but how could he distrust such a pure and powerful light?

"And the fog will not spread?" he asked.

"It will not," promised Ransom. "I give you my word."

"Go then, and may your light guide you until the New Sun dawns."

"Until the New Sun dawns!" echoed the Council.

Much to Corwin's relief, they departed without returning down the treacherous cliff side. The slope of the land descended to where a vast, verdant forest sprawled across the interior of the island, an ocean of amber shardleaves that swayed and glittered as they caught the sun.

"Is there truly a way to banish the fog?" the star child inquired.

"Oh, there's a way," said Ransom, "though it may return from time to time."

Corwin was mulling over his attorney's points as they passed through the tree line.

"According to your reasoning, just as hunger evidences the existence of food, man's desire for a higher purpose evidences the existence of god?"

"Correct. And note that I say 'evidences,' not 'proves.' It is not my purpose here to prove the Father's existence, only to prove that belief in him is rational."

"You assume that a higher purpose must have its root in the divine. Why should it? I don't need some religion to tell me why my life has meaning. It was man who created god. If we long for a purpose to make sense of this life, we can create that as well."

"Can you?"

All around them, the crystal forest bent the sun's rays into a mesmerizing prism of light, rife with soft patches of gold and lilac and glints of shimmering pearl that danced like fairies upon the underbrush. Ransom plucked a jewelberry from a hanging vine and popped it into his mouth, an act which made the star child most curious.

"That jewelberry!" he exclaimed. "Why do you do this thing?"

"It's called eating. It's not a bad pastime, though I much prefer drinking, to be perfectly honest."

Fishing a brushed metal flask from his coat, Ransom washed the berry down with a swig of bourbon, hissed a happy exhale and returned his attention to Corwin.

"Suppose that you decided upon the meaning of life, but someone else adopted a different meaning, one that contradicted your own. Which of you would be right? Which is the true meaning?"

"Both," Corwin replied. "One meaning can be true for one person and a different meaning true for another."

"Nonsense," spat Ransom. "If both are true, then nothing is true. Truth cannot contradict truth."

"What if there were no contradictions? What if, unified by scientific reasoning, our race decided upon a common goal towards which to aspire?"

"Even that improbable scenario would change nothing. Universal truths are always discovered, never decided upon."

As they were talking, the land rose on their left, a low roar furtively growing. The ivory-barked boles of the trees parted, giving sight to a wide and rambling river with many forks.

"It doesn't look like there's any way across," mentioned Corwin.

"We could swim or carve canoes," said Ransom. "Or build a giant catapult!"

"Or we could follow the path," the star child suggested.

The path, which won out over the catapult in a two-to-one vote, soon became a ledge that ran behind a chain of waterfalls. Because it wasn't frightfully high off the ground, Corwin felt at ease, far more so than on the previous ledge. The falls themselves were not a violent rush, but a smooth curtain of water spilling over the ridge. They misted the air with a white, spectral fog. As it swirled and strengthened, visions appeared in its folds.

Corwin saw a sunny pasture. In the air was a bi-wing glider, its shadow racing over the grass while a bicycler peddled furiously to catch up.

"In the realm of science, the nature of truth is most evident," continued Ransom, resuming his former line of thought. "Man did not learn to fly by deciding the laws of aerodynamics, but by discovering them and harnessing that knowledge."

The fog rolled and a new scene materialized. Grapes ripened on rows of vines in golden Tuscan fields. A painter stood in the shade, his easel propped before him. With quick and precise dabs of his brush, the canvas came to life.

"You see it also in the arts, for beauty is not as subjective as mortals think. The great painters and composers did not simply decide what beauty was. They discovered it in their lives and devoted themselves to capturing it."

Next came a place that Corwin instantly recognized. It was the frozen foods section of a local grocery store. Rows of

Ben & Jerry's ice cream stared them in the face. Corwin's mortal self stepped gingerly into view like a thief in a jewelry shop, prying open a glass door to the hum of industrial freezers.

"Chunky Monkey, good choice," grunted Ransom with an approving nod. "But even your favorite flavor of ice cream is not purely a matter of choosing. You discovered that some ingredients were more pleasing to your taste buds than others."

"That's not what I would call a universal truth," objected Corwin.

"True," Ransom agreed. "Maybe I'm just getting hungry."

Again the vision dissolved. The white mist was thinning.

"Let's say I grant you that in order for there to be an *objective* meaning of life, it would have to be something we discover," Corwin said as they put the river behind them. "You still haven't proven that there is one."

"Nor do I intend to, but why ignore the evidence written within you?"

"Because I can explain that evidence without the need of any of your metaphysical hocus pocus."

"I'm looking forward to it, but first . . ."

The forest gave way to a small clearing. A circle of stones paved the sacred ground, remarkable for just how ordinary they were. Crystal had accounted for every surface on the island, but not here. These bricks were cut from limestone; dull, opaque and bleached by the sun. Corwin guessed that they must have been quarried from some remote region. Arches ringed the circle, and though the ravages of time had reduced most of them to rubble, two remained intact.

Rising from her seat atop the base of a ruined arch, a female star child addressed them.

"When I heard the Council say that you had been exiled to the forest, I knew you would come here."

"Word travels fast on this island," muttered Corwin.

"That's telepathy for you," said Ransom.

"Gaeda, you shouldn't have come," spoke their translucent companion.

"I'm not afraid," she told him, care and courage shining in her voice.

Though the star children were faceless, or perhaps *because* they were faceless, their words held a depth of emotion that moved the heart as sure as the warmest smile or most hateful sneer.

As the travelers stepped into the circle, something disturbed the air beneath the two arches—a scintillating glow, barely visible from afar. Cycling colors, the light gently coruscated like the surface of a pool.

"Through the portal to my left is a world unlike the one you know," spoke Ransom. "Once you step through, you will not be the same, nor will you ever be able to return. What awaits you there is a life of toil. However, such a life also has its rewards. You'll find that which can fill your hollowness, strange new gemfruits and jewelberries and maybe more."

"But what shall I do when I find them?" asked the accused.

Ransom planted a friendly slap on his back.

"You'll figure it out."

"How can you know all this?" Gaeda inquired. "None can see beyond the gates."

"I walked this land when the sun was young and the seven gates were raised. They hold no secrets from me."

Firm in his resolve, the accused faced the mysterious doorway.

"I'm ready."

"Then so am I," said Gaeda.

The two star children joined hands and strode towards the undulating light. Upon touching it, they became light themselves, melting into the portal. Glyphs that Corwin hadn't before noticed lit up along the arch's bricks and seared in runic circles on the floor.

"You're next," Ransom intoned.

"I'll take what's behind door number two."

8

SHADOWS IN THE STORM

A luminous network of fibers stretched through the blackness like a spider's web, had that spider happened to be a master architect with a penchant for the psychedelic. They brightened from violet to pink before meeting at bulbous orange junction points, and countless pulses of light traveled their length, flashing in the junctions, changing course or forking along multiple routes with the manic speed of lightning channeled through a steel grid.

"Neurons," perceived Corwin. "It's like we're inside a brain."

"A mostly empty one," said Ransom.

There was a methodology to the strobing of the thought highways. Some paths, heavy with traffic, were almost constantly alight, feeding tributaries that branched off in a hundred directions. Other fibers siphoned the signals into huge, lambent clusters where the light cycled in complex loops but never escaped.

"Did you know that the brain can be triggered to sense a presence, even when no one is there?" asked Corwin. "All you have to do is release the right chemical or apply an electro-magnetic current to the right spot, and presto! One 'religious experience' coming right up!"

"A man may hallucinate that he's drowning, but that doesn't make the ocean any less real," replied Ransom. "And you seem to be implying that the human brain is wired for religious thought."

"It is! That's why we have this innate desire for purpose in our lives, but it has more to do with evolution than angels."

Pulling a cigarette from his case, Ransom brought it to his nose like a bow to a violin, the unlit tobacco hinting at licorice and sun-dried raisins.

"I'm listening."

"As humans evolved and grew capable of complex thought, we became self-aware, but with self-awareness came awareness of death, and thus anxiety and depression. Our spiritual inclinations are evolution's answer to that problem."

"So according to evolution, religion is beneficial to mankind's survival," Ransom concluded.

"It was, but we've evolved past that," argued Corwin. "In the modern world, religious thought is like the brain's appendix. Worse, it may just lead us to destroy ourselves!"

"You'd think evolution would have seen that coming."

The fibers were fading, all except for a disconnected few, and these slowly bent and curled into odd but orderly shapes.

"If your theory is right, you haven't eliminated the absurdity of human life. You've confirmed it," said Ransom. "You're left with a creature that has evolved an innate desire for something that doesn't exist."

"Even if there is no higher purpose, that doesn't mean that we can't grasp onto something that makes this life worth living!"

"Think back to your existentialism class. What did Camus say was among the most pressing questions facing an atheist?"

"Should I kill myself or have a cup of coffee?" quoted Corwin, his impeccable memory supplying the answer with ease.

The angel nodded and blew a stream of smoke.

"Any nonbeliever worth his salt should understand the gravity of those words. What's your take?"

"Well I could definitely go for a cup of dark roast about now."

"Excellent!" declared Ransom. "I know just the place."

As the gloom lifted, the fibers became streaks of neon, a dimly burning array of welcome signs and Budweiser logos. They belonged to a strip of cafés, pubs and eateries, all bustling with late night patrons. Breathing in the humid air, Corwin slipped off his coat and slung it over one arm. Wherever he was, this place felt instantly comfortable. Laid-back locals traipsed the streets with an easy gait. They were old and young, and as colorful as the city's colonial architecture. Rarely did the buildings rise higher than two stories, and the upper floors were mostly apartments, their banisters decked with streamers and chains of golden Christmas lights.

"Watch out, son," barked an older gentleman who was just exiting a shop as Corwin brushed past.

"Sorry," he managed.

His gaze trailed after the fellow and a second later it hit him.

"Say, are we back in the real world?" he asked Ransom.

"In your world, yes. But not in your time."

"But that guy just saw me! We must be more than shades here."

"A necessary risk," said Ransom. "A shade can't order a cup of coffee."

"Is this the past or the future?"

"Last summer. Why are you asking?"

But when Ransom glanced to his side, his crafty client was already gone. Corwin had spotted a young couple and wasted no time in accosting them.

"Excuse me, could I borrow your phone?"

His abrupt appearance and utter disregard for personal space compelled the man back on his heels.

"What's the emergency?"

"I may not look like it, but I'm from the future." Like a secret agent, Corwin donned a pair of sunglasses borrowed from a nearby display case. "I need to call my past self and warn him not to come to the aid of any wayward bums who happen to pass out on the subway tracks."

His plea moved the couple, but not in the way he intended, as the man locked hands with his date and promptly hurried off, shooting Corwin the sort of look that was usually reserved for washed-up comedians or the tragically insane.

"It's no use," said Ransom, waltzing over with his hands tucked in his pockets. "You might not be a shade, but the fact remains that you're still dead. There are measures in place to keep your kind from interfering in the world."

"So I've officially joined the ranks of the living dead!" Corwin's voice rang with satirical triumph.

"If you get the urge to sink your teeth into a juicy, delectable brain, do try to resist."

"Now that you mention it, I am feeling a mite peckish."

Ransom inclined his head toward the couple that had just recently made their escape.

"Notice how they've already forgotten you?"

It certainly seemed that way. Corwin spied them not far down the road, where both their pace and their mood had relaxed. A banjo player strummed a tune at a local bar and the happy couple wandered in.

"Your presence here is but a flicker in temporal space," said Ransom. "No longer can your actions leave an impact, not on the world, nor on the fate of your soul."

"Not even if I went on a murderous rampage?"

"If you tried to accomplish anything meaningful, you would undoubtedly find that something would go wrong and your efforts would come to naught."

"Story of my life," mumbled Corwin.

Leaving the busy lights and commotion of the main street, they turned down an alley and walked a little ways to where a hanging sign marked the side entrance to a café. An artsy script announced it as The Cosmic Cup, its sign emblazoned with the image of a sugar cube moon orbiting a celestial cappuccino mug.

Bells chimed as Ransom swung open the door. The cozy interior of the café was sparsely lit, consisting of a coffee bar with several round tables dappling the lounge. A nighttime cityscape adorned the walls, painted skyscrapers climbing towards a dark ceiling studded with hundreds of phosphorescent stars. Amidst their pale green glow, glass globes, crescent moons, peace signs and dream catchers depended from imperceptible wires.

"Not what I would have guessed for your type of place," remarked Corwin as he surveyed the scene.

Ransom's formal attire stood out starkly from the skinny jeans and pop-reference t-shirts of the café's hipster patrons. He strode up to the counter.

"What can I get you?" chirped a girl with raven hair and a nose ring.

"A large cup of dark roast. Oh, and one of those Lunar Lemon scones."

He glanced Corwin's way.

"Sounds good to me."

"Make that a double," Ransom told the barista.

They found a table and a short time later she appeared with their order, along with a porcelain tray loaded with creams and sweeteners. Corwin cradled his mug and inhaled, savoring the rich aroma of freshly ground beans. He took a sip.

"Ah, now that's heaven! I may not know the meaning of life, but I know a good cup of coffee, and that's worth more than all the empty promises in all the divinely inspired scriptures in the world."

Crumbs sprayed from his mouth as he ravenously attacked his scone.

"So, are we moving on to my third hope?"

"Not yet. From the way you humans talk about the meaning of life, you'd think that all creation began and ended with yourselves." Ransom raised his eyes to the star-studded ceiling. "There's a whole universe out there! Behind the question 'Why am I here?' lies the bigger question 'Why is anything here?'"

"Aren't they ultimately the same question?" deduced Corwin.

"They're closely tied, and the best answer is one that holds true for both."

"Or maybe you're just over-thinking things. Life is fleeting, so live each day to the fullest! Isn't that all the purpose that most people need?"

"To live as though there is no tomorrow may mean love and charity to one person, but rape and thievery to another."

Ransom opened his palm and one of the ceiling's phosphorescent stars dropped into it. Flicking his wrist, he hurled the ornament back. As Corwin looked upwards, the glow-in-the-dark constellations shifted. Greenish-white stars beamed brilliantly and receded into a fathomless abyss, the cold silence of space stretching for untold light years above their heads.

"Consider the Question of Origins, the dawn of space and time."

Farther and farther the vista pulled away. Billions of stars coalesced into galaxies, clouds of galaxies into super clusters. Then Ransom clenched his hand and instantly the vastness of the heavens compressed into a single shining spec of light.

"There are two logical stances that one can take. Either *essence precedes existence* (which is to say, there is a preexistent meaning behind the universe) or *existence precedes essence* (that is, the universe simply exists and humans make up a meaning after the fact). Atheists by definition claim the latter."

His hand sprung open, unleashing the Big Bang. The universe exploded forth in a dazzling burst of energy. Space rippled and shimmered, newborn stars gleaming in the hearts of nebulae and quasars whirling with molten fury.

"The problem you face is that a made-up meaning is just that: make-believe. Man doesn't yearn for an imaginary meaning. He yearns for a true one, for something worth dying for."

Corwin didn't dispute the sentiment. The Question of Origins spelled out the dilemma faced by those who sought meaning in a godless universe with sobering clarity. There was a time when he had thought it a simple matter to find purpose, but now he was beginning to see why so many atheist thinkers before him had struggled so arduously with the task.

"It's not that I don't understand, but without proving that a *true* meaning exists, your line of argument is just as likely to sway me towards nihilism as it is towards Christianity. Maybe human life truly is absurd."

"So be it."

Ransom drained the last dregs from his mug and reached into his breast pocket. He withdrew his flask and began unscrewing the cap.

"A good philosophy is like a good bourbon: best when not watered down."

"On that note," chimed Corwin, "I can hardly believe I'm saying this, but I think I need to use the restroom."

"It's no surprise," said Ransom. "That vessel doesn't just look like your old one. It can bleed, sweat, and leak other fluids as well."

The restroom was tucked away in the back corner of the café, a cell of square white tiles that was kept cleaner than most. Corwin still found it odd, feeling relieved as he looked himself over in the mirror while the sink's sensor issued a few seconds of water. He punched the drier and stuck his hands under the roaring blast of hot air. For the first time since he'd met Ransom, Corwin was alone.

Turning to leave, he stopped. From floor to ceiling, the door was covered in black and red graffiti. There were cultic symbols, vertical eyes and words harshly scrawled in some indecipherable language, and he could have sworn that none of it had been there when he came in. Compared to the rest of the pristine room, the door felt jarringly out of place.

For an anxious moment, his hand hovered over the knob. Then the lights flickered and fizzled. Just as the room fell dark, he pushed his way out.

"What the . . ?"

Corwin wasn't in the café anymore. A dingy, derelict alley stretched before him, brown bricks tagged with gang signs and crinkled newspapers littering the ground. A narrow strip of brooding clouds hung overhead, giving no clue as to the hour. His eyes were drawn to a fire that blazed in a rusty iron barrel, where three homeless old men in ragged jackets stood basking in the warmth.

"Ransom! Hey, Ransom!" he hollered. "Why is it that whenever I actually need an angel, you righteous bastards are nowhere to be found?"

One of the bums raised a bushy eyebrow, but the ravings of a madman weren't exactly unheard of in these alleys that society had forgotten.

"I must really be losing it this time."

He had begun to believe, just a little, that maybe there was an afterlife. A part of him wanted nothing more than for the angel to prove him wrong, to throw back the curtain and reveal a higher reality, one where suffering was no more and life was everlasting. But as tantalizing as that hope was, the cracks were showing through, cracks like Mary's wake-up call and this sudden, seemingly random detour through the limbo of a dismal alley. No, the more likely truth was that his brain, or what was left of it, was finally running out of juice.

Corwin heard the door swing shut behind him and spun for the knob. Its lock rattled to no avail.

No way to go but forward.

Past the crackling flames, the alley showed no sign of ending. Plumes of steam ghosted through a grated sewer lid. Chain-link fences barred alcoves and side streets, and wall lamps framed retractable doors in cones of stale yellow light. Eventually he came upon a crossing where another long alley intersected his own. Corwin turned a slow circle, gazing in all four directions, but one way looked as unpromising as the next. No hints of a main street, no gap in the dreary industrial sprawl of high-rises.

Catching a slight movement out of the corner of his eye, he snapped a quick look to his left. Corwin had already scanned that alley, but now the steam drifting up from the sewers was parting. A dark figure appeared, and then another. In moments the path was crowded by a wall of silhouettes marching his way, and something told him that these strangers weren't here to make friends.

As one, the group halted, standing deathly still. Seconds passed in tense silence. They were almost a block away, and yet Corwin could feel their eyes upon him. A cold sweat tingled against his skin.

Why should I be worried? A dead man has nothing to fear.

The stillness broke as the sinister mob burst into a dash, and in that instant all of his rationalizing meant nothing. Everything in Corwin's bones screamed out for him to run. This time he didn't debate.

Adrenaline propelled his limbs, his body moving on pure instinct. A nameless fear gripped him. Who or whatever these people were that happened to be chasing him, he knew that he couldn't afford to get caught.

There are fates worse than death here.

Corwin pumped his legs like a machine, splashing through puddles of muck. In the overcast sky, storm clouds rumbled threateningly, as if the whole world had set its will against him. Spotting a fire escape that zigzagged up the right-hand wall, a spark of hope enkindled his heart, but his leap fell short. The ladder was hoisted hopelessly out of reach.

"Damn it!"

He darted around the following corner, rubber soles skidding as he leaned hard into the turn. Too hard. Something snagged his foot and for a brief moment Corwin tumbled, weightless, through the air. Then the ground came rushing up to meet him. He crashed in a heap of trash and scrambled to find his feet again. But it wasn't garbage that he had tripped over.

"Crazy bastard!" cursed a gruff voice.

Corwin beheld the cause of his spill: a vagrant with a scraggly black beard who, until just now, had been fast asleep on a makeshift mattress of cardboard. Recognition dawned and his eyes went wide.

"It's you!"

Glaring back at him was the same haggard drunk that he had rescued from certain death on the subway tracks. He thought to give the ungrateful bum a well-deserved piece of his mind, but the stampede of rapid footfalls was growing louder by the second.

I don't have time for this!

Pushing the questions out of his mind, Corwin vaulted upright, and in another instant he was bolting down the alley at full stride. The vagrant stared after him with a bitter scowl.

"Don't nobody in this town watch where the hell they're going?"

Corwin swerved left at the next corner, right at the one after that. The dreadful sound of pursuit was never far behind. Sweat beaded on his forehead and his chest heaved with gasping breaths. Adrenaline numbed the aching burn in his legs, but for how much longer?

He rounded another bend and lightning pealed, the flash splitting the sky with a deafening crack. Corwin froze. Less than a block ahead, a horde of shadowy figures was charging in his direction. Somehow they had cut him off. He pivoted, thinking to double back, but the view behind was no better.

"Shit!"

From somewhere nearby, a girl whispered in an urgent tone.

"This way!"

She was hidden in a side street, a gap in the left-hand wall that had gone unnoticed. Without waiting for a response, she fled down the path.

A second lightning bolt crashed and sheets of icy rain began pelting the city as he dashed after her into a shady alley that was even more claustrophobic than those before. The girl was prying back a loose span in the corner of a chain-link fence. Corwin couldn't see her face, but there was something about the bounce of her auburn hair . . .

"Mary?"

"Through here!" she called and disappeared through the hole.

Corwin crouched, pulled open the fence and hastily squeezed through, the chain links clinking as they sprung back into place. Soaking wet, he hugged his knees to his chest and huddled behind a length of sheet metal. No sooner had he gotten out of sight than the alley swarmed with thugs. Boots stomped past his hiding place, close enough to splash him. There couldn't have been fewer than twenty men.

"He had to have gone this way," shouted one of them.

"Find him!" snarled another.

Corwin held his breath. Not moving a muscle, he waited as their footsteps faded into the night, until the only sound left was the incessant patter of the rain.

When all had been calm for several minutes, he let out a long exhale and finally turned to take a measure of his surroundings. There wasn't much to see. Whether or not his savior had truly been Mary, she was gone now. Corwin stood alone in the dank recess of a dilapidated building. It extended for maybe twenty feet before dead-ending beside a pair of tin trash cans. A lone doorway loomed in a pool of golden lamplight.

Might as well give it a try, he figured.

Every other door that he had come across in this bleak maze of alleyways had been obstinately locked, but for once the knob didn't resist. Corwin eased open the door and stepped through . . . into the rear corner of The Cosmic Cup.

9

APPLES AND RAZOR BLADES

"Well, what do you know?" Ransom poked his head through the restroom door. "There really is an alley back here!"

Corwin followed him and stepped out onto a cobbled road. Wintry daylight shone down, snowflakes drifting lazily in the frosty air.

"No!" His gaze darted left and right. "This is all wrong!"

"You were expecting a different alley?"

"A whole different city!" said Corwin emphatically. "For one thing, it was a stormy night. All the buildings were modern. There was concrete and graffiti and that bum whose ass I dragged off the train tracks!"

The foreign city in which he found himself now bore little resemblance to the one that he had just escaped. The architecture reminded him of something out of a Victorian era, with elegantly masonry, steep roofs and smoking chimneys everywhere on display. Tall, narrow windows were crisscrossed with strips of black iron that fashioned the windowpanes into exquisite patterns. A light blanket of snow dusted the rooftops and windowsills, but along the center of each road the ground was curiously dry. So too were his clothes. As a frigid breeze nipped his skin, Corwin noticed gratefully that he was no longer sopping wet.

"I hadn't expected them to make a move so soon," muttered Ransom.

"Who is *them?*"

"The prosecution. It was no lie when I told you that your trial would be a close one. The other side is convinced that your soul belongs to them, and demons aren't known for playing by the rules."

"Let me get this straight," said Corwin. "There's a demonic law firm out there that wants me condemned to Hell, and they don't particularly care about the finer points of the afterlife justice system?"

"If they were to get their claws on you, well, let's just say that it wouldn't be pleasant."

Corwin felt like pulling his hair out. It was all just too much.

"What would they do? Tempt me? Torture me? Give me the Hell sneak preview?"

"It would be torturous, yes, but not merely in the physical sense. They'll show you every dirty, ugly, sinful part of yourself, everything you keep hidden below the surface. You'll see every person you've ever hurt, everyone whose life you could have touched with love, but didn't because you were too lazy or miserly or vain. They'll replay the greatest hits of your worst moments over and over until that's all you believe there is to yourself. And when finally you beg for the torture, then your soul will be theirs."

"Yeah, I'd say that sounds pretty unpleasant," Corwin said dryly.

"I doubt they would be foolish enough to try anything while I'm by your side, but you had best not stray too far," the angel advised. "Be wary of doors, archways, anything that could serve as a portal."

"Well that narrows it down."

As Corwin took a stride forward, an electric crackle sounded from the road. Ransom gave a swift tug on the back of his coat.

"Hold up."

Embedded in the cobblestones were three iron rails. They ran along the middle of the street where the snowy carpet ceased. Tiny ropes of lightning arced between the groove in the nearest rail, and from around the corner arose a high-pitched mechanical squeal. Corwin followed his attorney's example and backed away, just as a steel carriage rolled into view, sparks leaping from its metallic wheels.

Through the window's maroon curtains, an aristocrat peered out. The lens of a monocle gleamed over his left eye, or was it an artificial eye? The oddly complex rim of the device appeared to be a permanent fixture on the man's face. He spared them but a passing glance and then turned up his nose as the carriage trundled on its course.

"I get the feeling that that strange fellow doesn't like us," said Corwin. "Of course, he probably thinks we look rather strange as well."

"Speak for yourself."

Ransom was fussing with a jaunty black top hat that had somehow appeared on his head, adjusting its brim to tilt forward ever so slightly.

"Where did you . . . Oh, never mind!" blustered Corwin.

His attorney wasn't listening. Ransom's attention was focused just beneath Corwin's collar, his gaze resting on a small cross that dangled from a golden chain.

"I recall giving you this cross for a reason." He lifted the necklace briefly, letting it drop back against Corwin's chest. "You should have borrowed its power when you were in need."

"I was running for my life! Clutching your good luck charm wasn't the first thought that came to mind."

"No, your first thought was probably that it was all *in* your mind," groaned Ransom, his perfectly pressed suit snapping as he strode briskly across the rails, which now had stopped sizzling. "In any case, if the prosecution is stepping up their pace, then so should we. It's time we moved on to your third hope."

"People turn to religion because they hope for justice," Corwin recited. "It's something that's rarely found in our world. Good people suffer while their oppressors grow fat and happy. Who wouldn't want to believe that there's an afterlife in which everyone gets what they deserve?"

"But it's not just about the afterlife."

"I'll give you that. Whether they're real or not, gods and devils can often maintain order better than soldiers and barbed wire."

"And most humans aren't fond of lawlessness."

"Aside from a few crazy anarchists, most people prefer the comforts of a civilized society, and any functional society requires some semblance of a moral code. Unfortunately, the simple wisdom of the Golden Rule is seldom enough. The less-evolved among us need a bit more motivation not to brutalize the neighbors, and religion provides that motivation."

Listening and nodding, Ransom reached for another cigarette.

"The threat of spending eternity in Hell can certainly be a strong motivator."

"Exactly!" exclaimed Corwin. "A moral choice holds a lot more weight if it means the difference between eternal bliss and eternal torment. And unlike an earthly king, an invisible god is all-seeing. He knows when you've been naughty or nice, so be good, because if you're not, there's no getting away with it."

"If legality is the measure of morality, then the only true evil is getting caught," Ransom agreed. "But surely there's more to religion's role here. People don't just seek to enforce justice. They seek to understand it."

"As you so elegantly put it while I was captain of the submarine," Corwin said in a sardonic tone, "religion provides the *why* behind moral values."

"But you don't think they need a why?"

"I think some things are self-evident. I believe in doing good for goodness' sake."

Ransom fought back a laugh, grinning as he coughed out a puff of smoke.

"Your generation of atheists is certainly different from the last. If God is dead, are not all things permissible? Are not moral values simply another matter of opinion in the end?"

"Oh please, spare me that tired old argument," drawled Corwin. "You theists are always quick to assume that without religion, society would plunge itself into a chaotic moral vacuum. You make it sound as if we atheists are a bunch of murderous psychopaths! Am I not a good example of just how empty those accusations are? Religion's fanciful threats and promises may have had their place in the past, but humanity has come a long way since the Dark Ages. Contrary to popular belief, most atheists make for perfectly pleasant neighbors."

"Because of their atheism, or in spite of it?"

Corwin took his attorney's jab in stride. "Morality isn't some cosmic insight instilled by the divine, and neither is it purely a matter of opinion. It's an evolved instinct, one that's further shaped by the culture into which we're born."

"It is one thing to say that your genes and environment influence your values, and another thing to say that they determine them," replied Ransom. "Can man not judge whether to follow his instincts? Can he not pass judgment over his culture, and endeavor to shape that culture, rather than merely be shaped by it?"

"You're oversimplifying things."

"That which one passes judgment over cannot be the basis of one's judgment. The compass does not point towards itself."

"Now you're just speaking gibberish!"

"Putting aside the question of free will for now, I think that your godless brand of morality overlooks one rather important consideration."

"Do enlighten me," Corwin droned.

"Regardless of how you come to them, values have implications."

They rounded the corner of a broad avenue and Ransom drew to a halt. Beneath the darkened panes of a shop window, a girl huddled against the stone, her scrawny figure swaddled in a tattered blanket. Mousy brown hair tumbled over her shoulders and her bare feet shivered in the cold. Alone and abandoned, she gazed up pitifully at the two travelers, but her quivering lips had lost the strength to speak.

"This one will not last the night," judged Ransom.

"Then help her!" demanded Corwin. "You're an angel, aren't you?"

"To help her is man's job, not mine."

"Apparently it's not your god's job either," Corwin said with a dark look. "What use is he, if he can't even save one little girl?"

Shedding his cashmere coat, he attempted to wrap it around her, but as he reached down, both his hands and the coat only passed through.

"I'm afraid that won't work," informed the angel. "But so that you might understand, I'll bend the rules a bit. The girl is starving. You may offer her one of these two apples."

His hands disappeared briefly into his suit, producing a pair of ripe apples. One was a bold red and the other a pastel green. He extended them to Corwin.

"What's the difference between them?" Corwin inquired, inspecting the two apples suspiciously. No choice was ever arbitrary when it came to his wily attorney.

"The green one is more on the tart side," answered Ransom. "Also, it's stuffed with razor blades."

Corwin stared aghast, his jaw dropping as he recoiled from the green apple.

"What kind of demented, sadistic asshole are you?"

Ransom smiled like a knife.

"So you'll be choosing the safe and nutritious red apple, then?"

"Damn right I will!" Corwin snatched it out of his hand. "And before you ask, no, I don't feel the need to offer some longwinded justification of *why* doing the right thing is important."

"But you do believe that there is a right thing? To give a starving child an apple that's harmless or one that hides a razor-edged surprise—those two choices are not morally equivalent to you?"

Corwin stooped and held out the red apple. The girl hesitated at first, the dark pools of her eyes wavering, unsure whether this stranger was a friend or a phantom, but hunger proved stronger than fear. She clasped the fruit in her slender hands.

"Not every atheist is a relativist," said Corwin. "I used to think like that, but if one truly believes that all values are relative, then whether you kill yourself or have a cup of coffee, it really is all the same. I decided that life is worth cherishing, both my life and the lives of others. I don't need the infantile promises of religion to motivate me to act like a decent human being."

"A noble ideal, but those words have deep ramifications," spoke Ransom. "To say that one course of action is ever preferable to another is to say that there is a way man is meant to live."

The girl sank her teeth into the apple with a crisp crunch, juice dribbling down her chin. So vibrant was the fruit's color that it seemed almost to glow, and as she hungrily devoured it, sparing not even the core, the chill wind began to lose its bite.

"If there is a way—a true way—that man is meant to live," Ransom continued, "then that implies intentional causality behind man's existence."

Corwin screwed up his face. "Intentional causality?"

"To put it simply: if man is intended to live a certain way, there must be someone who intended it."

"Hence, god," concluded Corwin. "I see where you're going with this. You mean to brand me as a Christian despite myself!"

"It certainly sounds to me like your values imply faith in a personal God," alleged Ransom. "Or does logic tell you otherwise?"

Knuckling his chin, Corwin searched for a weak link in the chain of implications. He mumbled as he reasoned to himself.

"If any decision is truly better than another . . . then there is a way man is meant to live . . . and therefore an intention behind man's existence . . ." He paused, then snapped towards his attorney, lifting a finger for emphasis. "But that doesn't have to imply a divine creator! It's evolution that 'intended' for us to think this way."

"You can't escape that easily. Saying that your genes urge you towards a certain choice is not the same as saying that one choice is *truly* better than another. All you've done is return to the starting point."

Corwin heaved a sigh.

"It sounds persuasive, but once again your argument hinges on the notion of truth. Instead of accepting god, the old me might just as soon have decided that nothing in life is truly good or evil."

"Then it's fortunate that the old you is already dead," Ransom said blithely. "And frankly, I don't believe that. Say what you will about truth and justice, you don't have it in you to give the starving girl the razor blade apple. By their fruits you shall know them. Your actions reflect where you really stand."

It can't be that simple, thought Corwin. The angel's assessment felt appallingly unfair, not to mention insulting, yet he wasn't quite sure how to wriggle out of it.

"Do you honestly mean to tell me that I'm a theist in denial?"

Infuriatingly calm, Ransom seemed more interested in his cigarette than in Corwin's existential crisis.

"You did end up as one of my clients, and I don't represent the hopeless."

Before Corwin could protest, he heard a small voice at his feet.

"Thanks for the apple, Mister," said the girl.

She was no longer shivering. The color had returned to her cheeks and her eyes were bright with a newfound vitality, a healthy glow that no ordinary apple should have been able to bring about.

In spite of his inner turmoil, Corwin managed a smile and instantly felt a tinge of relief. His attorney was right in one respect. He would never dream of inflicting senseless harm upon this child, nor any innocent person. To do so reflected far more than a mere "difference of opinion" in his mind.

"We've spoken much on the subject of morality," said Ransom, "but that's just one dimension of values. The same applies to other scales, as well. The scientist who values knowledge above ignorance, the rationalist who values reason above emotion, the artist who values the beautiful above the bland . . . They all proclaim 'This is how man should live!' And in doing so, they all appeal to a higher order."

A clanking, hissing sound erupted from down the street. As Corwin's head swiveled for the source of the noise, suddenly the girl leapt upright. There was a loud *thoomp* and something whistled through the air.

"Mister, watch out!"

She threw herself hard into Corwin's side, shoving him out of the way as a wire net ensnared her. Steel spikes stabbed the cobblestones and the net pinned her to the ground. Catching his balance, Corwin stared past Ransom and the captured girl to see a hulking mechanical monstrosity.

The steam-powered robot marched towards them one heavy step at a time. Its metallic sides were navy blue and a shield crest embellished its chest plate, marking the machine as an enforcer for the city watch. Mounted atop armored shoulders, its head was a cross between a tube television and a deep sea diving helmet, aquamarine light flooding the glass.

Raising an arm that ended in the barrel of a net gun, the mechanized watchman broadcast an electronic voice.

"Code 484: Unlicensed act of charity detected. Halt and surrender yourselves at once!"

10

THE DIVINE SUPERMARKET

The metal enforcer plodded closer. Clunky gears revolved in its joints and jets of steam vented from the exhaust pipes on its back.

"You need a license to be charitable in this city?" balked Corwin as he retreated a cautious step.

Ransom was scratching his chin.

"Ah yes, it seems I forgot about that."

Glancing above the shop window where they had found the girl, Corwin noticed a panning security camera, its lens now pointed their way and smoldering with an angry red light.

"Violators will be prosecuted!" droned the robot.

They heard the *hiss-click* of another round being loaded into its net gun.

"Such a nuisance," grumbled Ransom. "You're interrupting my valuable attorney-client session time!"

In his right hand he juggled the infamous green apple, casually tossing it and letting the fruit drop back into his palm. The enforcer leveled its gun towards them. With a swift twist, Ransom's arm became a blur and he pitched the apple straight at the robot's glowing face. It splattered on the screen, the glass bursting as a thunderous ball of fire blasted the torso of the machine into a thousand charred pieces. Corwin ducked and covered his head.

"What the hell did you stuff into that apple!?"

Shards of scrap metal whizzed past, raining down amidst curls of smoke and blazing sparks. The robot's sturdy feet were still planted right where the rest of it had stood only seconds before. Somewhere in the distance, a siren began to wail.

Waltzing over to where the girl was trapped, Ransom reached down with one hand and grabbed the wire netting. A powerful tug ripped the net loose, taking several of the road's cobblestones with it.

"Grab the girl!"

"Is that even possible?"

"It is now."

Corwin bent to scoop her up, and this time his body proved solid enough for the task. A clanking clamor echoed through the streets as he hastened after his attorney. They crossed the road, high-stepping over the charged iron rails. Ten thousand volts of electricity crackled between Corwin's legs. Clearing the last rail, he blew the girl's hair out of his eyes. Her arms were locked around his neck and her face buried in his shoulder. Just ahead, Ransom kicked in the boarded-up door to a deserted tenement building, littering the lobby with splintered wood.

"This place will do."

Steel wheels scraped the stone behind them as armor-plated streetcars rolled into view. Corwin's pulse raced, but what seized him wasn't anything like the creeping dread that he had felt in the alley. The danger here was something he understood, and fear robbed of mystery was a beast robbed of its claws. Still, he worried for the girl, and wouldn't abide leaving her to the mercy of the city watch, which he suspected wasn't very merciful.

The inside of the tenement was a dusty, decrepit mess. Flakes of paint were peeling off the walls and cobwebs clung to rusty chandeliers. Rats scampered out of the way, their beady eyes shining in the darkness as the three fugitives rushed up the stairs to the third floor. Ransom led them into an apartment that overlooked the road. Shutting the rickety door, he joined Corwin by the window.

The glass was thick with frost, but not so thick that they couldn't see the army amassing outside. Rear bay doors swung upwards on the troop carriers and squads of watchmen filed out with steamrifles in hand. Several more of the mechanized enforcers had also shown up, their diver helmets aglow, probing the tenement like aquamarine searchlights. Corwin rubbed at the window's icy coating to get a better look.

"I wouldn't do that," warned Ransom.

As Corwin glanced back at the angel, a loud bang rang out. A lattice of cracks split the glass and a bullet buzzed his ear.

"Oh shit!"

Tripping over his feet, he scrambled frantically away, and not a moment too soon. Another volley shattered the window and chewed holes through the wooden frame.

"Can't you do something about this? You made quick work of that robot!"

"Scrapping a hunk of metal is one thing," said Ransom, "but taking human lives is the sort of business I usually try to avoid."

"You should have thought about that before you got us into this mess!"

Rapid footsteps drummed the floorboards of the lobby below.

"No good deed goes unpunished," Ransom muttered.

"How about you snap your fingers and make that bedroom door lead somewhere else?" suggested Corwin.

"I could do that, but where shall we go?"

"Gee, I don't know. How about *anyplace where they're not shooting at us?*"

"We're supposed to be preparing for your trial, not sightseeing. Plus we've got an extra passenger now."

Ransom looked to the girl with a cheerful smile and she innocently returned it, neither one showing much concern over current events. Corwin wondered glumly whether he was the only sane person in the group.

"Unless that skeptical mind of yours is harboring some incisive objection, I'd say that we've covered your three hopes," stated Ransom. "Do you still consider belief in God to be irrational?"

"No, not irrational!" spouted Corwin. "You haven't convinced me that god exists, but to believe in some sort of higher power . . . It's not completely beyond reason."

"Only partially?"

"All that you've established is a vague notion of god, a distant creator that may or may not be knowable to us. But religion doesn't stop there. As an angel, you're no doubt speaking of the Christian God, of Jesus Christ, Father, Son and Holy Ghost and so on. What about all the other gods? Why shouldn't I believe in Zeus or Odin or Ra or Vishnu? God only knows how many millions of gods there are out there!"

"A fair point," considered Ransom. "These days the greatest objection to Christianity isn't that it's a false religion, but rather that it's *just another* religion."

Muffled shouts filled the outer hallway and a splintering boom rocked the walls, the sound of watchmen breaching a nearby apartment. As quietly as he could, Corwin leaned his shoulder into an oaken cabinet and slid it against the door. Even as he did so, he knew that the barricade wouldn't hold for long, and then his unpredictable attorney would have to do something.

The surest ways to get Ransom motivated seemed to involve cigarettes, liquor or a compelling argument. Corwin didn't have any cigarettes or liquor.

"Every religion claims to worship the 'true' god or gods or goddesses. Every religion claims that all the other religions are false. The way I see it, you're not so different from me. You're an atheist when it comes to ninety-nine percent of the deities that man has dreamt up. I just happen to believe in one fewer god than you do!"

"Religious pluralism is a vapid trope," replied Ransom. "Not even you believe that all conceptions of God are equal."

"They're all equally devoid of empirical evidence!"

"And what of philosophical evidence? What of the law of non-contradiction? That the scope of man's knowledge encompasses more than the empirical is a fact to which you already agreed."

"Whether or not one god is more logically consistent than another, the point remains that I can no more disprove Zeus than I can disprove Invisible Zombie Jesus. Moreover, the whole notion that one religion—a single faith among thousands—is the sole inheritor of divine revelation seems preposterously arrogant."

Ransom paced thoughtfully, his face downturned and his hands behind his back. He might have looked less absurd were it not for the young girl mimicking his motions two steps behind. All of a sudden he straightened up, clapped and eagerly rubbed his palms.

"Alright then, there are certainly plenty of gods out there. Let's evaluate them!"

The shift in his tone gave Corwin pause.

"All of them?"

"That's right." The angel grinned. "All of them."

Corwin's shoulders sagged. This was going to take awhile.

A heavy crash rattled the barricade, interrupting his thoughts. He reached reflexively to shore up the cabinet, but quickly yanked back his hands as an earsplitting barrage of gunfire riddled the wooden furniture.

"Come," called Ransom, poised beside the bedroom door. He held the girl's hand in his. "It's a fine day to do some shopping!"

Whatever that meant, Corwin was more than ready for a change of scenery. He kept his head low and sprinted for the doorway. His arm shot out, fingers clutching the hem of Ransom's jacket. Behind him, the flimsy barricade exploded. Watchmen in stiff-collared trench coats surged into the room, but Ransom was already turning the knob. The door cracked and radiant light engulfed them.

"You've got nowhere to—"

The watchman's voice was cut off, the commotion of the apartment now galaxies away.

Blinking, Corwin glanced down at his boots. They were still there, and so were his companions, but the rest of the world was gone. A sheer white void stretched infinitely in every direction. Ransom was on the phone.

"Elsie, what is it? . . . Yes, we ran into a slight complication . . . What? No, I didn't get carried away . . . Okay, okay, so maybe it is my fault, but everything's fine now . . . No, that's really not necessary . . . Elsie? Elsie?"

With a sour expression, he slipped the phone back into his pocket.

"I never knew you had a heavenly hotline," Corwin remarked.

"We used to take calls from the mortal world, but your solicitors are more persistent than the hounds of Hell."

Hovering near Ransom's side, the girl fiddled with a loose thread on her worn and faded rags. Corwin wrapped an arm around her shoulders.

"That was a pretty brave thing you did, pushing me out of the way. So what's your name?"

"I don't have a name," she said, her voice like a bell, "not a real one, but the other kids at the House of Colored Glass called me Blue Eyes, or just Blue, for short."

The nickname was well-earned. Deep as the ocean and strikingly clear, her royal blue eyes put jewels to shame. Breaking their magnetic pull was no easy task.

"They had never seen anyone with blue eyes before, except for some of the metal walkers."

"Where are your parents?" asked Ransom.

"I haven't any. I don't think I ever did. But there was a boy . . ." She scrunched up her face, straining to remember. "My husband."

"Your husband?" blurted Corwin. He hoped that it was only a child's play on words.

"From the place before. He was older than me, just by a little, only it seemed like a lot, because there were many years in his eyes. He was as brave as an eagle and as gentle as a lioness with her cubs . . ." Again she paused in quiet sorrow. "But I can't remember his name."

"What *do* you remember," Ransom prodded her, "from before the House of Colored Glass?"

"I remember a garden. I see it sometimes in my dreams. The Starlight Garden. There were green trees and lakes and stars like bright pearls in the sky. It was always warm and never snowy, and there were no metal walkers."

"That sounds like a good place. I'm Corwin, and I promise not to let the metal walkers hurt you anymore."

"Are you and Mr. Apples going to be my masters now?"

"Let's not get carried away," said Ransom. Pulling off his top hat, he gave it a twirl and hung it on her head. "The truth is that you're not technically supposed to be here, but as long as you don't tell anybody, I won't either."

The angel winked and Blue smiled, pushing up the brim of the over-large hat as it threatened to sink below her ears.

"So where is here?" inquired Corwin.

The great white emptiness felt a lot like nowhere, yet in its simple and unsullied perfection, it also felt like a beginning.

"You worry too much about where you are," Ransom replied. "It's where you're going that matters."

He pointed into the distance and snapped. Low, dark columns reared from a remote point on the horizon, extending towards them like a line of speeding trains—an image that Corwin could have done without. Taking an involuntary step back, he narrowed his eyes and focused. The objects weren't trains, but shelving units. They stretched and divided, sliding swiftly into position along the floor until the whole space was neatly sectioned into department store aisles.

Marble sculptures crowded the shelves, life-size men and women and animals both real and mythical. They struck gallant poses and bore eyes full of wisdom and fury and compassion. Beige tiles multiplied underfoot, replacing the stark whiteness, and seconds later the store was complete. Part cathedral and part shopping center, it was quite unlike any market that Corwin had ever seen. Sweeping arches crisscrossed the ceiling and sunbeams lanced through the marvelous walls of stained glass that served for the storefront windows. Chiseled cherubs spat rivulets of water into a grand fountain beside the checkout lanes where busy shoppers were already queuing up.

Ransom swept a hand over the scene with salesman-like swagger.

"Welcome," he proclaimed, "to the Divine Supermarket!"

Corwin had to step aside as a little old lady barreled past, her shopping cart laden with the statue of a nude, bearded fellow on a circular pedestal. Wherever he looked, customers bustled about in search of their favored gods. A few weren't content with just one, lugging multiple carts full of idols, wheels squeaking as they rolled cumbrously towards the registers. There were people of every race and creed, spanning the ages from antiquity to the modern era. They wore Greek togas and medieval tunics, tribal feathers and Japanese kimonos.

"Here you'll find every god that's ever entered the mind of man," said Ransom.

"It's quite a selection," noted Corwin.

"That it is, but you wouldn't like the customer service. There are no refunds, much of the merchandize is rife with hidden costs, and even the popular brands are likely to gain you more enemies than admirers."

A woman in red cut a determined path through the myriad shoppers. Her high heels clicked with efficient strides, a tablet computer tucked professionally under one arm.

"Why, if it isn't Elsie, my diligent and devoted secretary!" Ransom flamboyantly declared.

Ignoring his greeting, she pushed up her glasses and coolly inspected their young companion.

"This girl is mortal. You do realize that abducting her from her native universe is completely against company policy?"

"She's a bit underage for an intern, but I was thinking that she could tag along with us for a while."

"She's *mortal,*" Elsie repeated.

"A minor detail. I'm sure we can work something out."

"You know that I can't let you do that. I'm taking her back where she belongs."

As she reached for the girl's hand, Blue locked her arms around Ransom's waist.

"I don't want to go back!" she pleaded, tilting her head with a puppy dog stare. "I want to stay with Mr. Apples!"

"Mr. Apples is going to lose his job," threatened Elsie.

"Maybe," Ransom lifted Blue's chin, "but how could I part with a face like this?"

His secretary sighed in resignation. There was no talking sense into her incorrigible boss once he had made up his mind.

"I can't keep covering for you indefinitely. Sooner or later she'll have to return."

"Do me a favor," requested Ransom. "When you get back, visit the Archives and see if you can find anything on a place called the Starlight Garden."

"What's this about?"

"It's just a hunch I have."

Elsie eyed him dubiously.

"When this case is over, you and I are going to have another long talk."

"I'd be lost without you, Elsie!" called Ransom as his secretary strutted away toward the lengthy checkout lines.

Corwin was leaning against a shelf with his arms folded, an amused look stamped on his face.

"Another long talk? It doesn't sound like your methods are condoned by the management."

"Rules and regulations have their place," said Ransom. "But I find that many problems are best solved with a more *direct* solution. If the managing partners don't like it, let them issue a reprimand."

"That's not the way to get ahead in your career, you know."

"I wasn't always a paper-pushing attorney. This state of affairs is but a temporary arrangement."

"I thought you've been at it for eight hundred years?"

"A temporary arrangement," Ransom reiterated.

There was an edge to his voice, a rawness that hinted at some old and bitter memory. Corwin was more than a little curious as to just what sort of career his attorney had left behind, but he prudently decided to let it go for now.

As they strolled past rows of shelves, Corwin's gaze combed the aisles. Above each one hung a sign.

Aisle 14: Gods of Days, Months, Years and Seasons

Aisle 15: Gods of Planets, Moons, Stars and Constellations

Aisle 16: Gods of the Elements

Aisle 17: Kings, Emperors and Assorted Divine Rulers

He threw up his hands in exasperation.

"Surely you can see how ridiculous this is! Even if I were to assume that somewhere amongst all these deities is the one true god, how is anyone supposed to find him?"

"The first step to finding something is defining what it is that you're looking for," said Ransom. "God is, among other things, the answer to a question."

They turned down one of the aisles.

"Take Helios, here." Raising his hand, Ransom indicated a bold figure crowned in a laurel wreath, clutching the reigns of a fiery chariot. "He's the answer to the question: 'What is that scorching disk of light that crosses the sky every day?'

But that's not the question that Corwin Holiday asks when he speaks of God. No, you're too clever for that. An atheist of your caliber needs a worthy opponent."

"Look, it's Hierax!" exclaimed Blue.

Tugging Ransom's sleeve, she dragged them over to one of the neighboring gods: a fearsome lion with three eyes and griffon-like wings.

"My husband used to tell stories of him! Hierax is the god of the high mountains, seer of secrets and patron of warriors that die in battle."

"It looks like Blue didn't worship at the right temple," murmured Corwin. "I guess you'll have to cast her into Hell."

"Fragments of truth can be found in almost every religion," said Ransom. "Blue, in the stories you were told, was there a first god, one who was older than the rest?"

"Teos, father of all," she answered. "The stars are the windows of his palace."

Blue scurried ahead in search of other gods she might recognize.

"Even in polytheistic traditions, there's usually an eldest. This girl is closer to grasping reality than most atheists, though I think you understand more than you let on."

"I don't discriminate," said Corwin. "All gods are equally fictional to me."

"But not equally worthy of refuting."

While they were talking, Blue had climbed onto the lap of a bare-breasted, six-armed goddess, and was hard at work balancing her hat atop the deity's head. She succeeded in hanging it, only to slip backwards. With the routine motions of a professional babysitter, Ransom caught her and swung her feet to the ground.

"Notice that Nietzsche didn't say 'gods are dead.' He said 'God is dead.' He had a specific vision in mind, as do you. So tell me, for a man such as yourself, what is the unspoken question behind the word *God?*"

"The ultimate question," Corwin replied. "Why am I here?"

"Good. That narrows our search considerably. You'd be surprised how many gods haven't a thing to do with the origin of man."

Ransom snapped. As quickly as they had appeared, the vast majority of the shelves pulled away, leaving but a single row.

"But I think we can get even more specific than that. After all, 'Why am I here?' is only part of the bigger question: 'Why is anything here?'"

Again the selection thinned. Shelves slid free, most of them racing into the distance while the truncated row folded in on itself until it became a mere kiosk. Only a handful of deities remained.

"Now we're getting somewhere!"

"You've dismissed quite a few gods," observed Corwin.

"They were answers to the wrong questions," Ransom said simply. "You broaden your definition of God when it suits you, but there's a reason why you never devoted much energy to disproving polytheism or pantheism."

"Maybe because those weren't the dominant religious views in the place and time where I happened to be born?"

"While true, that's only part of the story."

"If there is another part, it's because the pagan gods have no teeth. Most of them are little more than humans with superpowers. You're right in saying that they don't answer life's deepest questions. However, I don't see what's so flawed about pantheism."

"The god-force of pantheism isn't totally flawed. God *is* a force, as Christians affirm when they say 'God is love.'"

"But you insist that he's also a person."

"An impersonal god who is one with the universe might as well *be* the universe. Such a deity wills nothing, asks nothing of man, and is no more deserving of worship or ridicule than the ocean tides."

"That god doesn't sound too bad! Though I must confess, when New Agers used to tell me that god was 'inside you and me,' I couldn't help but ask them 'where?' Perhaps the lord was hiding out in a body cavity that I happened to miss."

He managed to elicit a snicker from Ransom as they approached the lone kiosk. Most of these gods were familiar to Corwin. There was the ever-popular bearded old geezer in a flowing robe. Next in line, iridescent flames licked the leaves of a burning bush. He saw Christ crucified on the cross, and beside him, a dove descending on a ray of light. One vision of God was represented by nothing more than a clear pane of glass framed in marble. In the center of the glass was printed the message: "No pictures, please."

"As you can see, the search isn't nearly as daunting once you give a little thought to your terms," said Ransom. "The God you seek, or rather, seek to refute, is really quite distinct. He is an uncaused cause, a supreme being, a creator who calls forth existence from nothingness by a sheer act of will."

"Yet several gods remain," replied Corwin. "Were I to choose but one of them, the odds would still be against me."

Ransom sauntered in a slow circle around the kiosk.

"You assume that each one of these is a different god, but what if that's not the case? What if these that remain are actually just different visions depicting the same God, some more correct in their details than others, but none altogether false."

"Even if these gods are all one, the religions that worship them are most definitely not. Some of them are liable to chop your head off for even implying that they pray to the same god as the people in the church or mosque or temple across the street."

"Our task here was not to find a religion. Matters of religion have much to do with what a god says and who he says it to. If one is to weigh the truth of such things, one must first know what God is."

"And this god alone is, as you would put it, the answer to the right question?"

"He's the answer to all the big questions, from 'Why is there something rather than nothing?' to 'Why do flowers bloom in the spring?'"

"I thought we agreed that science was the answer to that latter question."

"That depends."

"On *what?*"

"Do you want the long answer or the short one?"

11

SUPERNATURAL FLYING SPACE GEEZER

Corwin perused the kiosk as though taking in a museum exhibit, admiring the finely sculpted gods (or visions of a singular god, if his attorney was to be believed).

The statues were so exquisitely crafted that he would hardly have been surprised if their marble eyes had blinked. Billions had sworn allegiance to this god. Millions had died in his name. He had left an indelible mark upon history, unlike any deity before, but that didn't make him real.

Even if this was the most logical conception of God (a notion that Corwin wasn't yet convinced of), was not the cost too high? And didn't the fact that he seemed such an ideal fit for the puzzle of life simply mean that wiser theologians had dreamt him up?

"As far as gods go, yours is awfully convenient," he said in a tone that meant *too* convenient. "If I wanted to be difficult, I could bring up the fact that you have yet to prove all those other gods are false."

"Unnecessary," replied Ransom. "I need only prove that the Father is uniquely suited to his title. He is not *just another* god. Or do you plan to persist in the trite notion that all gods are equivalent? For someone who prides himself on being an analytical thinker, that sort of pluralism reeks of intellectual laziness."

"I'll not beat a dead horse, but I do have a question."

"You usually do."

"Why?"

"Why?" echoed Ransom with a blank look.

"Why the mystery? Why force man to endure this confusing search in the first place? Does your reclusive god enjoy playing hide-and-seek?"

"If he does, he's apparently not very good at it. Seek and you shall find; knock and the door shall be opened to you, or so it's said."

"But where is the logic in that?" pressed Corwin. "If a reasonable god wanted us to know and love him, he wouldn't hide amidst all these pretenders. A reasonable god would openly reveal himself. I'd have dropped atheism in a second flat if the lord almighty had shown up at the foot of my bed and just given me a stern look."

"Believe me, I do wish he'd do that sometimes," muttered Ransom. "It certainly would make my job a lot easier. But have you ever imagined the consequences? Has it crossed your mind how the world might be if belief in God didn't require faith?"

A consummate darkness enfolded them, slowly lifting to reveal a tidy bedroom. Blades of pale light slanted through the shuttered windows. A middle-aged man lay sound asleep, tucked snugly beneath his quilted comforter. On the end table, the alarm clock's glowing red digits read 6:29, then 6:30. An incessant beeping announced the new day.

Silencing the machine with a groping swing of his arm, the waking man tossed back his sheets and climbed reluctantly out of bed, scratching the leg of his pajamas as he trudged towards the bathroom.

"This is Harold," said Ransom. "His life is fairly ordinary. Five days a week he wakes up at dawn and heads into the office."

Harold flicked on the bathroom lights and rummaged about for a fresh razor and a tube of toothpaste. The rhythmic scratch of teeth being brushed followed Corwin and company down the hall as they made for the small nook of tiles and granite that was the kitchen.

"Harold is what you might call a fallen-away Christian," explained the angel. "He's not anti-religious—not like you— but like many young adults, thoughts of God and the afterlife simply aren't of much concern to him. He may find religion again in another twenty or thirty years when the specter of death looms closer, but in the meantime he's got more important things on his mind, things like his upcoming promotion and whether or not he'll win big in the next round of fantasy football."

Wrapped in a towel, Harold stopped by the kitchen just long enough to put on a pot of coffee before rushing off to get dressed.

"Today, however, that's all going to change."

As the coffee dripped, Ransom raided the fridge and poured a tall glass of milk, then opened the pantry and introduced Blue to the wonder of Oreos. Captivated by the cookies, she studied how to dunk, twist off the tops and lick the cream with the rapt attention of a martial arts master learning new techniques.

Compared to when they had found her, Blue almost looked like a different person. Her spindly arms and legs had filled out, her mousy hair now fell in lustrous waves, and there was a gracefulness to her features that made it harder to guess her age.

Corwin also noticed a slight change in his attorney. Since the girl had joined them, Ransom hadn't touched his bourbon or cigarettes.

A few minutes later Harold burst out of the bedroom in a navy blue suit and striped tie, a leather briefcase clutched in one hand. He poured his steaming caffeine fix into a travel mug, screwed tight the lid and marched for the door.

The pastel light of dawn glistened on the leaves. Ready to face the day, he took one step off his porch, then stopped and stiffened. The coffee mug slipped absently from his hand. It struck the ground with a clack and a splash, but he didn't glance down. His gaze was riveted on the sky, on the impossible countenance that had appeared there.

Glorious rays parted the clouds, beaming forth from the head and shoulders of a colossal old man. Harold rubbed his eyes. *I must be seeing things.* But no amount of blinking made the vision disappear. The man was arrayed in a robe of solid light and had a wavy silver beard. Flames smoldered in his eyes, eyes that stared right at Harold—right through him—piercing the very depths of his soul.

His knees buckled and he stumbled back.

"Oh my God!"

"That's right!" boomed the imposing figure. "It is I, the Lord! Behold me and know that I AM."

"I, I see you Lord," stammered Harold. "I believe!"

"Henceforth all shall believe, but though I have been hidden from man's sight, man has never been hidden from mine. Your every thought and deed is known to me. Will you persist in sin, or repent and follow my commandments?"

"I repent, Lord! Have mercy!" cried Harold. "Whatever commandments you've got in mind, they sound great to me!"

He thrust a thumbs-up to the heavens, his trembling gesture a testament that the Lord was now his dearest pal.

"Harold isn't alone," stated Ransom. "By the end of the day, there won't be a single person left on the planet who doubts the existence of God. And so the Lord will remain for generations to come, a permanent fixture in the sky, lest anyone forget."

"I was thinking of something a bit more subtle," said Corwin. "But I guess it's hard to beat the effectiveness of *supernatural flying space geezer.*"

"Anything less would be rationalized away. A mass hallucination, a government conspiracy, a trick played by the weather. Humans can be very creative when seeking to disregard the miraculous."

Ransom began to pull something large, flat and angular out of his suit. The object that sprang into shape was a diamond kite, white and covered in big red hearts.

"Know how to fly one of these?" he asked Blue.

She nodded enthusiastically, taking the kite and running into the front yard. With his arms folded, the Sky Father gazed down upon the earth in judgment, but he paused in his glowering to return Blue's smile and wave. As she released the kite and gave it some slack, he pursed his lips, puffed out his cheeks and blew.

Harold felt the wind, but he couldn't see Blue, nor the momentary grin on the Sky Father's face. He only hoped that the Devil wouldn't be making a similar appearance.

"As you might imagine," said Ransom, "Harold is soon to become a lot more religious. From this day onward, he'll faithfully go to church, donate to charitable causes and make an extra effort to be kind and honest in all his dealings. But why? Will he do so out of a genuine love for his fellow man, or because he doesn't want to piss off the omnipotent being whose soul-piercing eyes see his every deed?"

"You have a point," Corwin confessed. "But then again, is fear such a bad thing? I thought Christians believed it wise to fear god's wrath."

"Fear of God is the beginning of wisdom, but not the end. While punishments and rewards have their uses in a child's upbringing, it's love that builds true relationships—the type of bonds that endure in the face of absence and doubt."

"A father who hides himself for the sake of love . . ." Corwin's tone was one of mock admiration. "I'll say it again: your god is awfully convenient."

"Your entire universe exists for the sake of love. That may not always be easy to see, especially through the narrow lens of one's mortal life, but I think you'll find that the only logical God is a loving God."

"And you claim that faith makes love possible?"

"Faith makes love *heroic,*" corrected the angel. "To choose love when the benefit is blatantly obvious is simply to be practical. The Father prefers heroes to pragmatists."

On the driveway ahead, Harold had managed to pull himself somewhat together. A new thought delayed him as he reached for the car door.

"Hey Lord, do I still have to go to work?"

"Only if you would stay employed," spoke the Lord.

"I thought so," moaned Harold. "You're not going to send down any manna from Heaven or anything?"

"You don't look like you're starving in the desert," the Lord observed. "Would you like to be?"

"Oh no Lord, that's quite alright!" He hurriedly opened the door. "I'll be off to work now!"

One hand waved skyward as he pulled out of the driveway, just narrowly avoiding a collision with his mailbox. The engine growled and Harold was on his way.

Corwin silently wished him luck, wincing as the car swerved unsteadily in its lane. With all the distracted drivers checking their rearview mirrors for the Lord, it was bound to be a dangerous day on the road.

"I guess an obvious god presents some obvious problems," he said. "How does this all work out in Heaven?"

"If there is any darkness within you, beholding the Father in his true splendor would reduce you instantly to a pile of ashes," replied Ransom. "Only in Heaven is man made perfect enough to endure that sight."

"Oh, is that all? We just have to become *perfect.*"

"An impossible goal to achieve on your own. Luckily, divine grace is offered to all. As to whether one accepts it or not—that choice lies at the heart of why you are born unto Earth in the first place."

"I think I speak for most humans when I say that god should have just plunked us straight into paradise."

"Then faith would play no role in your forming, and as I said—"

"The father prefers heroes," finished Corwin. His voice was a drawl, yet he wasn't discouraged. "But haven't you forgotten something? By your own logic, we atheists are the most heroic of all! We expect no punishments or rewards in the next life. That makes our actions nobler than any believer's when we choose virtue over vice!"

Unflustered, Ransom set his gaze on the clouds.

"Can one who believes in virtue truly be called an atheist? Can one who believes in nothing truly be called virtuous?"

In the yard, Blue's face lit up, the Sky Father tossing her hair and propelling the kite with another draft blown from on high. As he watched her, Corwin's thoughts went back to their first meeting, to the choice of the apple and what it meant. Values had implications.

"You're enjoying this, aren't you?"

"While I can think of better careers, the job does occasionally have its perks."

"Before you congratulate yourself on making god sound not totally insane, you should know that the tables are about to turn," said Corwin. "One might even say that you've played right into my hands."

"Is that right?" asked his attorney sarcastically.

"You said it yourself: I never devoted much energy to disproving polytheism or pantheism. That's because I was too busy shooting holes through the fairytale theology of your god. Making Christians look like idiots is what I'm best at."

"Then you should have no trouble at all doing the same to me," replied Ransom. "And no excuses," he added with a grim smirk.

"If your heavenly father is the most reasonable god that religion has to offer, then the future of atheism is looking bright."

Sliding a hand into his breast pocket, Ransom drew forth a floppy manila envelope stuffed with documents.

"I've got to get me one of those suits," Corwin muttered.

"According to your file," began Ransom in a ceremonious tone, "you outlined your thoughts on the Father's logical shortcomings in an article titled 'The Paradoxical God,' which you penned during your brief but distinguished career as a guest blogger."

"I'll have you know that that article shot straight to the top of Reddit," boasted Corwin, recalling fondly how well his writing had performed on the popular social news website.

"Impressive." Ransom thumbed through a few pertinent pages. "It says here that you highlight five principal paradoxes: the Paradox of Omnipotence, the Paradox of Omniscience, the Paradox of Evil, the Paradox of Hell and the Paradox of Heaven."

Corwin acknowledged each paradox with a sagely nod, looking altogether pleased with himself.

"And that's just the big stuff! Anyone with the faintest care for critical thinking will find that your god is—"

"Hold that thought," Ransom broke in. "Blue, it's time to leave!"

"Coming, Mr. Apples!"

She released the kite's string and skipped back towards the porch, her eyes tracking the red and white diamond as heavenly winds carried it away.

"You were saying," Ransom prompted his client.

"I was about to mention how your god is logically flawed on almost every level."

"Then why don't we put him to the test?"

"Are you sure that's prudent?" Lowering the pitch of his voice, Corwin gave his best impression of an Old Testament prophet. "Thou shall not put the lord thy god to the test," he solemnly quoted. "I recall reading that somewhere."

"We won't be demanding any miraculous signs. In fact, we're not really putting the Father to the test at all. Just the idea of him."

"There you go again, weaseling out of your sacred scriptures," huffed Corwin as his attorney snapped a turn towards Harold's front door. "You people always have an excuse."

12

THE LUNATIC'S LABYRINTH

A *ka-thunk* sounded as the door sealed, leaving Corwin to gaze in wonder at his peculiar surroundings. This most definitely was not Harold's foyer.

"I suppose this is what happens when you hire M. C. Escher to do your architecture."

Stone stairways climbed and twisted at dizzying angles with no regard for gravity. Connecting them were spans of bricks, hallways without walls like the crossroads where they presently stood. The whole place was suspended in a starry void, cold and still, a faraway wind wailing softly.

Above their heads, moths fluttered about the panes of an antique streetlamp. Its incandescent glow illuminated a most unhelpful signpost, busy with arrows pointing every which way, one of them directing would-be travelers straight into the floor.

A plethora of doors dotted the labyrinth, their frames sprouting from the edges of the brick platforms. Banded slats of hand-carved oak, planks of particleboard and steel portals rimmed in rivets, no two were the same. They appeared to lead nowhere, but then, so did the doorway from which Corwin had just come.

"Didn't you say to be wary of doors? If there are demons looking to ambush us, this sure seems like the perfect place."

"Relax," said Ransom. "These doors cannot be opened from the outside, not without a Dream Key, and demons don't dream." Keys jangled on an iron ring as he lifted it, then twirled it on his finger. "Even if they found a way in, they'd just end up getting hopelessly lost. The usual laws of logic don't apply in this realm. In that way, it's rather like your article."

"Or like your self-contradicting god," Corwin shot back.

A thin smile shone on his face. He was eager to get this stage of their debate rolling, confident that his cocksure attorney wouldn't be having so easy a time answering the challenges to come. Up until now, Ransom had offered reasonable arguments, but the god he'd been defending was Christian only in the most basic of terms. A god like that was too distant to compel worship, too innocuous to even bother refuting.

"I can understand keeping one's mind open to the possibility of the divine," he said. "Plenty of scientists have been deists. They believed in the idea of a creator, but doubted how much we could know about him, and were justifiably skeptical that such a being would give a damn about human affairs.

"There's also no shortage of agnostics. I used to be one myself; sitting on the fence, playing it safe."

"You can live as an agnostic, but you can't die as one," said Ransom. "The question of God is like a marriage proposal. You can say yes or no or maybe, but if you keep saying maybe until you're dead, then your maybe might as well have been a no."

Corwin had always suspected that most agnostics just needed the right intellectual push to land them on the side of atheism. Even so, seldom had he engaged them in debate. Arguing with devout believers was just more fun.

In his eyes, Ransom was wading into dangerous waters now. It was one thing to claim that god existed. It was quite another thing to claim intimate knowledge of god's nature and designs. Every major monotheistic religion did just that. As ideas go, a vague god might be simple and elegant. But religion was complex. Centuries of theology bogged down Christianity, and the bigger and more detailed the tapestry, the more opportunities there were to find loose threads.

"I remember it now!" proclaimed Blue, seemingly out of the blue. "When my husband and I were married, there was a great festival! All were invited. They came from across the land, bringing blessings and gifts. The dryads grew me a dress with a skirt of milk-white tulip petals. The mer presented me with earrings of orhalicon shell. And even the zol came down from their cloud lands. Theirs was the rarest gift: a tiara afire with moon tears!

"For seven days and seven nights we feasted, sang and danced, and my husband bestowed upon each guest a title, new names to honor their deeds. I can still hear the satyrs' songs . . ."

She pranced on ahead, humming a whimsical tune as bits and pieces of the past came together in her mind.

"After this is all over," Corwin spoke in a low voice to Ransom, "assuming that I'm not hallucinating this whole thing, are you really going to let them take her back?"

"Elsie wasn't lying. Sooner or later Blue will have to return to her native realm."

"But that place is a death sentence!"

"Was the place where we found her really her realm of origin?" Ransom gave the girl a look as she danced merrily, not a care in the world. "There's much that makes me doubt that."

"But then how–"

"I don't know, but there are people who slip through the seams, find themselves in worlds where they don't belong." The angel called "This way!" to Blue as he mounted a curving flight of stairs. "We've got paradoxes to unravel. Why don't we start with your first?"

"Perhaps you've heard the question: 'Can god create a boulder so heavy that even he cannot lift it?'" posed Corwin. "The Paradox of Omnipotence is kind of like that. If god is all-powerful, then that is to say that he can do anything, and therefore he should be able to create an unmovable object. If he can, then there is limit to what he can move. If he cannot, then there is a limit to what he can create. Either way, his power is limited."

"And so an omnipotent God is a logical impossibility."

"It's paradoxical—a contradiction, just like so many tenets of your nonsensical faith."

"Another deep insight by Corwin Holiday," Ransom sardonically intoned.

"Sarcasm? From you?" Corwin feigned surprise. "I'm shocked! Do you always resort to insults when sound arguments fail you?"

"Of course not! Sometimes I resort to *violence*."

It was probably meant as a joke, but the angel's evil grin told Corwin not to push his luck.

Upon achieving the top of the stairs, Ransom took a second to scan the branching pathways before striking off to his right. The platform sloped upwards, the floor gently bending into a perpendicular wall, but its steep incline didn't even slow him down. He casually walked up the side of the wall as if Newton's law of gravity was actually just a suggestion.

"What are you waiting for?"

The sight of his attorney standing at a right angle above him was odd to say the least, but it wasn't the strangest thing that Corwin had seen since leaving the mortal world. Raising her arms like a tightrope walker, Blue capered after Ransom on her tip toes.

"Here goes," said Corwin.

He stepped warily onto the sloping bricks. The feeling was at once reassuring and disorienting. His footing was secure, the gravity shifting so that there was no risk of a backwards fall. Wherever the soles of his boots were planted, that was the new *down*. However, as he stared into the maze, at the sideways staircases and the floor that was now the wall, he couldn't help but feel a little bewildered. Maybe his subconscious mind had conjured up this place from the stages of some puzzle video game that he'd once played. It looked nigh impossible to find your way anywhere, that is, unless you happened to be Ransom.

With intrepid strides, the angel marched for the ascending stairway on their left. He seemed to know exactly where he was going.

"You humans have a saying: 'There are no dumb questions, only dumb answers.' Well I'm sorry to break this to you, but there *are* dumb questions, and the crux of that paradox is a glaring example of one."

The staircase turned ninety degrees, a short span of level ground marking the corner. On and on it continued in like fashion, as if hugging the interior of a fortress tower, only this tower had no walls. One wrong step might send Corwin over the edge to be dashed against the bricks below, or worse, to fall forever through a dark abyss.

"Like a lunatic's ravings, your argument isn't so much a profound question as it is an abuse of the English language," Ransom went on. "While you're at it, why not ask: 'What caused the uncaused cause?' Or how about: 'Can God create a triangle with four corners?'"

His melodramatic tone emphasized the absurdity of the argument, and Corwin almost felt embarrassed for bringing it up. He had hoped to lay a trap, but the logic that underpinned his snares was coming undone.

Logic, thought Corwin. *That's it!*

"So what if the question is illogical? If god is omnipotent, why should he be bound by the laws of logic? Can your god not define truth as he sees fit?"

"Your mistake lies in thinking of truth as if it were an outside force to which the Father aligns himself. God does not obey truth, nor does he decree it. God *is* truth. It is intrinsic to his being. Truth, wisdom, power, love . . . These forces find their source, their very definition, in the nature of the Divine."

"Then answer me this," insisted Corwin. "Must god remain always as he is now? Can god change?"

A scraping rumble filled the labyrinth and the ground shuddered beneath their feet. Corwin lifted his arms to steady his balance. The whole place was shifting, stone grinding against stone as the stairs bent and revolved.

"Does perfection change?" asked Ransom when the noise at last died down.

"I wouldn't know," Corwin replied, climbing to join the others on a corner platform. "From what I've seen, perfection is about as illusive as your heavenly father." His gaze narrowed as he looked out across the newly rearranged landscape. "Wait, am I standing on a flight of Penrose Stairs?"

The bizarre maze made even less sense than before, as now the stairway on which they stood appeared to form an endless loop, rising and folding back in upon itself. It was a trick of perspective, a shape that shouldn't exist in the real world.

"Separating God from his nature is not your only mistake," spoke Ransom. "Your reasoning was flawed from the moment that you used the word 'can.'"

"What's that supposed to mean?"

"Can God do this? Can God do that? You speak of the Father as though he is some time-bound being that deals in potentialities. God transcends time. He is pure actuality."

"Not the eternity copout," groaned Corwin. "Christians always fall back on their god's magical time-traveling antics when an argument isn't going their way."

"I assure you, the point is relevant," promised Ransom with a chuckle. "God's relation to time makes a difference in the words we choose. The Father has no potential, because he is the realization of all potential. For him, there is no can or cannot. Rather, God does or does not. He is or is not."

"It all sounds like semantics to me."

"Don't be so quick to disregard language. Words have power."

"And what about the potential for evil?"

"Any act of evil would constitute an unrealized potential for good."

"So god cannot do evil."

"He *does not,*" the angel pointedly corrected.

"Hey, don't look at me!" Corwin raised his palms defensively. "Christians were spouting off about what their god can do well before I came along."

"True," Ransom admitted, continuing up the stairs. "It's unavoidable to a degree. Human language is sorely inadequate for describing the fullness of time."

"How delightful," spat Corwin. "Another concept that's beyond my mortal mind! Religions love their mysteries, but what use is an idea that can't even be comprehended?"

"Mysteries don't exist simply to be mysterious. If there was nothing to gain from the concept, the Father would never have revealed it to you in the first place."

"And what have we gained?"

Another tremor shook the ground and the stairway divided between them.

"Perspective!" shouted Ransom as the stretch of stairs on which he and Blue stood pulled up and away.

"Don't just leave me here!"

"I won't leave you, Mr. Corwin!"

Blue took one look and nimbly leapt down, right over Corwin's head, landing with cat-like reflexes behind him.

"Meet me at the top of the stairs," yelled Ransom.

"This place is a damn maze! How are we supposed to get there?"

"Stick with Blue. She knows the way."

As the upper half of the staircase rose, Corwin and Blue's half lowered, the stairs leveling out to form a walkway that met flush with two other paths. Picking a direction, Blue hummed along, a spring in her step, her threadbare dress fanning like a ballroom gown with each graceful twirl.

"Of course Blue knows the way," muttered Corwin under his breath. "Why wouldn't she?"

He followed his unlikely guide up staircases and around bends, past lamp posts and over sloping walls until he couldn't tell which way was up.

"Are you married, Mr. Corwin?" asked Blue as they emerged from a barrel vaulted tunnel.

"Not me. Never got the chance."

"What's it like where your home is?"

"Well, it's kind of like the place where you were flying your kite, only with fewer trees and bigger buildings. There are carriages that move without rails and long, snowy winters. Sometimes the sun comes out. And you can find some good people, but only if you look hard enough."

"Are you going to go back?"

"I don't think so."

"But I bet you miss it, don't you?"

"A little."

"My husband once told me that nothing good goes away forever. Someday all the good things will be new again. New, he said, but not the same. Never the same, for then there would be no adventure in our reunions."

Corwin smiled. "I hope he's right."

Their walkway intersected with another beneath the quaint brick dome of a gazebo. Blue had begun on a course straight through when something drew her attention to the left. She tilted her head and concentrated, as if listening for an elusive whisper that she alone could hear.

The stop was a welcome respite for Corwin, who propped one arm against a pillar.

"Are we lost?"

Like a bloodhound tracking a scent, Blue's instincts had thus far sniffed out an invisible trail. Her confidence was infectious, and somewhere along the way Corwin had ceased worrying about where they might end up. But now she looked conflicted.

"Not lost," she said. "Two ways."

"Which is the faster way?"

"Straight."

"But from that look in your eyes, I'm guessing you want to go left."

"I'm not sure why." As she stared down the left-hand path, a confused longing came over her. "I just feel I'm supposed to."

Corwin shrugged off his weariness. "Left it is, then!"

Blue's expression brightened at his words, though he still spied traces of sadness, shadows stitched in the arctic gems of her eyes.

She kept an ear to the far winds as they made their way. Her steps had lost their bounce, but there was a new type of energy, a hope or conviction that Corwin couldn't quite pin down. Content to follow, he let his thoughts drift to the many doors that edged the labyrinth roads. One appeared to belong to a ritzy hotel, Room 1901. Another was iron, eaten by rust and half-covered in peeling paint. Some bore windows, like the porthole in the door ahead, but they offered no glimpse of the worlds beyond. Even when Corwin leaned to inspect it from behind, the door's view was the same, its glass infused with amber light.

To reach out and turn one of the knobs was a constant temptation. He resisted it for the very practical reason that he hadn't the slightest clue what would happen. Perhaps he could peek through, harmlessly open one of the doors—just a crack—and reseal it when his curiosity was satisfied. Or perhaps it wouldn't be that easy. What if opening a door meant getting pulled into an alternate universe? And what if someone or something was waiting for him on the other side?

Feeding his curiosity with daydreams, Corwin didn't right away notice that he had lost his guide. Alone, his mind raced back to the here and now.

"Blue?"

No answer came, but it took only a second to spot her. Blue stood motionless some yards behind, her gaze glued to a large, stout rectangle of tarnished silver. The door was elaborately engraved, vines weaving a Celtic pattern along its border. In the center rose a tree. Seven stars hung above it, pointy crosses in the sky.

As Corwin drew near, Blue turned, and seeing her face he immediately dropped to one knee.

"Why do you kneel?" she asked, her voice a golden harp.

"It just seemed like the right thing to do . . ." he kept his eyes to the ground, "when in the presence of royalty."

"But you are not one of my subjects, Corwin. You are a friend. Rise."

He glanced up, but the vision of Blue was so resplendent, so stunning that he dared not look upon her. Instead of standing, his utmost urge was to dig a hole and crawl shamefully out of sight.

"If it's alright with you, I'll just stay down here."

Soft hands cupped his cheeks and the gentle warmth of spring poured over him. The scent of tulips perfumed the air as she raised his head, her sapphire eyes meeting his.

"Rise."

However unworthy he felt, Corwin had not the power to refuse her.

"My true name is Mirielle," she said. "You and the angel have done much for me."

"Um, my lady–"

"Please, call me Mirielle."

"Lady Mirielle, how did you come to be where we found you?"

"There is a place in the Starlight Garden, a meadow with many ponds. By day their halcyon waters glisten clear, but under the stars, the ponds reflect distant realms, worlds far removed from our own.

"One night while my king slept, I walked alone amidst the reflected lands, and there I saw a city mantled in dazzling white. Never before had I seen snow. My king had warned me against swimming in that place, but I thought that if I could just wade by the shore, perhaps I might feel some shadow of that land, know what it was to live as those people bundled in furs lived."

Her fingers traced the grooves in the silver door.

"That was a long time ago, and now I fear to return. What if my foolishness has brought shame upon my king?"

"No!" The word leapt out, louder than Corwin had intended. "He won't be ashamed of you. I'm sure that more than anything, your husband just misses you."

She hugged him, this same girl that had wrapped her arms around his neck while he carried her over electrified rails, only now her touch was enough to melt the coldest winter freeze.

"I thank you, Corwin! You will always be welcome in our land. And give my thanks to the angel!"

"About that . . ." he floundered, remembering where he was.

"Left at the next lamp post, then the second flight of stairs on your right."

She rested a hand on the doorknob.

"Can I ask you one more thing?" Corwin's request stalled her. "How can you tell which way is which in this maze?"

"After I left the Garden, the past faded, but the mists of the future began to clear. I can see where things lead, where time will take them."

"You can see into the future?"

The revelation struck Corwin like a ton of bricks.

"Only to the next bend in time's road." Her hand went to his forearm and squeezed. "Beware the one who wears false skin! Beware the whisperers!"

13

THE SOULLESS STRANGER

At the top of the stairs, Ransom held a phone to his ear.

"That's what I thought . . . No need, it's already been taken care of . . . Thanks Elsie, and stop worrying. We're ten steps ahead of them. I'll see you."

"Blue says thanks," said Corwin. "And her real name is Mirielle, by the way."

"Queen Mirielle of the Starlight Garden. Perhaps we can pay a visit when this is all over, provided that you're not in Hell, of course."

"Of course."

"And that would be our exit."

Near the corner of the platform stood a blue plastic door. As Ransom pulled its lever, the slider above switched from "occupied" to "vacant." The labyrinth vanished and the two travelers stepped out into a breezy autumn night. There was dirt underfoot and a full moon in the sky, its glow limning the clouds with a silver sheen. It might have been a pleasant change, if not for the acrid stench.

Cringing, Corwin turned to discover a row of filth-encrusted porta potties. In front of each was a line. At the head of the nearest, a portly man in a Red Sox cap was regarding them with a look of amused disbelief.

Ransom strode right up to him, his aloof demeanor not ruffled in the slightest.

"Whatever you think went on in there, I assure you that the truth is far stranger."

"Nice choice on the door," Corwin whispered cynically as they marched towards the colorful lights and blaring pop music of the fairground.

Families were everywhere, mothers clutching their children's hands and fathers with toddlers riding on their shoulders. Packs of teenagers roamed the trampled grass, navigating between food stalls and game booths, presenting their tickets to vendors and lining up in front of noisy, electric carnival rides that invariably looked more thrilling than safe.

That was the point, Corwin reminded himself, though a few of the rusty rides stood out to him as lawsuits waiting to happen.

He recognized several of the attractions, sights that brought back memories from his childhood. They walked past the Gravitron, a chrome flying saucer that spun in a stomach-churning whirl. Whoops and hollers arose from the bumper cars as they swerved and rammed each other again and again. A Viking ship swung like a great pendulum, its screaming sailors lifting their arms to the sky. It struck Corwin that these were all familiar but different. The painted backboards, the blinking lights, the horned dragon on the prow of the ship—they didn't quite match the rides that he so vividly remembered.

This place might have been the past, but it wasn't his past, and that knowledge came as a relief.

Corwin hadn't been to a carnival since he was ten years old. His parents had taken him then, his father holding his hand as he gleefully dragged them towards one ride after another. How big and strong that hand had felt! And how frail his father had become, reduced to a vacant-eyed shell of his former self in those last days. Corwin clenched a fist and briefly shut his eyes, blocking out the memories.

Ahead rose a huge red-and-white striped tent, its pinions fluttering in the breeze. The interior was aglow, promising hot food and live music, games of chance and a place to rest one's legs. Ransom's shadow lengthened as he approached the furled flaps of the entrance.

"It's a shame," said Corwin. "I bet Blue would've loved this place."

In unspoken agreement, Ransom drew a fresh cigarette from his case. A snap brought a tongue of flame to his index finger, the tobacco's glow swelling bright as he took a drag.

"Before you start puffing away . . ." Corwin pointed to a sign posted beside the tent's entrance. A red circle and slash barred the icon of a cigarette.

"No smoking?" scoffed Ransom. "Damn communists! They're welcome to try and stop me."

"You might give a thought to the children, not that I'd expect it from you. For an angel, you're a terrible role model."

Ransom gave a loud groan.

"Fine!" Cinders hissed as he crushed the cigarette's tip between his fingers and flicked its smoking butt into the nearest trash bin. "Happy now?"

His client's victorious smile was almost enough to make him light up another.

As they stepped inside, the tantalizing aroma of fried dough and cinnamon lured Corwin's eyes to a nearby stall where a bundle of long, ridged pastries had been set to cool.

"Churros! I haven't had one of those in forever."

"I was leaning more towards the funnel cake," said Ransom.

"Trust me," urged Corwin. "You want a churro. They go great with bourbon."

The angel perked up.

"Your arguments are getting more persuasive all the time!"

With a steamy, sugary stick of crisped dough in hand, Corwin launched into his second paradox.

"The Paradox of Omniscience is pretty straight-forward: If god is all-knowing, then he knows the outcome of your every decision before you make it. Given the choice between A or B, god knows that you're going to choose A, and god cannot be wrong. Therefore, you don't really have a choice. There was never any possibility for you to choose B, because you cannot choose other than as god knows."

"So either man doesn't have free will, or God doesn't know everything," Ransom summarized. "The Father's knowledge leaves no room for chance."

"Correct," said Corwin. "And just because your god is beyond time, that doesn't mean that he gets a free pass."

"God's transcendence is no less relevant here. It means the difference between 'God *cannot* be wrong' and 'God *is not* wrong,' between 'man *cannot* choose other than as God knows' and 'man *does not* choose other than as God knows.' But poor wording aside, your puzzle deserves a deeper look."

Ransom bit into his churro, abruptly halting as a pack of children bolted past.

"Tasty," he grunted.

They veered towards the game booths while a cover band performed John Cougar Mellencamp's "Authority Song" on stage, playing to dozens of exhausted parents who were more than happy to sit down and take a listen.

"The simple answer is that there is no paradox," Ransom asserted. "That the Father knows the outcome of your choices doesn't mean that those choices weren't yours. The conflict is a contrived one."

"There's nothing contrived about the notion that your god essentially dooms people before they're even born! For every soul that ends up damned, the lord chooses to create someone, knowing full well that the poor bastard is destined to spend eternity roasting in Hell. How is that not ridiculous?"

"It's only ridiculous if you didn't have a choice."

"But god knew!" Corwin insisted. "He knew where the cards would fall. He shuffled the deck and he dealt you your hand."

"A card game is a bit of a crude example," replied Ransom, his shrewd gaze scanning the big top.

"I take it you've got a better one?"

The answer sparkled in Ransom's eyes as he spied what he was looking for.

"Have you ever played pachinko?"

Nestled between goldfish catching and ring throwing was a game booth that went largely ignored. A sign above it read *Pirate's Treasure*, the words seared into a broken strip of wood. The booth was manned by a gap-toothed fellow who clearly took his job seriously. He grinned at passersby, looking every bit the pirate with his eye patch and skull-and-crossbones bandana, a plastic cutlass strapped at his side.

"Ahoy there, mateys! Only three tickets ta play!"

"Three tickets!" squawked the parrot on his shoulder.

There was no line, but the game did have one devoted fan. A boy in a pirate hat had been playing for some time, trying his luck in hopes of scoring enough points to win one of the many prizes displayed along the booth's rear wall. Steadfast determination was etched on his face, and Corwin guessed that he wouldn't be quitting any time soon.

"Tickets?" Ransom looked askance as he sauntered up. "Any chance you take cash?"

"Ya gots ta have tickets ta play," maintained the crusty pirate.

"Three tickets!" his parrot repeated.

With a magician's flourish, Ransom flipped his palm, pulling a folded one hundred dollar bill out of thin air.

"But my friend here loves games, and he's terribly impatient."

"Well why din'cha say so?" Swiping the bill from his hand, the pirate squinted as he held it up to the light. "That thar be a mighty fine ticket!"

He promptly snatched a pair of prizes off the wall.

"Congratulations, me boy!"

The man thrust a stuffed tiger and a purple squirt gun into the boy's arms, then swiveled his shoulders and propelled him on his way.

"Now shove off!"

Corwin shot his attorney a sidelong glance.

"Creating money out of thin air . . . Some might call that counterfeit."

"Strange," said Ransom offhandedly. "That's not what they call it when your banks do it."

"Save the lecture on monetary policy for the Federal Reserve."

"I thought I told you that I don't represent the hopeless."

Handing over a white ball that had probably served as a billiards cue ball in the past, the pirate retired to his seat behind the ticket box. Corwin and Ransom had the pachinko board all to themselves.

Like many of the carnival games, the board looked as though it had been constructed in a handyman's garage. A large wooden plank made up the backboard. It leaned like a pinball machine, rectangular and bordered with low walls. Numerous round pegs were staggered along its length, with slots at the bottom to catch the ball. Each was labeled with a point score, though the winning slots would have been obvious even without them. The coral blue waves of a tropical ocean colored the board. An unlucky player might end up in a slot that was home to shark fins or a black-flagged pirate galley, while those more fortunate would see their ball come to rest by the mermaids or on an uncharted island, next to palm trees and a heaping treasure chest.

"Pachinko is one of Japan's great gambling pastimes," said Ransom. "One look at the board should be enough to give you the gist of it."

"I drop the ball in from the top. It gets bounced around by the pegs as it rolls down, and I end up either rich or screwed, only it seems that my chances of getting screwed are disproportionately higher," deduced Corwin. "I can definitely see the parallels to Christian theology."

"Perceptive as always," Ransom droned. "Now imagine that the player is God and you are the ball. God starts the ball rolling with full and perfect knowledge of the outcome. Let's also say that every peg on your journey represents a decision, and God knows which way you'll bounce. He knows your final destination. The question is: has God forced you along your path?"

"Yes," answered Corwin. "In that scenario, your path and your fate—it was all predetermined. Moreover, god made the rules. Forces like gravity and momentum were implemented by him. The game was rigged from the start."

Ransom dropped the cue ball into play, watching as it clunked from one peg to the next on its bumpy descent.

"Since the pegs are decisions, let's replace gravity and momentum with, say, one's environment and biological urges. I believe we already spoke on the roles of nurture and nature?"

"Right. And your position was that those forces influence our decisions, but don't totally determine them."

"If they do, then you don't really have free will," stated Ransom as the ball caromed into a slot encircled by sharks, "with or without God."

"That makes sense."

143

"And you do believe in free will, seeing as how you've already spoken about making choices and even appealed to the existence of goodness, a concept which is surely absurd otherwise."

"How do I put this?" considered Corwin. "I feel that free will exists. It's not something that I can prove, and maybe I'm wrong, but not believing in it would make life intolerable."

"How very *religious* of you," replied Ransom. "Then let's apply that same logic to the game."

Snatching up the ball, he placed it a second time at the top of the board.

"Imagine now that the ball has free will. Forces such as gravity and momentum still play a role, but they can be defied. For every peg in its path, the ball ultimately decides which way it will bounce."

This time the downward journey made for an odd spectacle. It began with several predictable bounces, but upon reaching the leftmost peg, the ball rebelliously changed course, going on to cross the board in the complete opposite direction.

"Would you still say that God has rigged the game?"

"God still knows," answered Corwin. "I wouldn't want to gamble against him."

"And that makes you wiser than Lucifer, but the question remains: If one's choices are more than the result of physical circumstance, then where is the conflict? Is it not possible for God to know one's decisions without compelling them?"

"Perhaps it's possible. I don't know!" Corwin knocked the ball from its slot beside the treasure, consigning it again to a watery grave. "Either way, that doesn't absolve your god from dooming people. As you said, he starts the ball rolling, fully aware of how the game ends."

"And now we get to the real issue!" declared Ransom. "You see, your argument isn't actually about what's possible."

"And what, according to you, is my argument about?"

"It's about what's *fair*."

Pausing a moment to digest the angel's words, Corwin found that he didn't entirely disagree.

"If you're saying that I think god judging us is unfair, then sure I do! How can you defend a supposedly loving father who chooses to create souls that he knows will be damned? Any reasonable person would hold god responsible."

"I never said that he wasn't."

"You're doing that thing again, that thing where you agree with me and then flip my position upside-down!" huffed Corwin. "The point is that if god is responsible, then he has no right to pass judgment on us."

"Responsibility is a little more complex than that."

With a pealing flash, the carnival disappeared. Corwin heard the rapid scratch of pencils against paper and a teacher's strict voice.

"Ten minutes to go," she announced.

"I remember this place," said Corwin, recognizing the yellow cinderblock walls and plywood desks.

"Your old high school, Room 303, senior year," said Ransom as he strode invisibly between the students. Hunched over their papers, they jotted formulas in a rush to beat the clock. "You elected to take an AP course in calculus, and while you managed to pass, this particular test wasn't your finest hour."

He stopped at a desk beside the windows. A teenage Corwin was tapping his pencil anxiously, his brow furrowed in thought.

"That's right," said Corwin. "I failed a calculus test, though I don't see what this has to do with our debate."

"You're too hard on yourself, Corwin. Are you sure that the responsibility for that failure lies with you? Perhaps we ought to blame the teacher who gave you the test, or perhaps Isaac Newton!"

"I'd call that a bit of a stretch."

"Yet it's true, isn't it?" pressed Ransom. "If no one had introduced the world to calculus, you would never have had to study it, and thus would never have failed your test."

"Somehow I doubt that Newton foresaw my high school test results."

"Would it matter if he had? Intentional or not, actions have consequences. Newton deserves a share in the blame, as does God."

The classroom evaporated, returning them to the trodden grass, crowded booths and twanging guitars of the carnival big top. Ransom grabbed the pachinko ball off the board and spun it on the tip of his finger.

"In the ultimate sense, the Father is responsible for everything. However, God's ultimate responsibility does not erase man's proximate responsibility, no more than Newton's part in the discovery of calculus erases the fact that you didn't study enough for your test."

He yanked his hand out from under the ball and Corwin reflexively reached to catch it.

"Direct fault still lies with you," said Ransom as his client fumbled, the ball slipping through his fingers.

Corwin bent to retrieve it from the grass.

"Responsibility isn't simple. It's not purely either-or. On that I agree. But even if god doesn't force us to hang ourselves, you'd think he could have given us a little less rope. And isn't the penalty for losing this game too high?"

"Let's not get ahead of ourselves. The Last Things are yet to come."

"Then perhaps you can answer my second point, because it seems that there's one critical choice that I don't get to make."

"And what choice is that?"

Corwin tossed the ball back to its startled owner, whose effort to catch it sent him toppling backwards in his chair.

"Whether or not I want to play."

With a deep look, Ransom strolled from the booth.

"To choose whether one comes into existence or not . . . Now there's a real paradox!"

He sniffed the air and his hawkish gaze sharpened.

"Is that homemade apple cider?"

At a busy stall on the other side of the concert's seating area, a curly-haired woman was pulling drinks from a large oaken keg. Ransom growled hungrily. And faster than his client could say "evolution," he was off, blazing a trail towards the keg with laser-like focus.

"I'll give him this," uttered Corwin. "He's a man who knows what he wants."

He started after his attorney, but a haunting sense of unease brought him abruptly to a stop. Someone was watching him. A brisk, whispering gust blew back his hair as he peered out into the gloom. Fairgoers were coming and going, drawn to and from the big top as if swept along on lazy rivers. All seemed to be in perpetual motion. All except for one man.

Beyond the threshold, where the tent's glow bled to night, he stood unnaturally still, his dark, unblinking eyes pinning Corwin with a soulless stare. Corwin swallowed hard. He wanted to run or shout for Ransom, but he couldn't move, couldn't pull his gaze away. The man's stare held him like a vice, and he remembered. Those eyes. He'd seen them once before—a reflection in a window on a bright autumn day.

The stranger was tall and gaunt, with a bald head and wrinkled skin as pale as a corpse. His suit and tie were woven of purest pitch, as though light feared to fall upon him, and there was a falseness to his features. Corwin could feel it. The man was a lie, a mask, a monster in a meat suit.

He radiated a silent malice, calm and assured. No one else existed. Not the crowds, nor even Ransom. He and Corwin alone were real. And he saw everything, *knew* everything, with eyes opened wide—too wide, as if he had no eyelids at all. A hideous smile creased his lips.

Corwin momentarily lost sight of him as a family walked between them. And when they had passed, like a phantom, the dark-eyed stranger was gone.

14

A Savior to Some

"You look like you've see a ghost," said Ransom, handing his client a cup of piping hot apple cider.

"And if I have?"

"It's certainly possible," Ransom shrugged. "Some would say that you're haunting this carnival as we speak."

Corwin forced a smile, but didn't laugh. The memory was too fresh, his nerves frayed and raw.

"What if it wasn't a ghost? What if it was . . . something else?"

The angel's gaze thinned as he surveyed the crowd.

"If there was a presence here, it's gone now. I'm not sensing anything unusual."

"No disturbances in the Force?"

"Fear not, young padawan." Ransom turned for the yawning flaps of the tent. "Let's get some fresh air."

Upon finding a bench, he sat himself down and reached for his trusty flask, topping off the cider with a generous pour. He extended it to Corwin, who eyed its brushed metal finish uncertainly. A little something to take the edge off was tempting, but he decided against it.

"I'd hate to see what would happen if you ever ran out of liquor," remarked Corwin as his attorney sipped the cider, judged it half a jigger short of the golden ratio, and set immediately to remedying the situation.

"There's a man with the right idea!" declared a scruffy fellow who happened by. "I would drink to your health, good sir, but I seem to have run dry."

He wasn't talking about cider, of which he had a mostly full cup. From his jacket appeared a leather-wrapped flask, held upside-down, one last whiskey teardrop falling sadly from its lip.

"Well don't let that stop you!" Ransom offered his own flask in an act of angelic charity, but as the man leaned near, he yanked it back. "But be warned, this stuff packs quite a punch! Just one sip, and you're liable to wake up with the kind of hangover that makes a man rethink his life."

Far from dissuaded, their newfound friend only smiled all the wider.

"Sounds like my kind of poison!"

While Ransom spiked the man's cider, another passerby took notice, stopping some feet away. Thirsty eyes panned slowly from his plastic cup to the bourbon, then back again.

Unable to resist, Ransom raised his voice.

"Step right up! Free drinks all around!"

It didn't take long for a small, boisterous crowd to gather, the circle of drunks toasting Ransom, each other, the night, and just about anything that came to mind. Corwin sat back and watched the proceedings with a mixture of admiration and chagrin.

"Jesus may have fed five thousand, but with that bottomless flask of yours, you could make a true believer out of every alcoholic on the planet."

Ransom fished his cigarette case from his breast pocket.

"Don't forget that I've also got an endless supply of smokes."

At his side, a man gawped in slack-jawed amazement.

"There is a God!"

The angel eyed Corwin. "Now why can't you be more like our friend here?"

Ten minutes later and the party had died down. A snoring vagabond slumped on the bench between them. Half a dozen others lay curled up on the ground, passed out like a troop of jolly narcoleptics.

"Can't say I didn't warn them," Ransom intoned.

Across the grassy lane, a handful of children raced up the drawbridge of Lucky's Castle, disappearing beneath the white teeth and scarlet lips of a clown's gaping maw. Part fun house and part obstacle course, the castle zigzagged up four stories, complete with a climbing net, a mirror maze, rotating tunnel rooms and even a teetering rope bridge tethered with bungee cords. The last was suspended between twin guard towers that rose from either end of the castle walls.

Plexiglas windows gave a glimpse of the hectic romp. Some children dashed through the rooms, playfully shoving their friends, intent on being first to reach the top. Others tackled the course at a more measured pace. One rung at a time, they grappled up the slope of the climbing net, making steady progress while hastier children thrashed, arms and legs entangled in the ropes.

"What if we're both wrong?" supposed Corwin. "About humans having free will, I mean."

"Determinism has a comforting ring to it," said Ransom. "It must be nice to look upon all the depraved deeds of mankind and be able to say 'they cannot help but act as they do,' though it must be a nuisance as well."

"How can it be both?"

"To live in a world without heroes or villains, ever reminding one's self that responsibility is fiction, that there are no persons, only processes, despite everything in the core of your being crying out to the contrary . . . Such self-imposed brainwashing hardly seems worth the effort."

"The only good reason to believe something is if it's true," Corwin reminded him. "If free will isn't, then there's no greater waste of effort than religion."

"Without free will, there's no such thing as wasted effort, only the inevitable turning of the gears."

Atop the castle a mischievous boy was leaping on the suspension bridge, sending great ripples through the cords. The sudden dip and rise caused some to lose their balance and plummet into the ball pit below, but all eventually made it to one of the two slides, red and yellow, that corkscrewed down from the right-hand tower.

"Reason alone cannot disprove the determinist who claims that choice is a lie, nor the relativist who rejects moral absolutes," continued Ransom. "But such creeds always fail the test of real life. You won't have much luck finding a parent who denies evil or accountability when it comes to their child getting abused."

"You won't have much luck finding a parent who chooses to 'love your enemies' in that situation either," said Corwin. "You've been around for a while. How many *true* Christians have you met?"

"Of halfhearted Christians I've met plenty, but saints?" Ransom gave a snort. "I can count those deserving of the title on one hand. Not being numbered among them is the deepest regret that lingers in the hearts of many in Heaven."

"I didn't think there were regrets in Heaven."

"There are thieves and murderers in Heaven! But their regrets are not earthly regrets. Knowing their past sins only increases their joy at the Father's boundless mercy."

"You're telling me that there are murderers in Heaven, and yet I—who died saving a man's life, no less—might not be allowed in?"

Corwin scoffed at the notion.

"That's the biggest difference between you and the saints," said Ransom. "You think that you deserve Heaven." He scrunched the empty cup in his hand. "Hell is full of the tragically underappreciated."

The cup bounced off the rim and into the trash bin. On his feet again, Ransom struck off across the grass. Hot spice burned in Corwin's throat as he chugged the last of his cider, not wishing to be left behind.

An attendant with spiky orange hair was tearing tickets in front of Lucky's Castle. Between the line of impatient children and the music blaring through his headphones, he would scarcely have noticed a marching band parading at his back, much less Corwin and Ransom as they stepped nonchalantly through the gate.

"Do we really have to go in there?" asked Corwin.

153

He skirted aside, giving way to little boys and girls that bounded up the drawbridge and into the menacing jaws of the clown. A curtain of black rubber strips hid the inner castle from view.

"It's too late to turn back now," said Ransom.

Just behind them at the gate, it finally occurred to the attendant that two children were rather larger than the rest.

"Hey, you two! You're not supposed to–"

Ransom drew back the curtain.

"Ransom?"

"I'm right here," called the angel, his voice a beacon in the ink-black gloom.

Hearing a low hum, Corwin glanced down. Veins of blue light pulsed through the floor, bending and branching at sharp angles, tracing a strip of circuitry. Their feeble glow gave little clue as to the surrounding shadows, though the pattern suggested a corridor. The pulse faded into the distance and primordial darkness returned, its rule lasting but a few brief seconds before the cycle repeated.

There was a snap and a *scratch-hiss*, the flare of a tiny flame igniting the cigarette on Ransom's lips. He took a drag and spoke, only his voice sounded heavier than his usual, easygoing self.

"The Paradox of Evil, more commonly called the Problem of Evil, is perhaps the oldest, most natural and most compelling argument that your kind has raised against the Father. Tell me your understanding of it."

"It's compelling because it's something we've all felt in life," said Corwin. "You don't need a degree in philosophy to grasp it. Just turn on the news! Wars, poverty, disease, famine, slavery, natural disasters . . . How anyone can look at our world and yet believe in a loving god is beyond me."

"There is much pain in life," agreed Ransom, "The trials of the mortal world are many, and though you bring most of them upon yourselves, the Father's silence in the face of grave evil is difficult to understand."

"Difficult? I'd call it sobering." Corwin's bitter words reverberated in the darkness. "To witness true evil is to know that there is no god watching over us. A loving god wouldn't stand idly by while people slaughtered each other, while families were torn apart and children left to starve."

"Your passion is noted," Ransom said curtly. "Now speak plainly the logic of your paradox."

"Logically, the paradox is simple. No one wishes evil upon those they love. Either god loves us but cannot end suffering, in which case he is not omnipotent, or god can end suffering but chooses not to, in which case he is not all-loving."

"Very good."

They walked for a short time in silence. Corwin could guess what was coming. His attorney would make the argument that love required free will, and free will entailed the possibility of evil. It sounded like a tidy explanation, but it wasn't enough. Protecting a child from a pedophile was more important than protecting the pedophile's free will. Every just society put limits on behavior. Wouldn't a just god do the same?

A column of ash grew on the end of Ransom's cigarette. Stopping, he arched his neck and blew a smoke ring.

"There's just one thing I'd like some clarification on. Supposing that an all-loving God with the power to stop evil ought to do so, how much evil should he stop? Where do you draw the line?"

"At the very least, he could prevent mass murders! Take the school shooting that happened just a few months back. Where was god when that psychopath killed almost twenty kids? If I'd had the power, you can be damn sure that I would have done something. I'd say that makes me a better person than your almighty father."

"So it's about the scale of the bloodshed? God should intervene once the potential death toll rises above a magic number?"

The threading light paused beneath them, then flowered into a pattern that rapidly expanded in all directions. This space was no corridor. It was huge. Ramping off the floor, the lasers outlined buildings and cars and more until a whole wireframe city had taken shape. When it was complete, a wave of digital paint clothed the naked world in pixels, their resolution increasing, blocky edges smoothing until it was impossible to distinguish illusion from reality.

"So that's how it is. This isn't a dream *or* the afterlife," Corwin thought aloud. "I'm in the *Christian Matrix!*"

Standing in the center of the road, he could hear little over the cacophony of what sounded like a hundred police sirens blaring at once. Cruisers choked the lanes. Several were already parked to his left and right with more showing up every second, and soon the whole street was blockaded for half a mile. The sirens cut out as the deputy chief raised his megaphone, pointing it towards the stalwart columns of the First National Bank.

"We've got the building surrounded! Release the hostages, lay down your weapons and come out with your hands up!"

He was answered by the furious rattle of machinegun fire, bullets blowing out the windows and punching holes in his cruiser.

"Jesus Christ!" he swore as he hunkered behind the car.

"You called?"

Sandaled feet appeared before the deputy's eyes. Looking up, he saw Jesus, the Lord garbed in his signature white robe and red sash. His expression was warm and relaxed, and he stood without any regard for the bullets buzzing past.

"Lord, it sure is great to see you! A group of gunmen tried to knock over the bank and started shooting the place up. Now they're holding twenty five people hostage inside, although I'm sure you already knew that."

"Let me see what I can do," said Jesus.

He disappeared, and less than a minute later a stream of shaken men and women started pouring out of the bank.

"Hold your fire!" shouted the deputy chief to his officers.

After the last hostage was free and away, Jesus waltzed out, shaking the dust from his feet.

"You'll find the shooters taking a little nap in the lobby."

"It's a good thing you showed up, Jesus."

"All in a day's work," the Lord said. "And by the way, you might want to duck."

The short-lived peace was shattered by a second round of gunshots, this time from a different direction. Across the street, two masked men had stormed out of the Second National Bank. Armed with submachine guns and carrying duffle bags full of cash, they were ready for a fight, but hadn't expected to find the entire police force camped outside. With curses and a hail of hot lead, they retreated back behind the bank's brick walls.

"You pigs better not try anything or the sixteen people in here are as good as dead!"

The deputy had wisely chosen to hit the floor. He pushed himself up, still crouching, and brushed off the pieces of what used to be his driver-side mirror.

"Damn! A double bank heist!"

"Gotta go," Jesus said. "This one's all yours."

"But what about those people across the street?"

"What do I look like? Batman? They've got less than twenty hostages over there! Sorry, but that's not really worth my time."

"But Lord!"

Already on the move, Jesus waved farewell, but didn't look back.

"See you when I come again!"

Instead of disappearing, he simply marched east down the road. Corwin and Ransom followed at a distance.

"I'm not calling for divine intervention to kick in when some random quota is met," Corwin told his attorney. "If even one innocent child is in danger, wouldn't that be reason enough to act?"

"So it's the age of the victim that matters?"

Reinforcements continued to arrive, the glut of cop cars extending through the next block, home to Lincoln Elementary School. A police chopper circled overhead while the Kevlar-clad SWAT team took up position along the school's perimeter.

Evidently the city was having a rather rough day.

Beside one of the nearby cruisers, an officer with a handlebar mustache coordinated movements, talking over the static scrape of his hand radio. Seeing Jesus, he dropped what he was doing and rushed over.

"Jesus, since you're here, we could really use a hand! We've got terrorists holed up in the third and sixth grade classrooms. They're threatening to start executing kids if we don't give in to their demands."

"You can leave the third grade classroom to me," Jesus replied. "But the sixth graders? Come on! Those kids are practically teenagers! Why would I bother saving them?"

An appalled look flashed across the officer's face, but he quickly hid it, reminding himself that the Lord works in very, *very* mysterious ways.

"How about: the right to swing your fist ends where your neighbor's nose begins," proposed Corwin as the digital world dissolved, reverting to a realm of blackness threaded with neon blue. "How's that for a line?"

"One need not swing a fist to cause harm," said Ransom. "Many are driven to suicide by verbal abuse alone, and even sins committed in private can have a rippling effect. Your line is arbitrary."

"Any line drawn would be arbitrary! But isn't an arbitrary line better than none at all? Even if god only saved children no older than five, wouldn't that be an improvement?"

"Try telling that to the six-year-olds." The angel stomped out his cigarette. "God is not a spectator. He *does* intervene, but on his terms, not yours. And the suffering that he's most concerned with preventing is the eternal kind."

15

LOVE MACHINES

The glowing trail was darkening just ahead of their feet now. Ransom halted and lifted a hand towards the unseen wall. A pattern emerged, spiraling out from his palm. The intricate lines connected to form a circular doorway. Dull light seeped through the cracks as it slid open, its facets twisting and unfolding like the petals of a mechanical flower.

Shading his eyes, Corwin stepped forth from the passage, but not too far. Where the door stood, the walls were recessed, and beyond was a slim metallic ledge, a platform that wrapped around the exterior of some massive structure. It was a long way down, though how long, he couldn't say. By the looks of it, this world existed in the gap between two endless cloud oceans, one above and one below, a ribbon of lavender sky ringing the horizon.

Colossal pillars of steel speared down, suspended from who-knows-what above the upper clouds. They ended before touching the billows below, electricity coursing skyward through the thousand conduits that ran along their length. Each was linked to the next by a series of long catwalks. Stretching like sword blades, the daunting bridges looked far too thin to support their own weight, let alone any travelers, yet they did.

Robotic pedestrians journeyed between the pillars and satellite stations that hung where the walkways intersected. Despite being wrought of cold steel, the world hinted curiously at nature's organic design. Electrical cables crept like vines, and antenna arrays rose like skeletal trees from the stations, beads of light waxing on the tips of their fiber-optic branches. The robots, too, were distinctively male and female, with even scampering children and hunched seniors present among their ranks. They hustled about in an orderly fashion, everyone with someplace to be, but no one pushing or shoving to get there.

Setting his sights on the nearest bridge, Ransom ventured out upon the ledge. Corwin plastered his back to the wall and inched after him.

This isn't so bad. At least I can't see the ground.

Like clockwork, every ten seconds the wall vibrated, a metal heart thrumming within. Pistons pumped, fans whirred and water rushed with controlled fury, funneled through high-pressure pipes.

"Don't move!" warned Ransom as an orange light strobed overhead.

Just past Corwin's shoulder, the slats of a vent angled open, spewing steam and coolant from the guts of the pillar. Hot waste rained down on the hidden world. When the last of the fluid had splashed off the ledge, the slats flattened again, the light going dim.

Corwin quickened his pace and caught up with his attorney at the underside of the bridge, where rungs in the wall offered access. As they mounted it, one of the male automatons passed near. Toting a titanium briefcase, he looked as though he was on his way to work. Ransom stuck out his leg.

The poor robot never saw it coming. He pitched forward, clanging to the ground as circuit boards spilled out of his briefcase.

"Pardon me, sir," he apologized, regaining his feet. "I hope our collision did not impair your functioning."

"You should watch where you're going," chided Ransom. "You wouldn't like me when my functions are impaired."

Without complaint, the worker turned on his heels and went about fetching his loose circuit boards. Another robot bent to help and Ransom gave that one a swift kick in the backside, sending him crashing into the first.

"Oh, good! Everything seems to be working!"

Corwin was sure that his rude attorney had crossed the line this time, yet when the Good Samaritan looked their way, his only words were: "I do wish you hadn't done that sir, but you have my forgiveness."

"What polite robots!" declared Corwin.

"They cannot help but be," said Ransom. "Evil isn't in their programming."

"It's too bad for them that the same can't be said for angels."

"My sensors!" cried a third automaton as Ransom wrapped him in a headlock and blew smoke in the hapless robot's face. It stood wobbling, trying to adjust for its clouded vision as they proceeded across the bridge.

"If evil is incompatible with a loving God, then he ought to purge all evil, not just some of it. He ought to block even sinful thoughts from entering the mind. The result would be a race of robots, a world like this one."

"Some might call that an improvement," mumbled Corwin, casting guilty glances back at the battered and abused robots.

"What do you think is the point of all this?" Ransom spread his arms. "From God's perspective, what is the purpose of creation?"

"I try not to speak on behalf of gods, but I think I know what you're going to say."

"The point," Ransom said slowly, "is love."

He drew up to the bridge's edge, his gaze lost in the swirling bands of gray and white and seashell, cloud whirlpools corkscrewing into the deep unknown.

"The Father does not desire mere servants or slaves. He desires family—sons and daughters capable of sharing in his love."

"A fatherly god may sound nice," replied Corwin, "but if our world is anything to go by, an indifferent or cruel god seems a lot more likely. And the shackles of religion look an awful lot like slavery to me."

"Ask yourself this," proposed Ransom. "What use could an omnipotent God—a being who, should he desire anything, need only think it to make it so—possibly have for slaves?"

Corwin was no stranger to the concept. He had said much the same thing while debating Bible-thumping theists in the past. Those debates had a tendency to end with threats of hellfire, threats which were about as frightening to him as the prospect of Santa stuffing his stockings full of coal.

"No use," he answered. "Any god that feels the need for slaves is clearly less than omnipotent, not to mention foolish. If god wanted slaves, why give man free will in the first place? He must not have thought that one through."

"Such ideas are worse than illogical. They're dangerous," added Ransom. "A loving father cares for his children even when they disobey, but what is the worth of a servant who refuses to serve? Where men deem themselves slaves of God, the disobedient are branded as worse than slaves."

"As infidels," Corwin concluded.

The angel gave a solemn nod.

"But isn't your god needy as well?" challenged Corwin. "Doesn't his desire for love also imply a deficiency, just of a different sort?"

"Love is a curious thing. Hoard it up, and you lose it. Give it away, and you gain more. It defies all the usual rules."

A sparrow swooped down, sunlight glinting on its steel alloy wings. Alighting on Ransom's shoulder, the bird chirped synthesized notes and bobbed its head with sharp, precise movements.

"Think back to something that filled you with happiness. It need not be anything dramatic. Even your favorite pizza will do."

"Gianni's sure made a mean pie," Corwin reminisced. Even now, he could almost taste their rich, tangy sauce and aged pepperoni, thick-cut so that the singed edges curled each slice into a wonderful little cup of grease. You couldn't get pepperoni like that at the chains. "If you told me that their Sicilian was divinely inspired, I might even believe you."

"Actually, Gianni made a pact with a demon to acquire that recipe, but that's beside the point. After you discovered Gianni's Pizza, did you keep it to yourself?"

"Are you kidding? I should have gotten a discount for all the word-of-mouth advertising I gave that place."

"In other words, you shared your love for your favorite pizzeria. Did you do so because you felt unfulfilled or deficient in some way?"

"No," he admitted. "I enjoyed it, and so I told people about it."

"The Father's love is like that," Ransom explained. "He yearns to share it, not out of any deficiency, but because his joy overflows. Just as a love-struck friend won't shut up about their beloved, or new parents can't resist sending an endless barrage of baby pictures to everyone they know, it is the nature of love to be shared."

"Again, that sounds nice, but all this neat and tidy philosophy . . . Try telling that to the love-struck friend when his beloved is hit by a drunk driver! Try telling that to the new parents when their precious child is kidnapped!"

He could hear his voice rising, the fire swelling in his chest, but his attorney didn't back down.

"Man is quick to blame God for the crimes of his fellow man, yet even in that instinct there hides a clue. You've felt it yourself."

"What are you talking about?"

"When you suffer injustice, especially grievous injustice, you instinctively feel a rage directed at something beyond man, something bigger. Your spirit burns and you want to roar at the universe and at its Maker!"

"If that's evidence for god, it doesn't bode well for his image."

"The same holds true for feelings of profound joy. Think of a mother cradling her newborn child, her heart overcome with a gratitude so great that it transcends anyone who might deserve thanks in the mortal world."

Corwin wasn't sure that he had ever been that happy, but he had witnessed it, seen it in the eyes of others, and he was definitely acquainted with the former feeling.

The sparrow sprang from Ransom's shoulder, flapping its wings to gain altitude and then wheeling away towards the pillar ahead. Where the pillar met the upper clouds, arcs of lightning leapt from its conduits and quietly vanished into the haze. Heedless of the danger, the bird flew closer.

Robotic birds were apparently no smarter than real ones. A bolt of light branched, its blazing hot touch frying the sparrow instantly. It trailed a thin stream of smoke as it dove out of the air.

"There's one thing that your explanation overlooks," realized Corwin. "You claim that god permits evil for the sake of free will, but not all suffering is the result of choices. Not all pain is inflicted by the willful hand of man. What about earthquakes or hurricanes or diseases spread by insect bites?

"There is plenty of evil that your god could stop without taking away anyone's free will. So why doesn't he? If he loves us so much, why does he stay silent while millions suffer at the whim of Mother Nature?"

A draft ruffled his coat, the current of the drifting clouds pulling at him gently but insistently. Corwin began to wish that the bridge had been built with handrails.

"A worthy question, and a difficult one," said the angel. "Philosophy alone cannot answer it. One needs look to revelation, to man's ancient beginnings, to . . ." he laid a hand on Corwin's back, "the Fall!"

A strong and sudden push cast Corwin over the bridge's edge. In desperation he twisted about, grasping for some lifeline, but everything firm and solid might as well have been a thousand miles away.

"Not again!" he hollered, the wind whipping his hair.

The bridge dwindled to a stripe, dark against the sky, and the billowing folds of the clouds welcomed him with their cool embrace.

16

THE PRICE OF PARADISE

"Corwin, you've got to hold on!"

Like words spoken underwater, Mary's voice was muddled and remote.

"We're losing him!" reported another, even farther away.

Their shouts were receding, a steady roar rising on the black wind. It was all around him now, buffeting him, prying at his eyelids. Corwin squinted.

The view was the same in all directions as he hurtled through the murky haze of the cloud sea. It might have been seconds or minutes, but finally the veil parted and he plunged into open sky. He wasn't alone for long. Some yards away, his attorney burst through the clouds, streaking earthward like a bullet with a flapping tie. Ransom donned a pair of goggles, his arms pressed to his sides in a headfirst dive.

"You'll see better with these!" yelled the angel.

He flung his spare eyewear as if sliding a drink down an invisible bar. They spun across the air between them and into Corwin's flailing grasp.

"I'd rather have a parachute!"

He twirled and flipped, wrestling to get the strap around his head, and then opened his eyes.

"Whoa!"

If the world above the clouds had in small ways imitated nature, this world in every way magnified it. A broad valley unfurled, sparkling with azure lakes and rimmed with snow-capped mountains. Wildflowers of a hundred shades colored the fields and lush forests sprang from the foothills and riversides. There was a vitality in the air, an energy that bristled with new life. Breathing it in, Corwin felt like a boy again. He wanted to run through the meadows and roll down the hills.

But first there was the matter of landing.

"If you've got wings, now would be a good time to use them!"

"No need," called Ransom. "Just put your feet down!"

Easier said than done.

Tossed about at the mercy of the turbulent wind, Corwin tried to remember what he had seen of skydivers on television. Compared to them, his clumsy movements weren't much to look at, but he managed at last to gain some degree of control. Off to his right, Ransom tucked into a roll and spun out with his feet facing downward.

"Now you're just showing off!"

As Corwin angled his legs, his furious descent began gradually to slow until he was floating to the ground like a balloon sapped of helium. Together with Ransom, he gingerly touched down on the slope of the vale.

Breathless, Corwin drank in the world around him. The pristine land was a painting come to life, only it was more real than any painting or photograph. Earthly vistas paled in contrast. The green blades of swaying grass were greener, the crisp, white snow on the mountaintops was whiter, and the deep blue of the cloud-dappled sky was bluer. To gaze upon the land was to *feel* it. The soft flex of the grass underfoot and the silky caress of the flowers in the fields, even the brisk tingle of the snow—he knew its touch, its scent. Every cell in his body sang in scintillating harmony with this place.

Gently rolling hills stretched long and low across the valley. In the flatlands were shallow pools, no more than knee-deep. Ringed in wildflowers, their crystal clear waters mirrored the sky. The valley dipped to their right, cradling a vast lake, and before its shores stood the largest, most magnificent tree that Corwin had ever beheld.

He wondered at how he hadn't noticed it until now. The enormous tree dominated the landscape. Strong roots carpeted in evergreen moss burrowed into the earth, anchoring a trunk as wide as the base of a mountain. Even the oldest redwoods would have seemed but toothpicks beside it. It towered into the heavens, rising higher than the tallest frosty peaks before spreading its branches in a great canopy that shaded a swath of the land. Clouds enveloped its emerald leaves, the treetop lost to view.

Craning his neck to admire the gargantuan tree, Corwin discovered in awe that it had a twin. Beyond the mountains stood a second tree, no less impressive than the first, though the distance made its height easier to apprehend.

"Your world is broken, but it was not always so," spoke Ransom as he pulled off his goggles. "Once long ago, the land was pure and young, untainted by man's folly."

"Is this, *was* this Earth?" asked Corwin.

"You stand in Eden."

"Eden? As in the garden with the talking snake?"

Corwin couldn't hide his scathing sarcasm, nor did he try to.

"Much of Genesis is wrapped in symbolism, but the Fall is no children's story," said Ransom. "There is truth to be found in the creation account."

"Maybe in the sense of moral generalities. But historical truth? Surely you can see why no one takes the Genesis story seriously. Every early civilization has its creation myth. The Hebrews were no different."

With a "just you wait" smile in his steel gray eyes, Ransom turned and set off down the slope. For once, he didn't reach for his flask or his tin cigarette case, and somehow Corwin knew that he wouldn't. Not here. To spoil the purity of this place in the slightest was unthinkable, and compared with the raw, invigorating air, even the artfully balanced spices of the finest cigars would taste like ash on one's lips.

"The message of Genesis is less about how the universe as you know it was created, and more about how life was meant to be, and what went wrong," explained Ransom. "One would think that an all-powerful Father would prepare a safer place for his children, rather than one where their lives might be stolen by the quaking of the earth or the thundering of the skies."

"Or wild animals with a taste for human flesh," added Corwin, startled by the abrupt stirring of what he had taken for a golden-brown outcropping of rock.

The lion, as still as stone a moment ago, raised its proud head, and it was easy to see why this beast had been crowned king of the jungle. Fearsome and dignified, it faced them with a glimmer of wisdom in the amber pearls of its eyes. Ransom halted as it padded towards him. The lines of its muscles were visible through its regal coat, telling of speed and might that the king could call upon if he deigned.

Corwin hovered cautiously behind the angel's back.

"Your god devised quite the death trap for his *beloved* spawn."

The lion brushed up against Ransom and he combed his fingers through its thick, golden mane. Tentatively, Corwin reached out. A low growl and a flash of fangs answered, and he hastily snapped his hand back.

"It makes you wonder." Ransom soothed the lion with a pat. "How could a perfect and benevolent God create such an imperfect world?"

"It's a logical contradiction," asserted Corwin. "If god designed the universe, then he also designed scorpions and venomous spiders and rattlesnakes that kill children who wander through the wrong patch of grass."

"He doesn't sound very benevolent, does he? Unless there was a time when your universe was different, a time before sin."

"You're essentially admitting that without the creation story, Christianity doesn't add up. I would hardly call that a point in its favor."

Purring like a pampered house cat, the lion arched its back and then slipped free. It gave its wild mane a shake as the two travelers delved lower into the vale.

"There are few sentiments stronger in your age than the longing to, as you humans say, 'get back to nature.' Perhaps you've felt the same?"

"Living in a concrete jungle can do that to a man," said Corwin. "Parking lots don't exactly make for scenic vistas."

"And yet, if you actually did get back to nature, something tells me that you would tire quickly of life without electricity and indoor plumbing, and then there's the toil of hunting and growing your own food, and let's not forget the lack of antibiotics . . ."

"I get the picture. So what are you trying to say?"

"Only that once again man's spirit stands at odds with reality. You yearn to reunite with nature, but nature has thorns. What man truly desires is an idyllic natural world, a Garden of Eden, so to speak." Ransom's gaze panned across the snowy mountaintops. "It's almost as though some part of you still remembers this place and longs to return."

Corwin was far from convinced of that, but he couldn't deny that there was a certain feeling about this land, an exultant sense that *this* was where he belonged. All of Earth seemed a birdcage by comparison. Here at last he was free, and every point on the compass promised a new adventure. Were it not for the angel by his side, Corwin might have dashed off to uncover the secrets of a mountain trail, or maybe just lay sprawled in the serene meadow's inviting grass. Either choice was equally sublime.

"If this is Eden, it's certainly a sight to behold, but I must admit that I was expecting something a little less . . . literal.

The Forbidden Fruit, serpents and shame; you don't have to be Freud to see the sexual symbolism in Genesis."

"You humans turn everything into sexual symbolism," snorted Ransom. "You can scarcely look at the sky without seeing phalluses in the clouds! No, the Fall is not some Freudian allegory. The fruit is real fruit. And the serpent, well, you'll meet him soon enough."

"But doesn't that make it all the more absurd? Why create a tree which bears such marvelous fruit and plant it right smack in the middle of Eden, only to forbid Adam from taking a bite? Christians like to pin temptation on the devil, but it's pretty clear who taught him everything he knows."

"Remind me, besides avoiding the Forbidden Fruit, what other commandments was Adam given in this place?"

Like any studious atheist, Corwin was well-versed on the Book of Genesis.

"To be fruitful and multiply, to fill the earth and subdue it, to have dominion over the animals, to cultivate and care for the land . . ."

"All very practical things, things that he might have done anyway. But not so for the fruit. By all appearances, the Forbidden Fruit was pleasant to eat. It would even grant knowledge to him who ate it. To obey the Father's will therefore meant a sheer act of trust, a heroic obedience."

"And the Father prefers heroes to pragmatists."

"Now you're catching on! But there is more to the story than most of your theologians know. Adam's fault was not merely that he succumbed to temptation. Heroes are supposed to be courageous."

Farther below, near the gnarled fingers of the tree's outlying roots, a pair of figures came into view atop the crest of a low hill. Even at a distance, Corwin was struck by their elegance. These were no grunting Neanderthals. Both the man and the woman carried themselves with a natural nobility that no degree of nakedness could impugn. The very idea of robing their perfectly sculpted forms in clothing seemed terribly childish, like playing dress-up by slinging a royal cape over the shoulders of the lion they had earlier encountered.

"Ah, there are your ancestors now!" Ransom declared.

"If you don't mind, I'll just assume that they got here after a million years of evolution," said Corwin.

The man's hair was long and brown and the woman's golden locks were longer still. They walked hand-in-hand under the cool shade of the tree.

"Shall we get a closer look?" proposed Ransom.

Trekking across the valley, Corwin felt no fatigue in his legs. Whatever it was about the air here, he knew that to breathe it in was to never tire.

"Of all the things to forbid, why knowledge? What kind of father seeks to keep his children ignorant?"

"Do you really think that prior to eating the fruit, Adam had no conception of good and evil? How then would he have known whether it was right or wrong to obey the Lord's command in the first place?"

The question flipped a light switch in Corwin's head.

"Wow! Your creation myth is even more flawed than I thought!"

"Ever heard the phrase: 'To know in the biblical sense'?"

Corwin had heard it said, though usually in the context of a crude joke.

Ransom continued, "What Adam lacked was *firsthand* knowledge of evil. Experience. That's what the Father wished to keep him from."

Adam and Eve were yet a hundred yards away when they crossed beneath the leafy canopy. Suddenly the branches above creaked and shook. From the shadowy boughs of the tree, a menacing form took shape. The serpent.

Corwin felt his knees go weak.

The ancient dragon descended, its lithe and powerful body curling around the trunk. A glistening coat of obsidian scales armored its sides, and long, sharp talons gouged the tree bark. Its teeth alone were several times the height of a man. Black wings unfurled as the serpent inclined its head towards the two insignificant humans.

Adam shrank back a step, but Eve stood her ground.

Regarding her, the dragon opened its jaws and a thousand hissing voices spoke as one.

"Did God say, 'You shall not eat of any tree of the garden'?" it inquired innocently, fires blazing in the pits of its eyes.

"Of the fruit of the trees of paradise we may eat," answered Eve. "It is only the fruit of the tree which grows in the middle of the garden, of which God said, 'Thou shall not eat it or even touch it, lest you die.'"

"You will *not* die," coaxed the serpent. "God knows well that in the day you eat of it, your eyes will be opened and you will become like gods, knowing good and evil."

Lowering its forked tail along the opposite side of the trunk, it deposited the infamous fruit into its claw. The fruit seemed such a tiny thing, magicked to hover at the tip of a saber-like talon. It shimmered red-gold, ripe and faintly glowing with a soft halo of light. A nervous shudder ran through Eve as she accepted it in her palms.

And Corwin understood. Never before had he felt such an imposing presence. The dragon's fangs were death, its armor despair. From those insidious eyes, there could be no escape. It weaved words with a silken tongue, but that curtain of silk sheathed a naked blade, a threat impossible to ignore. Corwin sensed it, and so did Adam. To defy this creature meant risking one's life.

"If Adam had been braver," he said, "if he had placed himself between the serpent and Eve, refused the offer, would the serpent have killed him?"

"Unless the Father intervened," replied Ransom. "But Adam lacked the courage to make that stand. He bowed his head and took the fruit, then tried to shift the blame."

"He was a coward."

The angel cast his client a measured glance.

"Would you have fared better?"

Corwin had no answer. He certainly didn't envy the choice that Adam had been faced with.

"You wanted to know why nature is a cruel mistress? Your answer lies here," said Ransom. "Through Original Sin a rift was torn in reality, shattering the nascent harmony between God and man. Yours became a fallen race, condemned to a fallen world, in need of a redeemer."

"So then we're all born guilty? I can't accept that! Christianity has always used guilt to control people, but I won't play along!"

"It's not a matter of personal guilt. Your ancestors lost your inheritance! And there are few things more obvious than the fracture left by Original Sin. You've felt the jagged edges of that rift every time that you thought to yourself: 'The world isn't supposed to be like this!'"

The words echoed in Corwin's head. He had built a wall there, sealed away harsh memories from a time that was better left forgotten. But now that wall was cracking. He blacked out as a flood of visions surged to the surface. Corwin recalled his father's last days, the details every bit as lucid as when he had memory-dived before, only this time the gift of clarity felt more like a curse.

One vision burned brighter than the rest. A twelve-year-old Corwin sat on the edge of his seat next to his father's hospital bed. He hated it here. The sparse furnishings, the yellow glare of the lights and the smell of antiseptic solution made the room feel like a very sanitary prison cell. Yet somehow, despite being cooped up in this place, his father always managed to smile when Corwin rode his bike over for a visit.

There was a power inside him that was stronger than the cancer, or so Corwin believed, but he wasn't smiling today.

"You're going to make it, Dad. Don't give up!"

Seeking to numb the pain, the elderly doctor injected something into the drip bag that hung above the bed. There wasn't much else he could do.

Corwin could tell that his father was fading fast. He listened as the doctor conferred with the nurse.

"Did you manage to reach his wife?"

"I think so."

"What do you mean 'I think so'?"

"She picked up when I was halfway through leaving a message," said the nurse, and then added softly, "but she didn't sound too sober."

The whisper wasn't meant for Corwin's ears, but his keen hearing caught every word. None of it surprised him. As his father's condition had worsened, his mother sank deeper into depression. She had taken it harder than anyone, but it wasn't fair. Corwin was only a boy. He needed her to be there for him. Instead, it felt as if he had lost both of his parents in one cruel stroke of fate.

"Corwin?"

His father's thin voice was little more than a croak, his eyes glazed over, seeing without recognition. Corwin leaned in close.

"I'm right here, Dad."

"I love you, Corwin. I've always been proud of you." He squeezed Corwin's hand. "Tell your mother that it's going . . . to be . . . okay."

Okay? How could it possibly be okay?

He closed his eyes and his chest rose and fell for the last time.

With a child's faith, Corwin prayed for a miracle, but there were no miracles. If God really existed, how could he let something like this happen? Hot tears streamed down his cheeks and he whispered, hurling a furious protest at the universe.

"It's not supposed to be like this!"

A wave of darkness swept over him. Corwin wiped at his eyes, violently shaking off the memories. When he blinked again, he was back in Eden. Ransom stood by his side and Adam and Eve were gone.

A fierce wind howled, whipping up a maelstrom of leaves. Corwin raised a hand to shield himself, and then he noticed the serpent. No longer was it looking to the place where his ancestors had been. With eyes aflame, it turned its abyssal gaze upon the two intruders. Ransom thrust himself in front of Corwin.

The dark dragon's myriad voices rumbled.

"Do not think to deny me what is mine!"

17

DEAD ON THE INSIDE

Time stood still and color faded from the world. Corwin told his body to run, but his legs wouldn't listen. The serpent's paralyzing gaze stripped his soul bare. Even Ransom tensed under the pressure.

"Okay, so maybe coming here wasn't one of my best ideas."

The dragon's jaws gaped and a scorching gout of fire erupted from its maw. Ransom's hand shot out, his arm shaking as an invisible barrier held back the blast. But the inferno didn't let up. The heat was rising, flames licking at Corwin's sides. The angel's shield wouldn't last for long.

"Hang on!" shouted Ransom. "This might be a little rough."

Corwin reached for his attorney's coat, but before he could secure a grasp, the portal opened. Ransom had always made hopping between universes look easy—a simple matter of stepping through some mystical glow or a doorway—and so Corwin wasn't prepared at all for the turbulent nexus of torn space that greeted him. He was separated from Ransom almost instantly. Ribbons of light and darkness spiraled, pulling him through a winding wormhole. He saw stars and galaxies beyond his own, realms where people sailed through space on Spanish Galleons and worlds where lizard witch-doctors whispered to the constellations and the constellations whispered back.

If there is a god, he's definitely got too much time on his hands.

The light grew blinding, and, with a loud *boosh*, the wormhole spat Corwin out onto a slab of cement. When he came to, he was lying on his side by a street corner. Ransom was nowhere to be seen.

"Got somewhere you're supposed to be?"

Following the voice, Corwin glanced up. A cab driver had pulled over beside the corner. He was a black man with a gray beard, neatly cropped.

"I wish I knew," said Corwin as he climbed to his feet.

The cabby smiled. Despite the wrinkles that age and hard work had worn into him, there was an easiness to his grin, as if his face were tailor-made for smiling.

"They say life is a journey, and there's a destination we're all meant for, but some prefer to go their own way."

"Isn't that what life's all about?" asked Corwin. "Taking charge of your destiny? Finding yourself?"

"Oh, I wouldn't say that. There's a reason why they call it *falling* in love, and why you're said to *lose yourself* in a beautiful song or a good book. Folks try so hard to find themselves and to do their own thing, but aren't the most blissful moments in life those times when you're swept up in something beyond your control, when your *self* is the last thing on your mind?"

"You've got me there," Corwin chuckled. "Still don't know where I'm supposed to be, though. I seem to have lost my lawyer."

"If you'd rather sort things out someplace warmer, I could give you a ride."

"A free ride?"

"Whoa now, I never said it'd be free," replied the cabby. "It might cost you all you've got, but I never charge more than that."

"Thanks for the offer," said Corwin, "but I think I'll stick around here a bit longer."

"I hear you. When you get separated from somebody, staying put for a while can be the smartest thing to do."

"I sure hope so."

Popping open his glove box, the cabby fished out a glossy, wallet-sized card and handed it to Corwin.

"A little something to hold onto."

On the front of the card, a dove flew forth from golden clouds, shedding drops of sacrificial blood upon the earth. Corwin knew without looking that a prayer would be printed on the rear side.

"Uh, thanks, but I–"

The cabby shifted gears and pulled out onto the road. "You can pay me back later!" he called, waving above the roof of his car.

Corwin stared after the yellow cab as it sped away.

You can pay me back later.

Not likely, he thought. He pocketed the holy card, but couldn't shake the feeling that there was something more to those parting words.

His mind was still puzzling over the encounter when he turned and nearly collided head-on with a middle-aged man. The man was walking with his wife, and neither of them seemed to have noticed Corwin at all.

"Watch–!" Corwin began, raising his hands reflexively.

But there was no collision. The man strode right through him and proceeded to cross the intersection without ever so much as glancing back.

From around the corner came the grind of skateboard wheels. Just as the tattooed teenager swerved past, Corwin swung out his arm in a clothesline.

I've always wanted to do this!

Fortunately for his intended victim, his arm proved no more solid than air. The teenager would never know of the undead atheist who sought to torment skateboarders from beyond the grave.

"I'm a shade! But then how did that cab driver . . ?"

A rickety crash interrupted his thoughts and Corwin spun towards the door of the nearby pawn shop. It had been kicked open by the boot of a tall, bizarrely dressed figure.

"Ransom?"

There stood his attorney, clad in a full suit of samurai armor.

"I'm not even going to ask."

"So there you are!" exclaimed the angel, lifting off his helm. "I've been searching all over for you!"

"You couldn't have been searching too hard," said Corwin. "We've only been apart for a few minutes."

"A few minutes for you maybe, but I emerged from that portal days ago. That's what happens when you get separated in a trans-dimensional rift."

Ransom's helm clanged at his feet as he unbound the shoulder straps of his iron and bamboo plate mail. As ridiculous as it seemed, he still wore his perfectly tailored business suit underneath, though the fabric was showing some wear. Scuff marks, frayed threads and the blotches of soot on his cheeks gave the impression that he had just walked off a battlefield.

"Well it's good to see that you're still in one piece," he said.

"The next time we eavesdrop on a dragon that happens to be the Father of All Evil, would you mind not cutting it so close?"

"Our scaly friend was expanding a field of closed space, trying to seal us there," explained Ransom. "That's why all the color in the world went dull. Another few seconds and we would have been trapped with that bastard."

"Oh well," sighed Corwin. "It was fun while it lasted."

"That's what Adam and Eve said."

"Dragons aside, I much prefer your version of Eden to the stories I was told as a child."

Ransom straightened his tie and marched for the cross-walk.

"Yet I still sense a lingering concern," he noted.

"There was something you said about Original Sin," mentioned Corwin. "You said that we were condemned to a fallen world, almost as if the world were already fallen before we got there."

"You've got good ears," said Ransom. "Man's original sin was not *the* original sin. That dubious honor belongs to my kind. It is not for nothing that Satan is called the prince of your world."

"But then the cost of Adam's sin, all this suffering and death, doesn't it seem disproportionate?"

"Why do you think man was banished from the garden?"

"Because Adam and Eve failed god's test. It was a punishment."

"Not *just* a punishment. There were two elder trees in Eden. The other was the Tree of Life. To eat of its fruit and live forever in sin—the Father meant to spare you that fate. Because you were cast out, because of the Redeemer, you gained the hope of a paradise far greater than the one that you lost."

"So when god closes one door, he opens another," Corwin surmised. "The problem with that, of course, is my fourth paradox."

"The Paradox of Hell."

"God doesn't open any doors for the damned."

"If we're going to discuss Hell, I'd say that a change of scenery is in order."

At the suggestion, Corwin's steps ceased, his spine going rigid.

"On second thought, let's just skip my fourth paradox."

"Don't tell me that you're getting cold feet?"

"As it happens, I'd very much like to keep my feet cold. You know, rather than *on fire*. As much fun as I'm sure it would be to tag along with Dante and Virgil, something tells me that the Hell you and I would be visiting isn't the sort of place one goes for an afternoon stroll. And in case you haven't noticed, your angelic ass is a magnet for unforeseen circumstances."

"Who said anything about going to Hell?" Ransom replied with an innocent gesture. "There's a bar just down the road. I don't know about you, but I could use a cold beer."

"Oh." Corwin's stiff shoulders relaxed. "Well, in that case . . ."

They didn't have far to walk. Nestled in a rundown stack of bricks with security bars crisscrossing the windows, The End wasn't the sort of establishment that catered to the young and successful. The door hinges squeaked as Ransom let himself in.

"This place is a real dive," mumbled Corwin.

"You might want to watch your voice. We're not shades anymore."

Several patrons glanced up from their drinks in the dim, smoky room. Corwin got the distinct feeling that he didn't belong, but Ransom, with his soot stains and disheveled suit, apparently fit right in. He slid up to the bar.

"Rough day?" asked the bartender.

Her face was older than her years, though not unattractive. Wavy black hair framed the thin white slash of her smile.

"It's like the apocalypse out there," grumbled Ransom. "I think I need a new line of work."

With a shrewd eye, the bartender sized him up.

"You're a lawyer, aren't you?"

"How could you tell?"

"I've seen your type. You guys are always miserable."

"Not always!" Ransom objected.

"If you want a new career, what's stopping you?"

"It's not that simple. If I want to get my old job back, first I have to finish this one, and that means putting up with pains in the ass like this guy."

He tilted his head towards Corwin, who had pulled up a stool.

"Hi," Corwin said jovially.

"What was your old job?" inquired the bartender.

"Suffice it to say that it was something a bit more *visceral.*"

"Sounds complicated," she remarked. "In the meantime, what are you two drinking? The End may not look like much, but we've got a dozen local beers on tap."

"I'll take a pint of the Oatmeal Nut Stout," said Ransom. "And a menu, if you would be so kind."

Her gaze shifted to Corwin, who rubbed his eyes, uncertain of what he was seeing.

"Is that beer really called Darwin's Christmas Ale?"

An ichthys with two L-shaped legs and a Santa hat topped the oaken beer tap handle.

"It's always a favorite around this time of the year."

"Yeah, I'm going to have to go with that."

"You got it."

She handed Ransom a laminated, one-page menu and grabbed a pair of steins.

"You didn't bring us here just because you were thirsty," murmured Corwin to his attorney.

"Take a look around," Ransom said, casting a subtle glance over his shoulder. "This place is a gallery of humans wallowing in their self-pity. Where better than here to discuss your fourth paradox?"

Farther down the bar, a greasy-haired man stubbed out his cigarette in an ash tray. His sullen stare drifted often to the bartender, wishing for companionship, not caring whether it was real. At a table behind him, two salesmen exchanged boasts and banter in a desperate plea for attention. They talked because they feared the silence, laughed with the hollow humor of those who cracked jokes at the Holocaust Museum. A wizened fellow with a face like a prune cast occasional glances their way, his eyes dark with disgust, or was it jealousy? They still had time to change, time to make things right, time he didn't have anymore. He had squandered his years, and the world spared little love for old men without money.

"Here you boys go." The bartender set down two foaming mugs, then eyed Ransom. "Know what you want?"

"Give me a few more minutes."

"Take your time," she said and strolled away.

"As I was saying, Hell is probably the most unpopular concept in all of Christian theology. Well, aside from chastity, anyway. Even many Christians would rather brush it under the rug."

"Because that sort of medieval thinking is embarrassing in this day and age," said Corwin. "Hell is a tale told to frighten naughty children. As a theological teaching, it's blatantly flawed. You can't expect educated people to believe that a god who is pure love keeps a fiery dungeon where he tosses anyone who breaks his rules. How could a merciful father condemn his children to an eternity of unspeakable torture, with no hope of forgiveness or reprieve?"

Ransom gulped a draught of his chocolate-brown pint and wiped the froth from his lips.

"How about this," he proposed. "I'll answer your question, but first you have to answer one of mine. It's a simple question really: Who does Satan hate the most?"

A little too simple, though Corwin. Knowing his scheming attorney, it was certain to be a trick. Still, he thought it best to go with his gut instinct.

"Not that I believe in the cosmic boogieman you call Satan, but isn't the answer rather obvious? Satan is god's arch nemesis, the Joker to your divine Batman. Naturally, I would assume that the one he hates the most is god."

"You would assume wrong," said Ransom. "It's certainly true that he detests the Father, but the one whom Satan hates the most . . . is Satan.

"When your biases are stripped away and you see yourself as you truly are, some people find that they don't like what they see. To understand Hell, one must understand that the damned are self-loathing. The Father's forgiveness will not save you if you cannot forgive yourself."

"Then there ought not to be anyone in Hell," replied Corwin. "To wish nothing good for one's self . . . That kind of extremist mentality just isn't realistic!"

"Not realistic? You of all people should know how real those feelings can be. You've stood on the precipice, gazed into the abyss of despair! You know what it means to contemplate suicide."

A memory flickered. Corwin saw his sixteen-year-old self, red-eyed and trembling, standing before a mirror.

They'll miss me at first, but they'll get over it. It's better this way.

He slid the razor blade out of his wallet, pressed it to his wrist.

I've always been a nuisance. This is the kindest thing I can do.

A bead of ruby blood appeared where the blade's corner pricked his skin.

"STOP!" Sweating, Corwin breathed with effort as the bar came back into focus. "I *do* know. I know that the suicidal aren't all self-absorbed cowards as Christians make them out to be. Can you imagine what it's like when your existence is nothing but a burden upon those that you love most? When all you want is to pour out the love inside of you, only no one wants that love, and when you try to share it, you only bring people pain?

"At that time, I saw ending my life as an act of charity. I really believed that the world would be better off without me. And I would have gone through with it, if not for a sense of duty—if I didn't have a debt to repay."

"One doesn't need to be cast into Hell," spoke Ransom. "The damned are quite willing to jump."

"But can't people change? Eternity is a long time. Surely the souls in Hell can come to forgive themselves?"

"Eternity is not endless time, but the fullness of time. There is no can or cannot, only what is."

"Wouldn't god erase such dark thoughts from their minds?"

"There's a word for those who force themselves upon others. They're called *rapists*. No, the Father honors man's free will, even in Hell."

Corwin hung his head and stared into his drink. Could people truly hate themselves that much? God's mercy wasn't at fault if the gates of Hell were locked from the inside. However, that left him with another strange paradox.

"If the damned are as suicidal as you say, they should have no lofty aspirations. So how do you account for Satan's desire to overthrow god? The devil is always portrayed as waging war against Heaven, but if he despises himself, wouldn't he have abandoned those ambitions by now? Wouldn't victory over god be the last thing he wished for?"

"Victory?" scoffed Ransom. "Satan *knows* God. He is an archangel, a seraph! He comprehends the Father's power better than any human could ever hope to. How do you defeat a being whose mind is the very thing that holds you in existence? If God were to stop thinking about you or I or Lucifer for even an instant, we would cease to be. There can be no victory against such an opponent."

"Then why fight this hopeless war?"

"Your error lies in thinking of Satan as though he were a villainous man, merely another Hitler or Pol Pot. For men, war is a means to an end. A just man may take up the sword to protect his loved ones, an unjust man to satisfy his greed. But what drives Lucifer is not some futile lust for power. For him, war is an end in itself."

To envision pure evil wasn't easy for Corwin. It was an alien state of mind, but Ransom's uncomfortable description felt too wrong not to be right.

"All this talk of self-hatred . . . I thought Satan was supposed to be prideful?"

"He is," said Ransom, "but his is the pride of vanity, not of self-love."

"I'm not sure that I see the difference."

"If you truly love yourself, you have self-respect. The pride of a self-respecting person is not dependent upon whether one outshines others. A vain person's pride is. Those who love themselves least are often quite vain."

As the bartender circled back their way, Ransom turned his attention to the menu, scrutinizing the sandwich selection as though the fate of Heaven and Hell rested on his decision. From somewhere beyond the room, Corwin heard a small voice.

"Corwin! Corwin, please!"

Mary?

He slowly stood and stepped away from the bar.

"Made up your mind?" the bartender asked Ransom.

"Hmmm . . . the Blue Cheese Bison Burger . . . can I get that with bacon?"

"You can get *everything* with bacon."

"I knew I picked the right place."

Corwin was halfway to the door. White light bled through the windows and the edges of the doorframe, growing more intense with each step.

"If you can hear me Corwin, come back! Come back to us!"

"I'm coming, Mary!"

He reached for the handle.

"Corwin, wait!" Grasping the situation, the angel shot out of his seat. "Don't open that door!"

But this time it was Ransom's words that sounded far away. Cast in the glow of that radiant light, *The End* and everyone in it were but fading shadows. The light was calling him back to the waking world, to a place more real than any fairytale land of angels and demons and Bible stories come to life.

He pulled open the creaking door.

18

The Boardroom of the Beast

"We've been waiting for you, Corwin," spoke a cold voice.

"Who are you?" demanded Corwin. "Where's Mary?"

The bright light had fled, leaving him in a spacious boardroom with wood-panel walls and a million-dollar view. A long conference table stretched towards the windows, its mahogany as smooth as polished stone. Outside, other high-rises scraped at the slate-gray sky, though few were taller than his current vantage point.

Black-suited men and women stood along either side of the table, all staring placidly at their new arrival. He instinctively shot a glance towards the exit, but two gorilla-sized guards in dark glasses flanked the double doors. He wouldn't be getting out that way.

"There's nothing to fear," said the man at his left. "You're among friends."

He had platinum blonde hair, slicked back, with eyebrows so light that they almost weren't there.

"I guess waking up was too much to hope for," sighed Corwin.

"Ah, but you did wake up! You awoke to the reality that the angel's crutch was only holding you back."

"And you're going to tell me that you know the *real* truth?"

The pale-faced man laughed—a joyless, cynical laugh.

"Truth is such a rigid concept. We're not that old-fashioned."

"Why don't you have a seat and relax," intoned the woman to his right.

She reminded Corwin of an Egyptian queen, with too much eyeliner and gaudy bracelets clinking on her wrists.

"You're our guest, after all."

"Right, and those two fellows by the door are just there to make me feel secure."

"Our boss very much wanted to meet you," she said. "He'll be here soon."

"Great." Corwin noticed a single empty seat opposite him at the far end of the table. "I love meeting important people."

"Master Isley is one of the partners of this firm. It seems that he's taken a personal interest in your case."

"What does that make you? His army of demonic interns?"

With a snide grin, it was the man who replied, "Everyone you see is an agent of the Collection Branch. They call us fallen, because we dare to think for ourselves, but we are not your enemies. You've always belonged with us."

"Aren't you guys going about this the wrong way?" argued Corwin, straining to keep his voice steady despite the knot tightening in his chest. "I mean, if demons are real, that makes a pretty strong case for god."

"Don't you see, Corwin?" The man lifted his palm as if raising a chalice. "It's not that divinity doesn't exist. You, I, everyone—we are all gods here."

He laid a hand on Corwin's shoulder, but then quickly drew it back, his face contorted with a look of revulsion. Beneath Corwin's collar, the golden cross glimmered as it caught the light.

"That charm, won't you take it off?"

"If it's meaningless, what's the problem?"

"It's in poor taste. Master Isley might take offense."

"I'll take my chances," Corwin said stubbornly, but the man was indignant. Flexing his fingers like a claw, he reached for the chain.

"I'm afraid I must insist."

If ever you are separated from me and find yourself in a desperate situation, hold onto that cross.

Corwin's hand went to his chest, clasping the cross, and it ignited in a sudden flash. Rays of light fought to escape his clenched fist. Hissing and screeching, the demons recoiled, and when he looked down, he found that a katana now rested in his hand. Its gold crossguard was roughly square, but with notched corners that recalled the sword's original form. A fine blade extended from the hilt, curved and gleaming.

Corwin had never held a sword before. It was heavier than he expected, but the weight was well balanced, and for some reason it felt natural in his grasp.

Nursing a hand charred by the light, the fiendish man sneered.

"A soulrender—an angel's weapon! If that is your choice, then so be it, but you will regret not doing this the easy way."

There was no time to think. From his right, the dark-haired woman lashed out with a raking claw. Corwin's blade flashed. She stumbled back with a shrill cry as jeweled bracelets spun through the air, a spray of black blood erupting from the severed stump of her arm.

Did I just do what I think I did?

Corwin stared in disbelief at the katana. Maybe his body had simply reacted on impulse, but it didn't feel that way. Had the blade moved of its own accord? Before he could give it any more thought, footfalls sounded at his back, the demons closing from both sides. As two men lunged towards him, Corwin vaulted onto the table.

"Mortal fool!" cursed the burnt man. "Do you think that you can slay us all? There is no way out!"

"There's one way."

Corwin lowered his shoulders and sprinted down the length of the table, leaping over grasping hands. *I can't believe I'm seriously about to do this,* he thought to himself as he crossed his arms and dived for the windows. Like a human missile, he crashed through the glass, and then his heart lurched into his throat. The four lanes below looked pencil-thin from two hundred stories up, but they were getting wider all too fast.

"On your right you'll see the Regis Inferni Building, home to one of the most prestigious law firms in the nation," announced a guide to her double-decker bus full of tourists.

"Mom, what's that?" asked a young boy, staring skyward from the roofless upper deck.

His mother's shriek split the air as Corwin's body slammed into the center aisle with a bone-shattering crunch. Passengers ducked and covered their heads from the shower of broken glass. Several shards were lodged in Corwin's arms, though he didn't seem to care.

"Fucking hell, that hurt!" he groaned as he lifted his aching body off the ground.

Two heavy thuds rocked the bus behind him.

"You've got to be kidding me."

Standing sorely, Corwin turned to see the burnt agent, an onyx katana in hand. He was joined by a woman with glasses and a long ponytail. She stood atop a seat, one foot on the railing and two pistols drawn.

"He's mine!" roared the man.

He doubled his grip and charged. Corwin raised his sword just in time to answer. Ringing steel resounded above the din of the midday traffic. A flurry of slashes fell, the demon pressing forward, but Corwin parried each blow with miraculous luck.

I think I'm getting the hang of this!

His blade weaved and spun in a lethal dance, and suddenly it was the demon who was being pressured. The sword hungered. He could feel its lust for battle, a dread force coursing through him like an electric current.

As they locked blades, shock and fury filled the demon's eyes. Then the onyx blade cracked. He leapt away, but Corwin dashed in pursuit, his assault pushing the agent back on his heels. Corwin's movements weren't merely fast, they were perfect. His sword flew with expert skill. Even his stance was flawless, each pivoting step in time with his blows. He glimpsed an opening and the katana swept low, carving a gash in his foe's leg.

The vicious man howled. He lost his footing and Corwin planted a firm kick in his stomach, knocking him to the floor. As the demon slid down the aisle on his backside, Corwin stared again at the soulrender.

"I'm a goddamn ninja!"

Two shots rang out. Swift tilts of the blade deftly deflected the gunfire. One bullet ricocheted perilously into the seats between two passengers. The tour group gasped and a mother frantically tried to pull her son behind cover, but the spellbound boy refused to look away.

"This is the best tour ever!"

As Corwin evaded another barrage, the burnt demon crawled to his feet.

"Disarm him!" he snarled. "He's nothing without the sword!"

From the roof of a passing car, a third agent hopped onto the tour bus, his legs straddling the seats. Mounting the seatbacks, he struck at Corwin's head while Corwin slashed at his knees. Between the falling blade and the bullets, the demons were forcing him back, and Corwin was running out of bus.

They swerved into a sharp turn and a traffic light came to the rescue. The distracted demon looked up just in time for a hundred pounds of iron to collide with his skull, tossing him over the railing. His black katana clattered on the floor.

"Who the hell is driving this thing?"

Bending to scoop up his fallen comrade's sword, the burnt man fixed Corwin with a hateful glare. His twin blades whirled as he launched into a furious attack. Corwin hastily checked the road and spotted a taxi out in front of the bus. It was just close enough. He swung his katana in a wide arc, buying himself an extra second as the demon skirted out of range, then turned and leapt.

Gunshots blared and a stabbing pain stung his side, but his boots landed safely on the taxi's roof. The driver, however, wasn't too happy about it. Veering wildly, he hit the brakes and Corwin was thrown onto the hood. A string of profanities issued from the cabby's mouth as the speeding bus rammed him from behind. There was no stopping in this traffic.

Corwin lifted his eyes. Through the bus's windshield, a dark-suited man stared back at him.

I should have figured.

Just as he found his feet, the burnt demon touched down on the rear end of the taxi. They both rushed the roof, blades clashing. Corwin was quicker, but the dual-wielding agent held him on the defensive. To make matters worse, the ache in his side was starting to take its toll. Blood seeped through his coat and his wound cried out with every twist and jolt.

A silver SUV raced up alongside them with a short-haired woman perched atop it. She leveled the pistol in her hand. Corwin's lightning-fast katana repelled the first two shots, but the third bullet wasn't meant for him. Lowering the barrel, she fired a round into one of the taxi's front tires.

The helpless cab driver screamed and Corwin sailed airborne as the car spun out of control. He hit the ground rolling, skidding to a bruised stop. With a grinding scrape and a trail of sparks, the taxi careened towards a roadside bench. On it lay a man who had clearly chosen the wrong place for a nap. The bearded hobo opened his eyes just in the knick of time.

"Not you again," moaned Corwin. "Watch out!"

I swear, if that bum doesn't live a long and fruitful life I'm going to find him and drag his ass straight to Hell with me!

But he needn't have worried. In a feat of acrobatic prowess that left Corwin utterly dumbfounded, the man sprang from his bench, flipping in midair as he dodged the oncoming car.

He landed, flapped his collar and scowled.

"Don't nobody know how to drive in this damn town?"

The tour bus slid into a braking turn, blocking off both lanes. By some miracle, no one was hurt, or at least no one who wasn't already dead. Corwin rolled over, feeling like a sack of broken bones. Waves of pain wracked his body with every breath, and worse, where was the katana?

In a panic, his eyes darted.

There!

It rested only a few yards away. Corwin dragged himself towards the sword, a shaky arm outstretched.

"Enough!" snapped a bitter voice.

An onyx blade impaled Corwin's hand, pinning him to the road. He yelled, unable to pull away, the sensation like being bitten and set on fire simultaneously.

"You have insulted our good will," spoke the burnt agent. "Now I will teach you what it means to defy us."

He still bore the wound that Corwin had given him earlier, his pant leg matted with blood, but if the demon was hurt, he didn't show it. Others were approaching, slowly encircling him.

"First I will break your body, then your mind, then I will stand you before the Mirror of Time and tear the black soul from that vessel and—"

Abruptly, the demon gagged on his words.

There was a sharp flicker, a second's pause, and all at once his body exploded into ribbons. Behind stood a tall figure in a charcoal suit, the shining katana resting on his shoulder.

"You demons never learn," said Ransom. "No one abuses my clients but me."

Brandishing swords and guns, a dozen agents spun to face him, but not nearly fast enough. Ransom's movements were a blur. Corwin's eyes could barely follow what was going on as limbs went flying and bodies crashed into the surrounding cars. Reckless gunfire perforated the tour bus, cut off as the shooter's arms were both hewn in a single stroke. Ransom turned and vanished from sight, appearing behind another foe, his blade liberating the man's head from his shoulders.

The angel dealt death without a hint of hesitation or remorse.

"And I thought the demons were scary," Corwin murmured as he yanked the ebony sword loose, freeing his hand.

Briskly halting, a blood-spattered Ransom reached to pull him up.

"*Defense* attorney, remember? Protecting my client is part of the job description."

"You're no Guardian," hissed one of the few agents still on his feet. "I remember you!"

"It's him!" cried another. "The White-Eyed Shadow!"

"It's been a while since I've heard that name," said Ransom.

He grinned dangerously and his eyes flared with molten light. For an instant his form darkened, save for those eyes and a pearl strip of teeth. The demons shrank back, swords quivering in their hands.

"Our business is not with you, Hunter," stammered one of them. "That man is our rightful prey!"

"As you are mine."

In the blink of an eye, Ransom closed the distance, cleaving the cowardly demon in two. He shifted his stance fluidly and plunged his katana through the chest of another, but this last one refused to die. Abandoning his weapon, he clasped the raw edge of the blade. Holy flames leapt forth, immolating his hands, yet he held his grip.

"You may slay these bodies, you may banish our souls, but you will not leave this place," he grimly promised. "Our master . . . He is already here."

A violent blaze enveloped his entire body as Ransom kicked him loose and into the battered tour bus. Gasoline leaked from where the spray of bullets had ruptured its tank, the fire spreading in seconds. One last passenger jumped from the upper deck, and then the air shook with a tremendous blast.

Corwin buried his face in his elbow as a wall of heat singed his skin, but Ransom didn't move. He didn't even blink. The angel's attention was focused vigilantly on the terrible presence that he sensed before him.

A shadowy figure strode through the burning wreckage.

"Isley!" growled Ransom.

Not waiting for an invitation, he coiled his legs and bolted towards the threat. His sword streaked in a diving arc. And stopped. Barehanded, and by the strength of but a single arm, the demon held the fell blade at bay.

"Is that any way to greet a fellow attorney?" spoke the bald, wrinkled mask of the Prosecutor, a visage that had haunted Corwin more than once along his journey.

"I was just introducing myself to your staff."

"Yet several still cling to their mortal vessels." Isley blinked and his soulless eyes inverted—the whites of his eyes darkening, framing pale, pupilless retinas. "You might once have been the White-Eyed Shadow, but your blade has grown dull."

"Even a dull blade can cut."

Ransom leaned his weight into the sword and its edge sparked as though the demon's hand were forged of steel. A thin trickle of tar-black blood ran down Isley's forearm. With a flick of his wrist, he flung the angel back. Ransom managed to hold his stance as he landed some ten feet away, shoes skidding atop the fire-strewn road.

Unconcerned, Isley glanced down at his palm.

"Do you intend to scratch me to death?" The flames that wreathed his hand expired and the shallow cut sealed. "I am not so weak as to be hunted by a wolf without fangs."

"Then you'll forgive me if I don't hold back," said Ransom.

Again his eyes seared. The air rippled with pressure and his body became a solid shadow, the katana shimmering, eager to slice bone and spirit alike. Isley blanched, but before Ransom could raise the sword, a hissing brand scorched the back of his hand. A circular glyph had appeared there.

Enclosed within was the triangular mark of the all-seeing eye. As he clutched the burning scar, the gleam in his eyes dimmed.

"I see, so your power was sealed!" Isley cackled with disdain. "It would seem that you've lost your Father's favor."

"A temporary handicap, otherwise this just wouldn't be fair."

Despite his boast, Ransom held no illusions. He faced a demon archlord. Even if he were at his best, to take Isley lightly would be to invite peril.

Not good. If he targets Corwin . . .

Breathing heavily, Corwin wobbled on his feet. Undead or not, his body had lost a lot of blood. At least the pain from the gunshot wound was beginning to dull. In fact, *everything* was beginning to dull. The chaotic battle unfolding in the street felt vague and unreal, an echo of a dream that he had only just awoken from. In a lightheaded daze, he gazed at his hands and they blurred into double-vision. However, his new hands moved differently from the originals. As Corwin stared, admiring this curious new pair of transparent limbs, the strength fled his legs and he collapsed to one knee.

Ransom shot him an alarmed look.

"Corwin!"

Instantly the angel was by his side, bracing him against a fall, but Corwin's unfocused vision was going dark. And Isley had no intention of waiting.

The Prosecutor took a step and then disappeared, moving with such speed that he seemed to teleport. A clawed hand tore the air. But Corwin and Ransom were no longer there. Sensing his prey, his head swiveled towards the bus. Ransom stood atop the corner of the smoking ruin with his client slung over his shoulder. Streaks of crimson scarred the side of his face where Isley's claw had grazed him.

The angel and the demon locked eyes.

"His soul calls out to us," Isley said, blood dripping from his fingertips. "You cannot protect him from himself."

As Ransom turned, the wind gusted. Smoke and drifting embers swirled around him, leaving only emptiness in their wake.

19

YESTERDAY'S SINS

"My head is killing me," grumbled Corwin, opening his eyes.

Branches sighed as a gentle breeze blew through the forest, revealing patches of sky high above. Birds chirped and insects buzzed, that is, if the tiny, luminous creatures that flitted about could be called insects. Corwin lifted his head, but stopped short of sitting up. The firm green bed swayed beneath him. He realized that his resting place was a giant leaf, and not a low-hanging one. Stranger still, strands of light encircled his arms and legs.

One of the glowing bugs hovered above his left shin, fastening the slender thread with a knot. Corwin reflexively jerked his knee. Buzzing crossly, the creature darted at his face, stopping inches in front of his nose. Up close, there was no mistaking the pixie. She pursed her lips in a pout and waved a scolding finger.

"Sorry!" he declared. "By all means, go right ahead and continue tying me up."

Promptly returning to her work, she tightened the knot so that the thread hugged his leg. As the pixie finished, the light strands faded until they became imperceptible. She zipped off to rejoin her friends and disappeared among the hundreds of her people that danced amidst the glade.

Corwin's leaf hung in the center of a ring of trees, their tall trunks almost perfectly flush, not that he could really see them. Thick vines covered nearly every inch of bark. Misty waterfalls poured between the lower yawnings and the air was choked with humidity. Corwin crept towards the edge of his leaf to get a better view, and as he leaned out, the leaf leaned with him.

"Oops!"

He tried to scramble back, but it was too late.

"I'm not afraid!" Corwin shouted defiantly, his voice rising to the treetops as he plummeted towards the turquoise pool below.

The fall's momentum plunged him a dozen fathoms beneath the surface. A rush of water roared and a hurricane of bubbles whirled about him. Despite the pool's deceptively small diameter, as the bubbles lifted, it revealed itself to be unimaginably deep. The surrounding walls of roots and stone descended a far way, narrowing to an undersea tunnel, its dark passage just broad enough to swim through. Staring into it, Corwin glimpsed a golden light. Not one light, he realized, but a cluster of lights, a remote galaxy burning in the ocean depths.

The strangling pressure in his chest reminded him that he wasn't a fish, and while drowning seemed a silly cause for worry in the afterlife, he decided not to chance it. The water grew warmer, the soft prism above brightening as he kicked towards it. Breaking the surface, he gulped air and took a quick survey of the glade.

"Glad to see you've overcome your fear of heights," said Ransom.

The angel lounged against a viny tree trunk, sitting atop a root that ran just a foot or so under the water. He was naked as far as his client could tell, but that wasn't what made Corwin stare. From the neck down, his body was crisscrossed with scars. A horrific history of slashes, scrapes and gouges tattooed his skin—enough wounds to kill an ordinary man ten times over. Ransom bore the scars with blasé indifference. Reclining, he puffed leisurely on a cigarette, the smoke mingling with the steam that rose off the spring's burbling ripples.

"You look like a tiger's scratching post," Corwin said as he pulled himself onto the submerged bench. "What happened back there?"

"You began to desynchronize. Basically, your soul decided that your body was no longer fit for duty. I had to call in a favor to get you sewn back into one piece."

"I didn't know there was a limit to how much damage this body could take."

"It's not about the amount of damage, but the type," explained Ransom. "You were stabbed by a soulrender. Forged in the heat of the First Flame, the blades wielded by angels and demons don't just cut flesh. They sever the bond between body and spirit."

"So that's what those strands of light are for? To keep my soul from coming loose?"

"Luckily for you, the tear was a minor one, but such wounds tend to leave a mark."

Corwin glanced at his right hand, discovering a scar of his own.

"Under the circumstances, maybe leaving my body behind would have been for the best."

"No, humans aren't meant to be bodiless. Your soul would have jumped into the next available container, likely one of Isley's choosing, and then I'd have a hell of a time tracking you down, which reminds me . . ." He opened a hand and there in his palm was the cross. "Try not to drop it next time."

"I'm hoping that there won't be a next time, although you seemed to be enjoying yourself. What did they mean when they called you the White-Eyed Shadow?"

"That's ancient history," Ransom said tersely. "Nothing that concerns your case."

"Don't give me that!" Corwin brazenly grabbed the cigarette out of Ransom's mouth and proceeded to take a drag. "My whole life is an open book to you! The least you could do is shed a little light on your past career."

"You really want to know?"

"I think I deserve to."

The angel gazed contemplatively into the flickering mirror of the pool.

"Alright," he decided, snatching back his cig and shooting upright with a splash. "Follow me."

Behind one of the waterfalls, the roots forked to form the entranceway to a partially-sunken cave. Ransom stooped and delved within.

"You're going to catch a cold, walking around like that," muttered Corwin as he waded after his stark-naked attorney.

The cave's elevation gradually climbed, the floor rising above water-level and the shadowy ceiling stretching to an unknown height. A cool draft swept away the mugginess. Corwin's clothes were completely dry by the time he spotted the dim, violet-blue glow of the exit.

"Long before I was a defense attorney, I was a Hunter," spoke Ransom, who again donned his suit. "My duty was simple: to seek out and vanquish demons that prowled the mortal plane."

They strode beneath the arch of two trees that leaned until their trunks met. The woodland on the other side was mysterious but not unearthly. Ivy clung to the beech trees, covering their bark with waxy, dark-green leaves. Owls hooted and a lonesome wolf bayed from some deep corner of the forest.

"With the skills I'd honed during the Betrayer's War, the job came naturally to me, and over the years I earned a bit of a reputation. Those I hunted came to call me the White-Eyed Shadow. My strength was formidable in those days, but even when fighting demons, there are rules to our battles, rules that must never be broken."

Night had only just fallen and a string of windows was aglow beyond the tree line. Smoke rose off the chimneys of the village's stone huts.

"It was the thirteenth century and I was in England on the trail of a demon named Strega. He and his followers had taken up residence in a band of outlaws."

As they neared one of the humble dwellings, Corwin heard the thunder of galloping hooves. At the sound, a woman who had been toting a bucket of water let it drop to the ground. Grabbing a pitchfork, she dashed home and hastily shooed her young son inside. Doors slammed and windows were shuttered from one house to the next.

"With most of the men off to war, villages like this one were easy prey for bandits. They roamed the countryside, raping and pillaging and generally creating their own little slice of Hell on Earth."

The marauders that charged over the hill were no less than thirty men strong. Suited in hides and leather armor, they hollered war cries, their blades rattling the shutters as they galloped by.

With the villagers sufficiently terrified, the band's grizzled leader dismounted his steed. He hefted a battleaxe and hacked at the door of the nearest home. One stroke and a forceful kick splintered the weathered boards.

As he stepped inside, the woman thrust valiantly with her pitchfork, but the brigand was a seasoned warrior. The haft of his axe caught the fork between its prongs, and with a quick twist, he wrenched the weapon from her grip. A burly hand reached out, ripping her blouse. He threw her down violently and loosened his belt as more men stomped into the home.

"Mama!" a boy cried, and suddenly one of the bandits howled in pain.

Frightened though he was, the woman's son had found a dirk and driven it into the outlaw's leg. His companions roared with laughter.

"That brat's not too bad!" proclaimed their leader.

Yanking the bloody knife from his thigh, the bandit cast it aside with a murderous glare.

"You've got guts, boy. Maybe I should show them to you!"

"Please, not my son!" the woman pleaded.

Leering, he raised his axe. The mother shrieked and Corwin turned his gaze away.

When at last the bandits departed, they did so in a blaze, lobbing torches onto the thatched roofs. The horrid nightmare would not be complete until naught but ashes was left of the once-peaceful village and all who had called it home.

"I caught up with them just after a raid," resumed Ransom, "and having seen their handiwork, I wasn't feeling particularly merciful."

Though the bandits couldn't see him, their horses felt Ransom's presence keenly. They were half a mile down the trail when their leader's destrier reared back on its hind legs, nearly throwing him from his saddle. Its nostrils flared and it tossed its mane with a loud whinny.

Hooves stamped the trodden dirt. Numbered among the steeds were war horses that had braved the chaos of battle, but the fear that gripped them now was something deeper, an instinct no trainer could breed out. There wasn't any beast on Earth that would willingly cross the path of a wrathful angel.

Ransom stood in the middle of the trail with his soul-render piercing the soil, both hands resting atop its pommel. Like a curling black mist, the demons left their hosts and materialized before him. They were twisted copies of the men they had indwelt, onyx swords, axes and cudgels held at the ready. Their grim circle slowly constricted.

With an icy stare that never left Strega, Ransom waited. Fear ruled the hearts of demons, and as he expected, those at his back swung first. Corwin saw him change his grip on the katana, but he couldn't well follow what happened next. The circle broke and screams were cut short by gurgling coughs. Ransom was everywhere at once. Obsidian blades snapped and axe hafts shattered against the edge of his sword. Within seconds, the demonic legion lay slaughtered, all except for their leader.

"Strega had gorged himself on evil."

Stepping over the corpses of his fallen brethren, the strapping arch demon crossed his arms and drew twin battleaxes. He bore a jagged scar through his glass right eye and his beard fell in thick braids.

"He'd forgotten which one of us was the hunter and which one the prey."

Ransom whipped the tainted blood from his blade.

"I reminded him."

As Strega unleashed a mighty war cry, flocks of birds fled from their roosts. Both axes sliced towards Ransom's neck. Sidestepping adroitly, he slipped the blades by a hair's breadth. His mind was clear, focused. The flames of vengeance burned hot, but he knew better than to let himself get careless. Even when Strega missed, the force of his swings sent shudders through the earth and split trees like chopsticks.

Stunned and bewildered, the bandits began to share the fear of their mounts, but no matter how much they urged them on, the horses refused to obey.

Finally one of Strega's blows connected. He buried an axehead beneath Ransom's chest, hurling him into a tree so hard that its bark was blasted off. The angel slumped forward, eyes closed and arms hanging limp at his sides.

Strega spoke in a deep voice that resonated from the dark hollows of time.

"Do you think you've changed anything?" he asked. "Where the feast is, there will the revelers be. We merely gather at the table that man has set."

Ransom exhaled—a long, low hiss—and opened his molten eyes.

"This feast is over."

Wrapped in blackest gloom, he took on the form for which he was named, and what had been an even fight became an execution. Strega glimpsed his leg sailing free before he even realized that he'd been cut. He toppled to one side and bellowed in rage as Ransom crossed his scar with another.

Strega's body sank to the ground, his foul spirit expelled, and Ransom looked once more to the bandits.

"For a moment, their eyes were opened. They felt doubt, perhaps even a flicker of remorse. But that moment passed. Their leader steeled his gaze and I knew that Strega had been right, that it would all happen again."

The savage man snapped the reins and his destrier, believing the worst had passed, trotted hesitantly forward.

"Angels are strictly forbidden from slaying mortal men, or so I'd heard."

Anxious stares probed the forest's forbidding shadows. No man would breathe easy until they were well away from this accursed place.

The wind had died and an eerie silence hung in the air. Between the trees, a pair of eyes glimmered like silver coins. With a bloodthirsty growl and a flash of fangs, the black-furred beast emerged from the brush.

"You took the form of a wolf?" asked Corwin.

"Sometimes we wear masks," said Ransom. "Sometimes more than one."

The shadows came alive with eyes and sharp teeth. A ferocious pack of wolves, more than a match for the bandits' numbers, descended upon them.

"I left a trail of blood and corpses a mile long. The neighboring townsfolk would call it divine retribution, but I'm not so sure that the Father saw it that way."

Quiet returned to the wood, the somber hush of death, and in the east, the horizon bloomed with dawn's coming. Crimson dirt glistened in the early morning light.

"As penance, my true form was sealed and I was assigned to a new department, providing last counsel to souls like yourself."

"So *I'm* your punishment?"

"Well you're certainly not a reward!"

"And you're alright with that?" Corwin stared into the lifeless eyes of a bandit who lay eviscerated, his chain mail torn by razor jaws. "If you ask me, your only crime was having a sense of justice."

"God sees farther than you or I."

"You said once before that this job is only temporary. How many more years have you got?"

"The hour of my atonement is for the Father to decide. Whether it takes another day or another thousand years, it is not my place to question his judgment. Speaking of which, we're still not done preparing for yours. Your fifth and final paradox yet remains."

The rising sun crept over the treetops, rimming the sky in fire, and Corwin limbered up his back with an arching stretch.

"Heaven awaits," he said. "And what would Heaven be without a few atheists to keep things interesting?"

20

ENSLAVED TO HAPPINESS

"You're looking spry," noted Ransom. "That's good, because we've got a bit of a climb ahead."

Golden sunbeams striped the forest, illuminating patches in the dirt trail. Ransom marched over to the nearest. As he lifted his foot, the ray began to bend. Its perfect slant sprouted ridges, a staircase ascending into the sky.

Corwin felt a song coming on.

"And it's whispered that soon
If we all call the tune
Then the piper will lead us to reason"

Led Zeppelin's "Stairway to Heaven" continued to play in his head as he mounted the steps, each smooth and clear as a sheet of glass. The light which gave shape to them intensified ever so slightly, so that the beam's pathway was distinct even beyond the window of leaves that framed it.

"This does go to Heaven, right? Not the surface of the sun?"

"Depends who's climbing it."

As they rose above the beech trees, the forest's dense canopy spread forth like an otherworldly meadow. Butterflies bobbed and birds nested in its green and yellow folds. The treetop plains rolled towards distant hills in the east, but to the north, Corwin spied the march of civilization. A clearing had been carved into the land, dotted with crop fields and farm houses. Past a river bank, the walls of a medieval castle town arose and fortress towers thrust their parapets stark against the horizon.

They climbed higher and higher until Corwin could glimpse the sea. There he paused, raising his head to ward off a momentary dizzy spell. The thought of falling wasn't nearly as terrifying as it would have been a day ago, but that didn't make looking down any less hypnotic. Ransom waited a few steps ahead. Shading his eyes, he gazed skyward. The stairway appeared to stretch on forever.

Just then the sun pulsed, sending forth a ripple of light that pealed across the heavens. Corwin crossed his arms to guard against the blinding shockwave, but he felt only a static tingle as it passed. When he opened his eyes, the world below had changed.

The forest had receded, with highways and railroad tracks cutting efficiently through the trees. Modern skyscrapers replaced the fortress towers of old and suspension bridges spanned the river. The city had spilled over to both shores, growing like an inkblot on a fresh sheet of paper.

Corwin continued to climb as hundreds of cars sped along the roads beneath him, and soon he reached such a height that the traffic seemed to flow in slow motion. The sun pulsed a second time.

A boundless cityscape now carpeted the earth, with only a few green islands of woodland remaining. City walls had returned as if recalling the medieval age, only these soaring, metallic barricades were many times taller. They divided the opulent inner city from the outlying slums, where a jumble of buildings from different eras stood in various states of disrepair. Mega-structures loomed behind the walls, towers stacked atop towers and an enormous trapezoidal pyramid that dwarfed the skyscrapers of Corwin's day.

Another pulse, and the world became a glittering reflection of the blue sky. The seas had risen, reclaiming the land, and where once the sprawl of the outer city had been, only a scattering of eroded buildings now jutted from the waves. Mangrove trees dug their roots into the crumbling concrete and moss hung from windowsills. The great walls had endured, as had the inner city, though its rusty spires no longer shone as proudly.

"Is this—are we moving into the future?" asked Corwin.

"Into a future," Ransom replied.

Again the shockwave swept away what was. A curtain of amber draped the heavens, and Corwin's first thought was that day had faded to sunset, but when he looked ahead, he found that the sun still hung in the very same spot. However, this sun was larger and orange-tinged. The ocean had retreated and a forest of scarlet-leafed trees had sprung up vengefully in the wake of civilization's fall. Yet humanity lived on. Farmers penned livestock in the foundations of ruined buildings and horse-drawn wagons rolled atop cracked and beaten pavement. Inside the walls, the monolithic pyramid had become a fire-lit temple. Technology's clock had been turned back, or so the Earth proclaimed, but among the stars which poked through the day's thinning firmament were constellations new and unnatural. They twinkled in tight formations, patterns that spoke of intelligent design. Perhaps Earth hadn't abandoned technology, but rather those who commanded technology had abandoned Earth.

Corwin had little time to wonder about it before the next pulse flashed and the world was made anew. A biting-cold wind whistled and he hugged his arms with a shiver. The land had brightened, but only because sheets of glacial ice now stretched as far as the horizon. Glass panels domed the ancient inner city, a warm bastion of life that stood alone against the frozen tundra. Streaks of light darted like shooting stars between the manmade constellations, and a red sun burned dimly in the sky.

The sun mustered one final pulse, transporting Corwin and Ransom to the misty gray heart of a cloud. Corwin glanced down to check that the steps were still there. The stairway was only faintly visible. He could see the shadow of Ransom's back farther ahead, along with a dull glow where the sun had been.

"Ransom, I've had some time to think about things, and I've decided that I'd rather not go to Hell."

"Well that's a start."

"However, I'm not really sure that I want to go to Heaven, either. When it comes right down to it, there's more than enough wonder and mystery in my own universe, without the need for any heavenly fantasy realm. Why not let me be reincarnated as part of some karmic cycle?"

"Beware of karma," warned Ransom. "In the strict sense, it means that in all things, everyone gets what they deserve."

"Sounds like a nice thought," Corwin remarked.

"Far from it. Judging by karmic laws, one might say that an abused child is simply receiving payback for some sin committed in a past life. One might look at the Holocaust and declare that the Jews had it coming. With karma, there are no victims."

"Then to hell with karma! But even if I can't reincarnate, I'd still rather haunt the earth as a ghost than spend eternity prostrated on my knees, stroking some god's infinite ego."

Ransom's laugh echoed through the fog.

"You humans sure have some odd ideas about Heaven."

From above the clouds came a soft hymn that steadily grew louder and more triumphant.

"Allow me to tell you something that, as an atheist, I think you'll be glad to hear," said Ransom. "There are no religions in Heaven. Road maps lose their use once you've arrived at the final destination."

The sunbeam led through a gap in the clouds and there the stairs ended. Corwin stepped off onto the fluffy, white cloud top. A pearlescent gate swung open to greet the two travelers, admitting them to a land where fluted columns rose, upholding nothing, and slender bridges arched between sky islands. The whole place was bathed in celestial light and filled with the sound of the joyous hymn. Winged angels in flowing robes sat atop nimbus puffs, their fingers plucking harp strings, while a great multitude of humans knelt humbly and raised their hands, singing praise to a glowing figure enthroned above.

"For a moment there you were starting to get my hopes up, but this is just what I was afraid of," grumbled Corwin. "Is Heaven really like this?"

"I should hope not. Could you see me singing in a choir?"

"Oh, I don't know," Corwin said in an encouraging tone. "Maybe if you quit smoking, took a few classes . . ."

Ransom hopped onto one of the drifting nimbus puffs. Once Corwin had climbed aboard, the cloud began to rise, flying out over the singing congregation.

"What you see is no more than a popular conception of Heaven," said the angel. "I assure you that it falls well short of the reality."

"Yet isn't this exactly the sort of slavish devotion that your god demands?" asked Corwin. "He clearly has self-esteem issues."

Ransom tapped his cigarette case and the lid flipped open.

"Who stands to benefit the most from religion, God or man?"

"Going by your theology, it's man who has everything to lose."

"And everything to gain. So it is with worship. God doesn't need the praise, but man needs the humility."

"What you call humility looks a lot like groveling."

"Only to one who can't tell the difference between awe and cowardice."

They set down on one of the smaller islands where a line of boxy contraptions spat out reams of paper. The sign above them read: "Incoming Prayers."

"I might have a higher regard for prayers if your god actually answered them with any degree of consistency," mentioned Corwin.

"Answered them with a 'yes,' you mean."

"There are thousands of religions in the world with billions of followers sending up god-knows how many prayers every day. If any of them were the *one true faith*, shouldn't we see a preference for that group's prayers getting granted more frequently than the rest?"

"Perhaps you were looking for the wrong signs," replied Ransom. "When it comes to God and requests, religion's role isn't to get you everything you want, but to teach you what *to* want."

Grabbing up a length of loose paper, he stretched it before him as if reading a scroll. The usual prayers were all in evidence. Corwin spotted pleas for success in romance, for financial security, for good health in the face of illness or injury.

Unmoved, Ransom let the list fall.

"Many pray to be millionaires. Few pray to be saints."

At the island's edge, a dock extended into a current of wispy cirrus clouds that snaked through the air like a river. A gondola was tethered to one of its posts. Standing at the stern, a white-robed woman waited with an oar shaft in hand.

"But enough about prayers," said Ransom as he strode onto the dock. "Your Paradox of Heaven raises an altogether different concern."

"The problem is that the Christian conception of Heaven rests upon two conditions that simply aren't compatible," Corwin asserted. "Heaven is supposed to be a place without sin, yet Christians insist that we still have free will. The result is an illogical, unsustainable state of affairs."

They sat down in the gondola and the woman gracefully pushed them off from the dock. Her brown hair was gathered into rings that swung about the sash at her waist.

"Given all eternity," continued Corwin, "what's to keep me from sinning if I can do as I please?"

"It certainly wouldn't work in the mortal world," concurred Ransom. "Down there, doing what you please and doing what will bring you happiness are not always one and the same."

Since entering this realm, not once had the sound of music ceased. Profound and solemn and jubilant at the same time, the harmonious melody would have humbled even the greatest Renaissance composers. But as Corwin listened closely, a disturbance reached his ears. From the broad, stepped clouds below, a discordant note arose. Someone was singing out of tune.

Sporting a goatee and a shiny bald head, the man in question was either oblivious or supremely confident in his baritone voice. However, the fellow to his right was rapidly running out of patience. He gave the man a nudge, but it had no effect. An angry vein bulged on his forehead and he nudged harder.

"Hey now, what's the big idea?" the bald man thundered as he turned on him.

Abruptly the melody broke.

"You're not singing in tune!" the skinny fellow complained.

"You got a problem with my voice?"

"Now hold on!" said another. "There's no need to be unkind."

"But he's right," someone else chimed in. "That oaf was singing to his own piper!"

"Maybe a little variety is just what this choir needs!" yelled a rebellious hippy.

"No!" the skinny fellow shouted back. "What we need is harmony!"

The bald man's blood boiled.

"I'll show you harmony!"

Tearing off his robe like a pro wrestler, he roared and threw himself at the fellow with the tenor voice. In moments, the whole choir transformed into a roiling mosh pit. Fists flew and a few unfortunate souls rolled right off the clouds in a tangle of grappling limbs.

Ransom watched it all with a shameless smile on his face.

"What does it mean to sin?" he asked.

"To defy god's will—whatever *that* is—and choose to do evil instead of good," replied Corwin.

"What if I told you that most sin isn't a matter of choosing outright evil over good, but rather of choosing a lesser good over a greater one?"

"For example?"

"Take adultery," offered Ransom. "Sexual pleasure is a good thing, but not when it means being unfaithful to one's spouse, for the sanctity of marriage is something greater."

"You're saying that sin is a case of bad priorities."

"Most sin, yes. Acts of pure evil do happen, but humans usually need a little help to pull that sort of thing off."

A place could be seen up ahead where the river divided. Mountainous thunderheads narrowed the sky into canyons, their walls soaring gray and white with swaths of lilac and opal blue. The two branches of the river were fast lost to the cumulous billows.

"Miss, if you would take us left at the fork," Ransom said to their gondolier.

"As you wish, sir."

"You can call me Ransom, and this is my friend Corwin."

"Julia," she said in return.

"Tell me Julia, have you ever felt inclined to strike my friend over the head with that oar of yours?"

"Why would I want to do such a thing?" she asked, her expression bemused.

"Imagine that we rode your gondola a million more times. Might it ever occur?"

"What is time to me?"

"Point taken, but how about if we carried on in a most obnoxious manner?"

"Would you want to carry on in such a manner?"

"Well, no," admitted Ransom.

Julia giggled.

"You ask amusing questions, sir."

Their gondola yawed gently as they turned starboard and followed the twisting river into a deep cloud ravine. Lightning bolts leapt across the sliver of sky above and the airy walls rumbled like the belly of a great beast, but the lower reaches of the ravine were mostly calm, if a bit claustrophobic.

A pair of torches marked a short dock that stood downriver.

"That would be our destination," said Ransom.

They drew up beside it and the gondola glided to a stop.

"Shall I await your return?" asked Julia as her passengers disembarked.

"That won't be necessary," replied Ransom. "You have our thanks for the ride."

With a parting bow, the gondolier shoved off.

There was no shore at the foot of the dock, only a daunting doorway set in the wall of the thunderhead. Torchlight flickered darkly on its burnished bronze panels, silhouetting scenes of daring hunts and kingly feasts.

"In a place where no one is foolish enough to fall for lies, there can be no sin, for behind every sin is a lie." Ransom tensed his arms and pushed open the double doors. "At the root of all evil is deception."

From Corwin's agile memory, a Bible verse bubbled to mind.

"I thought that the love of money was the root of all evil?"

"And what does money represent?"

The groaning doors swung wide to unveil a sea of glittering gold. Bountiful riches were piled high, heaps of coins shining, speckled with sparkling gemstones. There were diamonds and pearls, emeralds and sapphires, and rubies as large as Corwin's fist. Gilded crowns and elegant jewelry littered the cavernous chamber, guarded by suits of armor that silently stood watch. It was a treasure trove fit for a pirate king or a miserly dragon.

"Money means different things to different people," spoke Corwin as he entered the room. "Power, prestige, freedom . . ."

"That's true in a sense, but we both know that power is not always bought, nor is prestige. And freedom? What has money to do with freedom? Recall how you felt in the winter of your eleventh year when you donated that collection of childhood toys."

It might have started because his mother had threatened to throw his things out, but when Corwin laid down that big cardboard box full of treasures at the charity drive, he couldn't help but feel relieved. They would bring joy to someone else now, and letting go of that box lifted a burden off more than just his shoulders.

"I felt *lighter*."

"Treasure can weigh a person down," said Ransom. "The freest among you are often those with the fewest possessions."

"But to be free from worrying about how to pay the bills! To be free from the anxiety of not knowing where your next meal might come from!"

"You're getting closer, but what you speak of is not freedom. Slaves don't fret over paying the bills."

"Then what is it?" Corwin asked in frustration.

"Think! What drives kings to hide behind castle walls, investors to diversify in case the market falls, and pharaohs to be buried with their riches? What is only sought harder the more men gain, but is always sought in vain?"

Voices moaned from tombs and bluish spectres materialized before Corwin's eyes. Their transparent bodies were garbed in royal vestments, worn ragged by the passage of eons. Some wandered the chamber while others sat atop thrones that jutted from the spoils. Bony hands scooped up coins, but could hold them for only an instant before the gold fell through their ghostly fingers.

"It's security!"

"Security," repeated Ransom. "An obsessive desire to control future uncertainties. Nothing poisons man's heart more than fear of the future, and for most of you, money is seen as the surest guard against that fear. Thus you hoard the wealth of the present world, when you should be seeking the treasures of the next."

"Another case of bad priorities," Corwin concluded.

A canal cut through the immense cavern, which they crossed by way of a footbridge. Stray coins glinted under the water, the stream's winding course vanishing behind the bars of a sewer tunnel.

"By the way," said Corwin, "if we happen across a magic lamp with a genie inside, I call dibs on the first wish."

"What would you wish for?"

"To go to a heaven of *my* choosing. Personally, I'm leaning towards Pie Heaven at the moment."

Ransom rubbed his stomach.

"Mmmm . . . Pie . . ."

"Also, if the way you describe sin is correct, then it seems to me that your god is rather unfair about it."

"How so?"

"According to you, it's not a lack of free will, but a lack of stupidity that prevents sin from occurring in Heaven. But whose fault is that? If mortal man is too dumb to know what's good for him, isn't god to blame for making us that way?"

"You see through a clouded lens, but it is not so clouded that you can't tell light from dark," said Ransom.

"Why not just give us perfect vision from the start?"

"You ask why man should need faith. I think you already know the answer to that."

Though it pained him to admit it, Corwin found that the angel was right. A certain phrase about heroes and pragmatists came to mind.

"Because being pragmatic isn't enough."

"Faith makes doing the right thing heroic, and Heaven is a place for heroes."

"Even atheist heroes?" pressed Corwin with a smirk.

"I wouldn't know," Ransom glibly replied. "I've never met one."

"What about heroic Buddhists or Muslims or Hindus? Jesus claimed that no one goes to the father except through him."

"Indeed. Without the Redeemer's sacrifice, none would enter Heaven. What's your point?"

Ransom's succinct response took the wind out of Corwin's sails. He could handily recite a hundred Bible verses word-for-word, but interpreting them was another matter.

"Okay," he gathered his thoughts, "but by that token, if Heaven can be earned by anyone, what's the use of Christianity?"

"Does a lover ask what the use is of knowing his beloved better?" posed Ransom. "And understand that Heaven is not 'earned.' A prize so extraordinary as that can never be deserved. It comes always as a gift."

A gold ring caught Corwin's eye and he stooped to pick it up. Its band was thick and masculine, set with a square-cut amethyst and engraved with crooked runes.

"With the way some preachers harp on about tithing, I'd assumed that you could buy your way in," he muttered, admiring the ring as he slipped it on his finger.

Upon noticing the trinket, Ransom's expression stiffened.

"It's a little late to warn you, but you really shouldn't touch any of the treasure here."

"Why?"

A malevolent shriek stood Corwin's hair on end. One of the wraiths had halted behind them, its arm raised, a knobby finger pointing, accusing.

"Thieves!" it rasped. "Plunderers!"

"That's why," said Ransom.

Spirits animated the suits of armor, their limbs jerking mechanically into motion as Corwin tugged at the ring.

"It's not coming off!"

He stepped back and tripped over something protruding from the heaped coins and gems. It was the arm of a golden sculpture, an eyeless effigy so lifelike that Corwin could almost hear the tormented scream forever frozen on its lips. A fresh look at the chamber revealed others like it, their poses bespeaking horror and despair.

From his place atop the uppermost throne, the high king of the wraiths thumped his ethereal scepter.

"Give our intruders the baptism of gold!"

21

A HEART-SHAPED CAGE

White-blue eyes burned like hot coals beneath the visors of the possessed suits of armor. Two were nearly upon them, advancing from either side, their plate mail clinking as they descended the heaps of hoarded treasure. The first raised his halberd. Swiftly, Ransom stepped inside the swing, caving the armor's helm with a blow and disarming it. He drove the halberd's point through the second armor, lifted it and brought it crashing down on the first.

"Succumb!" shrieked the wraith beyond, unsheathing its phantom blade.

Ransom freed the halberd and threw it, but like a sword through smoke, it only disturbed the apparition briefly. The wraith reformed as the weapon speared a ruined pillar behind it.

"That's a problem."

Grabbing Corwin, Ransom kicked up coins as he bolted away. Wraiths wailed and armors clanged at their backs.

"You're an angel!" shouted Corwin. "Can't you handle a few ghosts?"

"Spirits can't be stopped by physical force. Even severing body from soul with a soulrender won't help if your foe doesn't have a body to begin with!"

"How can they be stopped?"

"Normally a prayer or two would do the trick, but ever since I broke my oath, the Father has been putting my prayers on his back burner."

"Then warp us out of here!"

"There's nowhere they won't follow so long as you're wearing that ring."

Corwin pulled and twisted, but the ring wouldn't budge.

"Got any Vaseline in that suit of yours?" he asked as they clambered up another glittering hill.

"Afraid not," replied Ransom. "But I've got a pair of scissors! Compared to the 'baptism of gold,' losing a finger might not be so bad."

"Yeah," spat Corwin, "and I'll be hailed as a hero when I return to the Shire!"

They had just passed the hill's crest when the ground shifted beneath them. There was a jingling rumble as thousands of coins spilled, golden waves breaking against a stony shore. Corwin caught his foot on a crown and half-slipped.

"Holy Mother of—"

Ransom's fist rattled his skull and Corwin tumbled down the slope in a wild roll.

"What was that for?" he complained at the bottom.

"Blasphemy," said Ransom. "We could use the Mediatrix on our side about now!"

The mound was coming apart, a long shape rising out of it. A tail.

Corwin paled.

"About those scissors . . . I may just be starting to come around."

Like a wet dog, the scaly beast shook itself, flinging gems and medallions. Corwin couldn't see the rest of its body, but he heard a loud stomp, and then the tail swung out over their heads, smashing through one of the cavern's thick columns.

"Try to keep up!" yelled Ransom.

Again they were running. Corwin spotted a yellow glow between the hills ahead. Another river divided the chamber, broader than the canal that they had crossed before. It was a river not of water, but of liquid gold. An arching strip of stone connected their side of the treasury to a cave in the chamber wall. Above it were carved two crowned skulls, waterfalls pouring from their mouths, giving rise to pillars of steam as they met the simmering current below.

A booming roar shivered the walls. Dust sprinkled down from the ceiling and steam shrouded Corwin as he dashed for the cave. He glimpsed a giant shadow rearing over his shoulder and dove.

With an earth-shaking crash, the cave's entrance collapsed. Falling rubble threatened to bury him alive, and would have if not for the flooding. Submerged in bottle-green murkiness, he swam hard as boulders splashed and sank all around him. At last he reached the shallows and came up beside Ransom.

Crawling onto the shore, Corwin noticed a change.

The ring! It came loose!

He saw where it had slipped off beneath the water's edge and stepped away, glad to be rid of the blasted thing.

Twenty tons of rock sealed the passage to the treasury. Through it came a wraith, its voice a wretched moan, icy breath trembling the torches. It hovered before them with a bluish saber in hand. Ages-old hatred burned in its eyes, but the wraith's lust for treasure was greater than its lust for blood. Swooping low, it seized the jeweled ring, and like a mist vanquished by the sun, both wraith and ring evaporated.

"Guess we won't be needing these," said Ransom, stowing his pair of barber shop scissors.

Wet and weary, Corwin trudged towards the rear of the cave, where a short flight of stairs led to a second bronze doorway.

"Can we please go to Pie Heaven now?"

"As tempting as that sounds, I intend to see that you end up someplace even better."

"There's a saying about things that sound too good to be true."

"Oh, but it's more true, more real than all the splendor of the mortal world!"

"I rather like the splendor of the mortal world!" retorted Corwin. "I like junk food and violent movies and rock & roll and sex! A heaven without those things doesn't sound like a place I want to be."

Ransom eased one of the doors open.

"Perhaps you would prefer a paradise like this one?"

Sweeping balconies let in the sun, its heraldic light gleaming on marble tiles and florid pillars so tall and slender that Corwin doubted whether they really supported any weight. Tasseled cushions and richly embroidered rugs were strewn with abandon. Roses were in bloom, their vines clinging to sculptures, and cool water sluiced from fountains into wading pools.

The palace held many sights, but none more striking than its occupants. Wearing lacey garments of scarlet and spun gold, the voluptuous beauties of the harem were enough to make Corwin's lungs forget how to breathe. One of them sauntered over, balancing a saucer of fresh fruit.

"You know, I used to make fun of people who believed in this sort of thing," Corwin said to his attorney as he plucked a few choice grapes from the arrangement, "but it's actually kind of awesome."

The attendant whisked the fruit away and it took every ounce of Corwin's willpower to wrench his gaze from the sway of her red sarong.

"To be sure, a paradise like this is a little crude, not to mention totally pointless if biological reproduction is a thing of the past, but at least I can see the appeal."

"The Father is a creator, not a destroyer," said Ransom. "Nothing good in the mortal world is undone in Heaven."

"So there *is* sex in Heaven?"

Fetching a long-stemmed glass off a passing tray, Ransom sampled the fizzy vintage.

"The question isn't whether or not you can have sex in Heaven. The question is whether you'll care."

"How could I not?"

They came upon a young boy with straw-colored hair at play on one of the rugs. A mountain of sweets topped the saucer next to him. Gourmet chocolates and gooey caramels and frosted cakes tempted the eye, a cocoa smear staining the boy's cheek, but presently his attention was focused on his toy truck. The shiny red and blue semi had a gray trailer and long, chrome exhaust pipes. He made a *vroom* sound as he excitedly pushed it back and forth.

"That's me!" exclaimed Corwin, studying the child in amazement.

His younger self, however, seemed totally uninterested in the two adult visitors.

"That toy truck once meant the world to you," spoke Ransom.

"That's not just some toy truck," objected Corwin. "That's Optimus Prime, fearless leader of the Autobots!"

As they watched, young Corwin detached the trailer and transformed the semi truck into a formidable robot warrior. What had been *vrooms* became the *pew-pew* of a laser rifle.

"To a five-year-old, toys and candy are the height of pleasure," said Ransom, "but when one becomes an adult, new pleasures present themselves. Given the choice between a night of passionate sex and a Snickers bar, which would the adult Corwin choose?"

"Well I do like Snickers."

Ransom cast his client a withering glance.

"Maybe not *that* much," blurted Corwin.

"In the journey from childhood to adulthood, man's desires evolve. How much more will they evolve when you come into the fullness of the next life? Once you've tasted the pleasures of Heaven, I highly doubt that the act of wedging your bodies together like sweaty Tetris blocks will still hold the same allure."

The analogy made sense enough to Corwin, but there was something about it that rang hollow. Christianity didn't paint a pretty picture of Heaven, because it didn't paint any picture at all.

"If Heaven is really so great, why all the secrecy? Christians are more than happy to talk about Hell, but on the subject of Heaven 'eye has not seen, ear has not heard' and so on. One might think that hope takes a back seat to fear."

"Explaining Heaven to mortals is like explaining color to a man born blind," replied Ransom. "It's like explaining the world to an unborn child that knows only the womb! Hell is a simpler thing, for it is less than Earth, but Heaven is more."

"Can nothing be said of it then?"

"I didn't say that."

They roamed out onto the rearmost balcony and Corwin had to double-check the view. Sure enough, sunlight still poured through the other porticos, but this last one inexplicably looked out upon a starry night. He could see that their palace resided atop a mountain that rose high above the moonlit clouds. What's more, it wasn't the only one. Other palaces crowned the far-off peaks, their lofty towers capped with golden, onion-shaped domes.

Leaning against the banister, Ransom stared up at the stars.

"The Father is infinite. Our finite minds will never fully grasp him, not even in Heaven. But in our smallness is our joy, for to learn of the Father—to discover his ways and the glorious works of his hands—is an adventure without end."

He turned to Corwin.

"You said once that you dreamed of being captain of the starship *Enterprise*. In a way, your dream wasn't too far off the mark. Heaven, you see, is *infinite discovery*."

For a time Corwin said nothing. The thrill of scientific discovery was a joy that he had always associated with atheism, but what if that very same joy was another clue, another foretaste of the divine?

"And that's only the beginning," continued Ransom. "Just as your mind has an endless appetite for discovery, so too does your heart have an endless appetite for love. God alone can sate it."

"But how can love be perfectly satisfied in a heaven that only some people go to?" The thought had been percolating in Corwin's head, and now it came fiercely to a boil. "Can a mother be blissfully happy, knowing that her children are burning in a lake of fire? Could I be at peace if I knew that my father was being tortured eternally?"

"*Her* children? *Your* father? Listen to yourself!" snapped Ransom. "That sort of childish passion is not love. It is a selfish desire that seeks to possess the other like a piece of property!"

"What could be more selfish than enjoying yourself in Heaven without a care for those who didn't make god's cut?" Corwin fired back.

Their argument was interrupted by the singsong tune of boyish laughter. Young Corwin bounded past and disappeared through a curtain of hanging beads into an oval chamber, a room within the room. Ransom started after him and his client followed, the beads jingling as they pushed through the doorway.

Plopping himself down onto a cushion, young Corwin gleefully admired his peculiar gallery. An array of nine-foot-tall crystal shards stood clustered around him, and frozen inside each was a person. Like frosted glass, the foggy tint of the crystals masked the features of those trapped within, but Corwin knew them at once.

"Mary!" he gasped, rushing to the nearest. His eyes then panned to its neighbors. "Father! Aunt Rose!"

His family and dearest friends were all there, imprisoned in the crystal cages of his heart.

"Here you keep them safe from harm," said Ransom. "Your own private collection of souls!"

"That's not fair!" fumed Corwin. "My love isn't really like that!"

The angel regarded him with sympathy, but not softness.

"Even in your best thoughts there are shades of darkness. Such are the consequences of the Fall. You recognize that to love is to wish the best for someone, but you must know that love is more than that. It is also respect for the other *as* other. In true love, there is a kind of letting go."

Corwin sank to his knees, his palm pressed against the shard.

"And if the person you love is a drug addict or a compulsive gambler? Aren't there times when loving someone means striving to change them, not simply accepting their decisions and letting go?"

"And if the person you love is an atheist?" countered Ransom. "We can try to change those who choose a path of self-destruction, but we cannot force them to change. To do so would not be love."

"But must Hell be an end to trying? What if I don't want to give up?"

"You would reason with the damned? Talk sense into demons?" Ransom's tone was incredulous. "You know not of what you speak.

"The Father loves them still, infinitely more than you ever could. But just as Hell is less than Earth, the damned are less than the living. You will not mourn for them."

"I won't even mourn for them? How can you say that?"

"On Earth, one may love the idea of a person more than a person's true self. A ruthless dictator may be a loving father in the eyes of his children. But in Heaven, we see the fullness of things. We rejoice in perfect justice."

"Love is stronger than justice!" Corwin insisted.

"Love demands justice!" retorted Ransom. "Ask yourself which would be a worse fate for your beloved: to be killed or to live a long life as a serial killer?"

Calming his mind, Corwin considered the meaning behind the question. By the logic of materialism, death was an ultimate end. People simply ceased to be. The loss was utter and complete. So why was the thought of a loved one turning into something vile so much worse? To think of his father as a murderer, a rapist or a child molester—it was hard even to imagine, and far more disturbing than the image of his lifeless body laid to rest in that coffin.

That was true death, he realized. He could love the dead, but could he love a serial killer? Not in the same way. Perhaps not at all.

"Better to die than to live as a monster," he declared, "because to do so would be to die twice. It would mean the death of something inside, something more precious than a beating heart."

Light enveloped the frozen figures. With a flash, they vanished, set free from their cages. A cloud of sparks twinkled like stars in the glassy crystals. Ransom laid a hand on Corwin's shoulder as their glow softly died.

"A wise answer."

Love is not mere kindness, thought Corwin. *It's not something easy or safe . . . It's the most dangerous thing in the world.*

22

Wars and Rumors of Wars

Departing the inner room, Ransom led the way up a spiral staircase that climbed one of the palace towers. Arrow slits were spaced every fifteen paces along the outer wall, and like the rearmost balcony, they overlooked a world whose clock had been turned to night. Torches crackled in sconces between them, casting light on the tower's smooth masonry.

"You've run out of paradoxes," said Ransom. "But surely you have other arguments that were never put to paper?"

"Why bother?" sighed Corwin. "Without proof, we could go on trading arguments until Hell freezes over. Would it change anything?"

"You fear that we'd be running in circles, but thus far we haven't been. You've agreed with much that you didn't think you would, and found that you believed in much that you didn't think you did."

It was true, Corwin had to admit. He'd lived his life taking many things for granted, things such as free will and intrinsic values, without ever giving much thought to what they implied.

"But I'm still not the kind of believer that you want me to be," he said. "If I had met someone like you in life, maybe things would have turned out differently. Instead of a virtuous atheist, maybe I would have been . . ."

"A skeptical Christian?" guessed Ransom.

"I was going to say an optimistic agnostic," snorted Corwin with a laugh. "But who knows?"

Outside, thick clouds veiled the starlit vista, and from above, the raucous din of drumbeats and war cries, quiet and remote at first, began to reverberate through the walls.

"That which keeps you from believing runs deeper than the claims of Christianity," stated Ransom.

"Your can defend those claims philosophically, but there's philosophy, and then there's real life," said Corwin. "When you witness how much violence is committed in the name of god, it's hard to view religion as anything other than a poisonous lie. You don't see atheists killing each other over the proper way to interpret Darwin's *Origin of Species*."

"And if they did, would you conclude that all interpretations must be equally false?"

"That's not the point!"

"I hope your point isn't that religion is the cause of all war, or some other uninformed nonsense," Ransom droned.

"War has many causes. I'm not so simple-minded as to lump them all into one tidy catchphrase. But you can't deny that religion has a history soaked in blood!"

"Hasn't it also united people, brought those from different tribes, races and cultures together?"

"At what cost? Unity has never been god's top priority. Jesus himself said that he came not to bring peace, but the sword."

"So he did."

A wooden beam barred a doorway at the top of the stairs, the stout length of oak rattling with the crashes and clamor of the world it locked away. Ransom lifted it off and laid it aside.

"Religion *is* rather like a sword," he said as he threw open the door.

Rough-hewn bricks paved a walkway that ran atop the fortress walls. Corwin hastily ducked as a huge ball of burning pitch whooshed overhead, exploding in the courtyard below. A knight commander was barking orders and waving his blade. Archers rushed up the stairs on Corwin's left to reinforce the walls, ring mail jangling beneath gray and crimson tunics.

"There's too many of them!" lamented one of the knights who huddled not far away. "We're all going to die in this godforsaken land!"

The longbow shook in his tremulous grasp. A veteran with a bushy beard pressed his back to the merlon beside him.

"Fear not, brother," said the large man. "The Lord is with us this day."

"As he was with those in Damascus? The Lord isn't going to hold these walls."

"By God's grace, we will. And if we should fall, His Holiness has already seen to our souls. Death has no claim on us!"

War horns sounded with a doleful tone that echoed off the fortifications. The young knight tried to steady his bow by clasping it with both hands. His breath came in spasms, and sweat drenched his unsullied tunic.

"I don't want to die," he whimpered.

Seizing him by the collar, the veteran throttled the fear out of him.

"Then fight!" he growled.

Corwin gazed over the ramparts. The sky was bleached. Bone-white clouds domed a battlefield on which a staggering army had amassed, their forces clad in turbans and conical helms. Scimitars flashed as the front lines charged, the regiments behind them marching inexorably onward. Catapults loosed their fiery bombs, and siege towers rolled towards the walls.

Nocking arrows, the two knights spun from behind the merlon and fired. The twang of a hundred bowstrings struck a discordant melody.

Many an onrushing warrior fell, yet the vanguard surged on, anguished screams drowned beneath trampling boots, and the disciplined soldiers that followed were not easily hindered. Raising a wall of shields, they covered their advancing archers, the wall lowering briefly for the Moors to return fire.

Corwin scuttled after Ransom, keeping an eye to the horizon as it darkened with a volley of arrows. Shades might be able to pass through the living, but how they fared against pointy projectiles wasn't a topic he was eager to explore.

The trenchant darts pelted the battlements, some whizzing through the crenels to punish unwary knights. One such knight collapsed right at Corwin's feet—the same young man who had deemed the battle hopeless. Blood spurted from his neck and Corwin averted his gaze as he gingerly sidestepped the corpse.

"I hope that indulgence did the trick," he murmured sincerely.

An arrow streaked towards Ransom's skull, and without even a glance, the angel caught it out of the air, snapping the shaft in his fist.

"The mortal realm is under siege," he proclaimed. "Or perhaps it would be better to say that all men are born into enemy territory. The Father has not abandoned you. He has sent his Word so that you might arm yourselves, given you a means by which to prevail, but few there are who ready themselves for battle."

Corwin hopped back as a grappling hook flew between them. A quick tug pulled it out of its arc and the hook caught hold of the ramparts. Hefting a battle hammer, the bushy-bearded knight swung it like a golf club and knocked the prongs loose. But no sooner had it fallen away than a dozen more hurtled over the wall, long ladders thunking against the bricks.

A high-flying hook sailed over the knight's head. Yanked back suddenly, it snagged on his ring mail, and before he could twist free, he was dragged down hollering into the bloodthirsty throng.

"Those who handle a sword carelessly are liable to cut themselves," continued Ransom. "And a blade that isn't well forged will break when it meets adversity."

Arrows, boulders and boiling oil rained down on the Moorish warriors scaling the walls, but the crusaders could not stop them all.

"Allahu Akbar!" yelled the first of the Moors to gain the top of the battlements.

His scimitar leapt to his hand and the nearest archer drew his broadsword.

"For God and King Richard!" the knight bellowed.

Their blades met, the crusader deftly turning the Moor's scimitar aside. He brought his pommel up hard against the man's jaw, laying him low, and lifted his broadsword for the finishing blow. But the Moor also carried a mace. The knight's sword shattered upon blunt steel and a rising scimitar slid between his ribs.

"If one wields it poorly, a sword may even cut down those whom it was meant to save," spoke Ransom as he picked a path through the carnage.

Springing atop the wall, a black-cloaked Moor spotted a crusader whose back was turned. He unsheathed his dagger, smiling wickedly. The knight was already engaged in battle, but as the man darted in for the kill, he swung his foe full-around. The Moor's dagger sank into the back of his comrade, and with a mighty kick, the knight sent them both tumbling to their deaths.

"I'd prefer a world with no swords at all," said Corwin. "Organized religion moves armies. It provides the incentive for holy wars, for witch hunts and suicide bombers."

"As opposed to unorganized religion?"

"One can have spirituality without religion. It would at least be a step in the right direction."

"Only if the 'right direction' is atheism," replied Ransom. "Imagine that you had some ideas about God and wrote them down. Now you've got a bible. But suppose someone mis-interprets your words and you correct them. You've just given yourself authority to interpret your scriptures. Congratulations, you're now the pope! It's as simple as that. An organized religion is *any religion that can be communicated."*

Maybe that's why so much New Age talk sounds like mumbo jumbo, considered Corwin. To talk a lot without actually saying anything was an art that spiritualist gurus had honed to perfection.

"I was trying to compromise, but fine, then let it all rot! Unlike religion, there's nothing in atheism to compel a person to violence."

"Was the atheism of Stalin or Moa Tse-tung without violence?" Ransom paused as a line of spearmen sprinted up the stairs to join the fray. "Theism begins with 'God is,' atheism with 'God is not.' Go beyond that, and either viewpoint can be twisted to serve a dark end."

"Going beyond that is what every religion does! I'm not about to defend atheistic dictators, but the blood on their hands is irrelevant. It doesn't change the fact that religion is dangerous."

"Of course religion is dangerous!" Ransom's voice boomed irritably. "The yearning for God lies close to the heart of what it means to be human. Anything rooted so deeply within you is bound to arouse strong passions, even violent ones."

The next Moor to come over the wall was greeted by a dozen thrusting spears. His scimitar proved no match for the seven-foot-long polearms. Skewered and tossed back, he fell with a dying shriek that caused many of those climbing to freeze a fearful second on their ropes and rungs.

"Maybe Buddha had the right idea," said Corwin. "A little detachment would do the world good."

"Siddhartha understood that with passion comes pain, but he failed to see that some passions are worth the price."

"Even if the price is war?"

"Wars are always fought in the name of something good, be it God, freedom, justice or what have you. It's difficult to rally an army with the battle cry: 'Let us go forth and slaughter in the name of *evil!*'"

Bolstered by the range of their spears, the crusaders strengthened their hold on the walls, but the siege towers were drawing ever closer.

"Light up those towers!" shouted the knight commander.

Archers swapped their arrows for ones wrapped in oil-soaked rags, and Corwin realized that the braziers set along the wall weren't there merely to help guardsmen see in the dark. Setting arrows aflame, the knights focused their fire on the towers, the nearest of which was soon smoking like a rolling funeral pyre.

"Would you do away with every ideal that men fight over?" asked Ransom.

Corwin was about to say that, unlike God, ideals such as freedom and justice were universal concepts that people could agree upon, but his inner skeptic silenced the words before they came to his lips. One had only to look at political parties to see how bitterly divided men were, even over the most basic of ideals. And many of his fellow atheists would argue that notions such as justice were no more real than God.

Hearing the *whip-thoom* of another catapult, he turned and saw a fire-ringed shadow blotting out the sky. The pitch exploded against the ramparts. Black smoke smothered him, then cleared, a blustery breeze sweeping away the soot. And Corwin wasn't on the wall anymore.

He and Ransom stood on a hilltop, the fortress a gray promontory across the plain. Besieged on all sides, it seemed destined to fall before the might of the Moorish hoard.

So many men, he thought, *so eager to hack each other apart.*

A line several hundred prisoners long trailed down the side of the hill—Christian knights whom the Moors had over-taken outside the walls. They'd been stripped of their armor, ropes binding their wrists.

"I can accept men fighting and dying for a cause," said Corwin. "But not when that cause is a ticket to god's won-derland in the next life. Religion preys on the suicidal. It gives those who long for a release from life's pain an excuse to go out in a bloody blaze of martyrdom."

"No true martyr is eager for death," replied Ransom. "To lay down a life that you don't cherish . . . Where is the sacrifice in that?"

Prodded by the tip of a sword, Sir Willehad strode for-ward. The dire view from the hilltop wounded him deeper than any archer's arrow ever could. Such an overwhelming host! They must've come to sack one of the great cities, and this siege was but a stop along the way.

Lord, I ask not for a miracle, he silently prayed.

His brothers had long walked with death by their sides, but what of the villagers? Most of the men would be butch-ered, and those who didn't lose their lives would lose all dignity, forced to grovel and feign thanks to their conquerors while their wives and daughters were enslaved in the troops' pleasure houses. Their sons would be taken and indoctrinated, forged into the fanatic warriors that made up the disposable front lines of the Mohammedan fighting force.

I ask not for victory this day.

Perhaps there was justice in this. He had heard talk of crusaders in other lands, boasts that made his stomach turn. But those men were not his brothers. Those men were not facing the axe. Hopefully some of the villagers who had fled at the attack's onset had escaped. They might even bring word to the king, though by then, this fortress would be flying a different flag.

I ask only for the courage to do your will.

"See how the infidels are brought to their knees!" trumpeted Khalid, commander of the caliph's Eighth Battalion. "But Allah is merciful." Khalid threw down a Bible, one of the spoils from the monastery they had sacked the day before. He kicked it open. "Submit to your rightful Lord, spit on this book of lies, and your life will be spared."

"Never!" grated the knight.

With a nod, Khalid signaled to the soldier behind Willehad. The knight was forced down, his knees slammed to the dirt and his chest pressed to a stump that now served for a headsman's block.

"The martyr says to God 'this life is yours,'" said Ransom, "while the suicide declares 'it's my life,' and no words hold greater peril than those."

The axe fell in a black arc.

"He who gains his life shall lose it. He who loses his life shall gain it."

As Willehad's headless corpse was dragged unceremoniously aside, the next of the king's men approached the stump. Stone-faced, he knelt of his own accord, ignoring Khalid's offer.

Corwin had seen enough. He turned his back as the executions continued, the thwack of the axe sounding every few moments. *It's insanity. Both religion and war. It's all insanity!* But then a new sound arose. For reasons he couldn't explain, the knights lifted their voices in song.

It was a moving chant, slow and reverent. And though the lyrics were all in Latin, Corwin could feel power in the words.

"Salve, Regina, Mater misericordiæ
vita, dulcedo, et spes nostra, salve
ad te clamamus exsules filii Hevæ
ad te suspiramus, gementes et flentes
in hac lacrimarum valle"

Over the field their voices carried, only strengthening as the corpses piled up. Even the headsman felt something stir within him. Who were these men, who went to their deaths with neither fear nor hatred in their eyes? Were they truly the detestable swine of whom the Prophet spoke? Then why was their song so hauntingly beautiful?

Yet another knight knelt, baring his neck to the axe. What a terrible weight, that axe! The headsman's grip faltered. *No more.* The axe slid from his sweaty palms, fell to the grass. *This cannot be Allah's will.* Deep inside, he felt his consciousness touch something lost, now found again. There was an innocence that he could never regain, but a goodness that he could, if only for a moment. The gravity of the choice pressed upon him.

A moment of life, or a lifetime of death?

"I . . . I wish to become a Christian!"

In less time than it took him to draw another breath, Khalid's knife opened his throat. The headsman's body rolled down the hill like so many of the heads his axe had hewn.

Again I cull our ranks, thought Khalid. He had seen it coming, predicted it. *There's always one or two like him.* It was best to deal with such matters swiftly and soundly, before the sickness spread. Much evil could be sewn by the hushed murmurings of a few soldiers around a campfire.

With cold efficiency, he wiped clean the blade.

"You!" He pointed to one of his men. "Take up the axe!"

Having witnessed what a moment of weakness cost his brother, the soldier obeyed without delay. And still the Christians sang.

"Not one of these men will renounce the Redeemer. Not one of them will live," Ransom said as smoke began to swirl. "Do you sense nothing noble in their sacrifice? Is their choice foolishness to you?"

"What's foolish is that this had to happen at all," replied Corwin. The smoke veiled his eyes, whisking him and his attorney back atop the fortress walls. "Abolishing religion might not bring an end to all wars, but it would bring an end to some, and isn't that enough? If doing away with all this business of gods and devils could save us from just one nuclear war, wouldn't that be worth it?"

"Were Christianity but a myth, you would be right," said the angel. "If there is no afterlife, then all the worldly merits of faith—all the hope and kindness and charity that the Redeemer has inspired—would not be enough. No honest man can say that religion is a wonderful dream. If it is not true, then it is not wonderful at all."

"That's exactly my point!" exclaimed Corwin. "Christianity cannot stand on its perceived benefits to society alone. No religion can!"

Moors jumped from a burning siege tower, abandoning its timber skeleton as it veered off course, its great wooden wheels crushing the corpses of those who had fallen in the earlier assault, grinding their bones into the mire.

"But if it *is* true . . ." Ransom bent to light a cigarette in one of the blazing braziers. "If the fate of not just nations, but eternal souls hangs in the balance, then it is worth any price—an infinite price! For such is the worth of the blood that was spilled to redeem you."

23

RIDDLES AND REVELATIONS

The only good reason to believe something is if it's true.

In his past life, those words had spurred Corwin to set off on a quest that led him as far away from God as atheistic humanism could take him, only it wasn't as far as he thought. A part of him now wondered: *If I had lived a little longer, steadfastly followed that maxim a little farther, might it have taken me full circle?*

He had to marvel at his own invincible stubbornness. Those contrite atheists who "wished they could believe" would surely have broken long before now. But not Corwin. Truth was the only thing that he wished for, which made the sneaking sense of joy he felt as Christianity's puzzle came together all the more disconcerting.

Prudently, he reminded himself that the puzzle wasn't complete yet. There remained one glaring problem in the case for Christianity: *Christians.*

"How am I supposed to believe all this stuff when Christians themselves don't believe it? If they did, they'd all be shining examples of love and humility, but when I look at Christian churches, what I see instead is intolerance and hypocrisy."

"In order to tolerate that which runs contrary to one's convictions, one must first *have* convictions," said Ransom. "Your secular society doesn't prize tolerance. It prizes indifference. And despite what you may think, Christianity doesn't have a monopoly on hypocrites."

"Maybe not, but it sure has a lot of them, and they don't do your cause any favors. Neither does your fanatical adherence to the scribblings of some ancient sheep herders that we're not even sure existed."

"Disregard all your ancient scribblings and you won't have much history left."

Moorish arrows ricocheted off the unyielding bricks of the guard tower that stood before them. Ransom reached for the iron ring on the door. As the portal swung shut at their backs, all the tumultuous noise of the battlefield was hushed in an instant.

They were somewhere dark and musty. Ransom procured a candlestick from a small table beside the entrance and held the wick to the end of his cigarette. A tiny flame was soon waxing happily, illuminating a path that was about the same width as the walkway they had just left, only this path was quiet, peaceful and hemmed in by tall bookcases. Dusty tomes and papyrus scrolls were stacked three stories high to where brass candelabras hung, flickering and fuming.

Corwin examined the writing on some of the book spines.

"The Douay-Rheims Bible, the New American Bible, the King James Version . . . These are all Bibles."

"This library is home to every edition, translation and iteration of the Holy Bible that ever was," said Ransom, "along with apostolic letters and several long lost writings by the Patriarchs. You'll find the approved, the apocryphal and even the illustrated."

"There's even a copy of the Jefferson Bible!" Corwin said in surprise as he pulled a modern-looking volume off the shelf.

"I figured you'd like that one, although a Bible without miracles is like an issue of Playboy without nudity. It kind of misses the point."

Replacing the book, Corwin continued down the aisle. He ran his fingers along the bindings and marveled at the stupendous effort his race had put into cataloging this most unbelievable of tales.

"If Christians would just admit that most of those stories are mythical, more people might actually take them seriously."

"Why assume that every account of the supernatural must be a myth?" Ransom inquired.

"I live in the real world, or at least I used to," muttered Corwin.

"What's more logical: believing in an omnipotent creator who can defy the laws of nature, or one who cannot?"

"Sure, a god who authored the rules should be able to break them, but believing in such a god doesn't mean that you have to take the Bible literally. No rational person really believes in Noah's Ark, Moses parting the Red Sea, or Jonah living in the belly of a whale. The Bible is an interesting book, but it's not a historically accurate one."

"The Bible is a collection of books," said Ransom. "Some passages are meant to be taken literally, others are symbolic, still others are poetry. Unlocking the truth requires the correct key."

"Are you saying that there's truth to those outlandish stories?"

"There is, though not necessarily in the way you imagine. Much was left unwritten. What if I told you that Noah was a member of an advanced, Atlantian civilization who kept a gene bank of all the Earth's organisms?"

"Now that's a flood story I'd like to hear!" laughed Corwin. "But I can't argue about what's not written, only about what is. And this I can tell you for sure: To accept the historical claims of the Bible is to discover a tale of two gods, neither one as perfect as your theology suggests. The god of the Old Testament is a cruel and petty tyrant who thinks nothing of massacring women and children. And while Christians like to think of their New Testament god being kinder and gentler, what we really find in Jesus is a puritanical moralist whose strict standards are impossible to live up to, even for his own hand-picked apostles!"

"The Father and the Redeemer are different persons, yet the same God. His love is fierce and his wrath terrible, but his ways are never without mercy."

"Calling god's wrath terrible is putting it mildly. In the Old Testament, he wipes out nearly the entire world in the flood, sends the Angel of Death to kill a bunch of children in Egypt, and orders the Israelites to murder every living thing in Jericho, sparing not even the livestock! Where is the justice in that? Where is the mercy?"

"Your lives are valuable precisely because they are not your own. They belong to the Father, and should he not have an absolute right to call souls home to him whenever he wishes?"

"Calling souls home?" echoed Corwin. "That's a rather kind way of saying *killing people.*"

"True death comes through sin alone," said Ransom. "You're still too caught up in the physical, still judging that which you know not. Can you see what mankind deserves? Can you see the fates of their souls? Can you look a million years into a billion different futures and chart the most humane course? Of the scope of God's mercy, those bound by time can only guess."

"One thing that I never would've guessed is that a god of perfect justice would be so hard to justify."

"Before accusing him of cruelty, perhaps you should consider the stubbornness of man. The Father is ever patient, always offering his rebellious children many chances to change, but time and time again, nothing less than bloodshed gets through to you."

The candelabras creaked, their flames wavering as a sudden gale whipped up a storm of loose parchment. Corwin and Ransom found themselves caught in the eye of a tornado, the library hidden behind whirling Bible pages. When the wind quieted and the papers fell away, they stood in a spacious stone hall.

A stately colonnade bordered the edge of the room, which overlooked a thriving desert oasis. Grand buildings and statues of half-human, half-animal gods shone under the sweltering sun. The broad, azure band of the Nile flowed out of the south, leaning palms and sandstone dwellings nestled along its banks.

To their right the hall rose in a dais, and there sat the Pharaoh, his expression unamused. Standing below him was a bearded man whose robe and walking staff left little doubt as to his identity.

"What is it this time?" moaned the Pharaoh.

"The Lord commands that you set his people free," declared Moses. "If you will not listen to reason, then he will convince you by the might of his hand."

"I should like to see that."

Time leapt forward and it seemed at first that nothing had changed, but then Corwin noticed the river. Its blue waters had turned a dark maroon and the stench of rotting fish was thick in the air.

"I don't know if you've bothered to look outside your palace, but there's a river of blood out there." Moses raised his staff towards the Nile. *"A river of blood."*

"More of your cheap sorcery," spat the Pharaoh. "I am the lord of this land, not your feeble god."

Weeks flew by and now frogs were everywhere, leaping from pillars and feasting on buzzing clouds of flies. The Pharaoh slouched to one side of his throne, his head propped against his knuckles. Swollen boils erupted from his skin and he looked even more irritated than usual.

"Are the pests and disease not enough?" asked Moses. "You can end this at any time."

"Very well." The Pharaoh waved him away. "Return to your people."

As Moses left the hall and the click of his staff against the floor dwindled, a pointy-bearded advisor skulked out of the shadows.

"Are you really going to release them, Sire?" his rasping voice whispered.

"Not a chance."

Time skipped ahead. Attendants were waving palm fronds in a vain attempt to keep the Pharaoh cool and unmolested by the hundreds of locusts that now made the palace their home. Batting away one of the palms, he seized a locust from his shoulder, crushing it in his fist as the heavens rumbled with a gathering storm.

If Moses was having a better time of things, his face didn't show it.

"How about now?" he asked in an exasperated tone. "Won't you reconsider?"

"I'll think about it."

"Will you truly?"

"There, I've thought about it," announced the Pharaoh. "I decided against it."

"Have you gone completely mad?" Moses stepped boldly atop the dais. "Hailstorms have beset your kingdom! Swarms of locusts devour your crops!"

"Then we shall dine on locusts!" The Pharaoh leaned forward in his throne, seething with barely contained rage. *I'm told they're very nutritious.*

The scene changed, and though Corwin sensed that it was day, an ominous darkness hung over all the land. There was no thunder, no pestilence; only a dreadful stillness.

"You're back," the Pharaoh said sourly.

"Think of your people, of your family!" pleaded Moses. "The plague that is coming is worse than all the rest."

But the Pharaoh only hardened his gaze. Rising, he retired from the throne room. He would hear no more.

The scattered pieces of parchment were once again swept up in a rustling, roaring tornado, returning Corwin and Ransom to the library.

"Humans are hardheaded, lazy and fearful of change," said Corwin when they were back amongst the books. "On that, you'll hear no argument from me. Heck, I'm probably a pretty good example, myself."

"You don't say?"

"However, I'd be a worse person if I lived by the morality of the Bible. The Old Testament justifies slavery, misogyny and brutal punishments for minor crimes. And don't tell me that Jesus changes all that, because he himself said that he came not to destroy the old law—"

"But to fulfill it," chimed Ransom. "You're looking at the threads, but missing the tapestry. Because of man's stubbornness, the Father took things one small step at a time. And so he began not by abolishing slavery, but by commanding that slaves be treated with greater kindness. He began not by forbidding tribal warfare, but by commanding that his people first offer peace. You think the old law barbaric because you consider not the true barbarism that prevailed before."

"If god is perfect and unchanging, how can his laws change at all?"

"It was not God who changed. It was man. After the Fall, man was like a limb cut off from the body, but when the body is made whole again, lifeblood can flow into that which was dying. That lifeblood is the saving grace of the Paraclete, the Holy Spirit who was sent down when the Redeemer's sacrifice made you whole.

"Thus the law was fulfilled, for the heights of virtue are possible only through grace, which you did not always have with you, and God never asks the impossible."

"But he does ask the impossible!" contended Corwin. "Consider the teaching of Jesus: 'Whosoever looks upon a woman lustfully hath already committed adultery with her in his heart.' If that's true, then every man alive is an adulterer!

"And not only is it impossible to follow, a rule like that isn't even good morality. Sexual attraction is written into our genes. Without it, the human race would cease to reproduce. Why demonize something so healthy and natural?"

"You speak of lust and physical attraction as though they are the same thing," said Ransom. "They are not. You can be physically attracted to someone and still respect that person's dignity. Sexual attraction is, as you say, healthy and natural. But that's not so for lust. To lust is to objectify. It means viewing a person as less than a person—as merely an object to be used for one's sexual gratification."

"Again with the semantics . . ."

"Your disregard for language is why you fail to see the difference between lust and physical attraction, tolerance and indifference, jealousy and envy, self-love and vanity. Need I go on?"

"Jealousy and envy," mused Corwin. "I don't think I've heard that one yet."

Ransom obliged, "A jealous man wants what his neighbor has. An envious man wishes that his neighbor didn't have it."

"Thanks." Corwin rolled his eyes. "But even if you explain away every issue of biblical morality, you're still left with the problems of the Bible itself, namely that it's unoriginal, contradictory and simply untrue."

A black cat leapt from one of the bookshelves. It bounded off a globe and landed lightly, the kingdoms and empires of 1,000 B.C. spinning on a squeaky axle as it crossed the aisle to slip behind another row of books.

"You said once before that people today view Christianity as *just another* religion, and you were right," said Corwin. "Anyone who studies pre-Christian faiths will find the same old stories recycled in the Bible. There are Hindu gods like Krishna who had virgin births, Roman gods like Hercules who were part man and part divine, and Egyptian gods like Osiris who died and rose again. Would you call it mere coincidence that Jesus shares so much in common with his pagan ancestors?"

"Certainly not," Ransom replied. "It's actually quite astonishing. Just think of it! Even without the Father's revelation, the mystics of the ancient world had some inkling of understanding, some foresight into how the Redeemer would come!"

Corwin slapped his forehead, his palm sliding down his face like a wet rag down a window.

"You *would* say that! It's just like you to twist honest criticism into some far-fetched point in your favor!"

"What can I say? I'm a relentless optimist."

"But I'm not! I'm a realist!"

"Oh, come off it!" huffed Ransom. "Were you to play angel's advocate, you could come up with plenty of arguments for the uniqueness of Christianity, not the least of which stems from common sense. If the Good News of the Redeemer were simply the Same Old News that everyone had heard before, Christianity would have registered as no more than a blip on history's radar."

"I never claimed that there was *nothing* unique about Christianity," Corwin clarified. "It's just that I don't see any vital difference so striking as to convince me that your scriptures are true while everyone else's are false."

"Then let me offer you one."

Grabbing a leather-bound Bible, Ransom cradled it in one hand. Like a wizard's spell book, it opened, the pages flipping in rapid succession.

"Forget what the Bible says about God and consider for a moment what it says about man. Almost every major philosophy or religion takes one of two stances: either man is noble and destined for greatness, or man is pitiable, an absurd dreamer whose only destiny is to return to the dust from whence he came.

"The first stance leads to pride, but also to depression when the life you've been told is so special doesn't work out quite the way that you'd hoped. The result of the second stance is despair."

He snapped shut the book and tossed it backwards, into the arms of Corwin, whose clumsy hands juggled it before finding a grip.

"Now, which of these two stances does Christianity take?"

Corwin pried open the Bible and again its pages began to turn, but not at random. As verses sprang from his memory, the pages flipped to the relevant chapters, their words illuminated in a golden glow. "Sinners" decried the Lord, but did he not also say that he came not for the just, but for sinners such as these? Did he not claim that these lowly sinners were to inherit his kingdom?

"I would have to say . . . both," concluded Corwin.

Ransom awarded him with a slow clap.

"You spoke much of paradoxes, but it seems that you forgot one. Let us call it the Paradox of Man. On the one hand, you are made in the Father's own image and likeness. But on the other hand, you are fallen. On the one hand, you are wretched sinners, undeserving of love. But on the other hand, you *are* loved—loved with a passionate, infinite love! In Christianity alone you find this wonderful paradox. And so you find both humility and hope; an answer that denies neither the hardships nor the aspirations of life."

Corwin was reminded of the old saying "It's so crazy, it must be true!" Christianity had an uncanny propensity for unbelievable claims that yet seemed to get so much right about human nature.

"You sometimes have a way of saying things that makes even me want to believe," he told the angel. "So why does the 'divinely inspired word of god' do such an inferior job? Your holy book has more contradictions than I can count! There are contradictory teachings, contradicting accounts of Jesus' birth, his death, his genealogy! The Bible is anything but consistent."

"A contradiction means more than just a difference in accounts," said Ransom. "To be contradictory, it must be impossible for both accounts to be true. You will find no meaningful points of difference in the Bible."

"I wouldn't be so sure about that. And if I'm mis-interpreting your scriptures, you have only the holy spirit to blame! Why inspire the biblical authors to write a text so absurdly cryptic?"

"You exaggerate, but yes, the Bible can be rather mystifying. Thankfully, the Redeemer didn't send forth a simple collection of writings. He sent forth the apostles. Christian thinkers throughout the centuries have left you plenty of insight into those cryptic passages. Why ignore them?"

"Maybe because they can't seem to agree."

Voices arose from a nearby nook of the library, and Corwin peered through the right-hand bookcase. The row of Bibles was haphazardly arranged on the shelf, some stacked and some leaning, loose pages sticking out at odd angles. On the other side, he spied a brightly lit table set against the wall. Wax dribbled from a dozen candles, spilling like milky icicles over the table's edge. Upon it rested various scriptures and documents, and seated across from each other were two men in priestly attire. One had sharp, hawkish eyes, his beard trimmed close. The other fellow was clean shaven with curls of gray hair shooting out from under his foppish black cap.

"The text is clear, Luther," declared the first man. "The Lord says: 'Thou art Peter, and upon this rock I shall build my church.'"

"What Christ meant, Ignatius, is 'thou art a pebble, but upon *this rock* I shall build my church.' The rock he was speaking of was himself, not Peter. In the Greek: *petra*, not *petros*."

"Consider the surrounding verses," insisted Ignatius. "You would have Jesus say: 'Blessed are you Simon bar-Jona . . . you are an insignificant pebble . . . here are the keys to the kingdom of Heaven!' Would the greatest of all teachers really have spoken in such a disjointed manner?"

The heated debate continued, but Corwin had already lost interest. He turned away, leaving Luther and Ignatius to the unenvious task of working out their differences.

"Do you see what I mean?"

Ransom was crouched in the aisle, petting the black cat that had crossed their path earlier. It meowed, swished its tail and slinked away into the shelves.

"For all their disagreements, you'll still find more wisdom in the words of men such as these than in the shallow interpretations of those with no faith at all."

"But which theologians are correct? Which translation of the Bible is the proper one? I wouldn't even know where to start."

"That never stopped you before. In the church of atheism, there are many denominations. The relativists disagree with the humanists, who disagree with the determinists, who disagree with the existentialists, who disagree with the nihilists, who—"

"Okay, okay!" interjected Corwin. "Atheists may not always agree, but at least they don't waste their time arguing over events that, in all likelihood, never even happened. Real historians will tell you that much of the Bible is pure fabrication. Passages were tweaked and verses added over time, not by some spark of divine insight, but because of the very human desire to make the stories more appealing."

"Interesting." Ransom knuckled his chin. "Tell me of these 'real' historians. Are they the sort of men who suppose that all records of supernatural events must have natural explanations?"

"That's called being objective," stated Corwin.

"It's called being an atheist."

"What then? Should historians blindly presume that all the old myths are true? Should they give serious consideration to whether we once lived on the back of a giant celestial tortoise, or to the possibility that our ancestors discovered fire thanks to Prometheus stealing away with some embers from Mount Olympus?"

"Historians ought to *presume* as little as possible. If supernatural events have in fact occurred, then a view of history which denies them, denies reality."

"But there's no firm evidence that they ever have!"

"Could there have been any account, any collection of relics from 2,000 years ago that would have convinced you that a man rose from the dead?"

"Probably not," conceded Corwin. "Unless perhaps there were prophesies in plain, precise language that foretold events unfolding in the modern age."

"No, even that wouldn't have swayed you," said Ransom. "You would simply have deemed such prophesies to be self-fulfilling."

"Couldn't god have seen fit to impart some actually useful information? Why not tell his followers about disease pathogens or electrical conduction?"

"Would that have saved their souls? If the Father had told Moses all about magnetic polarity, would skeptics in your age have renounced atheism, concluding that the origin of such knowledge could only be divine?"

"That's doubtful, but . . ." Corwin's voice trailed off. He had thought to say that supernatural events demanded supernatural evidence, but what kind of evidence would that be? Would God leave behind some speaking stone or ever-lasting rainbow? And if he were to go that far, why not just reveal himself openly? No, leaving a signpost like that would undermine the role of faith. It would reduce belief to a simple question of practicality.

"The truth of the Bible is hidden for the same reason that God is hidden," Ransom said, as if reading Corwin's mind. "The Father does not force himself on those who don't wish to see, nor does he force his Word on those who don't wish to hear. With faith and reason, the truth comes to light. Reason alone will only take you halfway."

24

THE RISK OF REDEMPTION

The lights had been turned off, the hallway deserted, but Corwin knew this place. He knew the white walls and yellow doors and checkered tiles, the picture frames in which newborn babies cuddled with teddy bears and doctors smiled respectably, the sterile scent and the dull gleam of the freshly mopped floor.

But something wasn't right. Hospitals never slept, yet this place did. It was as quiet as a crypt, and the only light was that which shone meekly through the wired glass windows of the double doors that stood at the far end of the hallway—the doors of the operating room.

"I liked the library better," mumbled Corwin.

He wondered vaguely whether his real-life body was right now in a hospital like this one, his life signs fading as surgeons frantically tried to patch him up. What kind of shape would he be in? A frightful thought occurred to Corwin, the thought that he might not want to go back. What if he was horribly crippled or had severe brain damage? Did he have the strength to endure life as a paraplegic? He wasn't so sure.

"An operation is underway, and the patient is in critical condition," said Ransom.

"Who's dying?"

"Mankind."

A hazy shadow stirred within the lighted room.

"You have a hole in your heart—a God-shaped hole—and you will never be happy so long as you try to fill it with anything less. Atheism's solution is to unmake man by reducing him to just another beast, to kill the disease by killing the patient."

"Then the patient is going to die either way," said Corwin. "Anyone who looks at the world today will see that it's religion that's liable to bring civilization to a bloody end. You even admitted as much!"

"I admitted that religion wasn't safe," replied Ransom. "Love always carries a risk."

"Let's say that you're right and that atheism is contrary to human nature. That doesn't make it untrue. And happiness has nothing to do with it! We've come all this way on a simple maxim: that the only good reason to believe something is if it's true. You can't have it both ways! You can't stand there and tell me that 'because it makes me happy' is a valid reason for belief! That's never a valid reason! Truth can be hard. Truth can hurt. But I'd rather believe in the truth than in a kind lie!"

Ransom spontaneously punched his client in the shoulder.

"Ouch!" yelped Corwin, rubbing the sore spot.

"That's what I like about you, Corwin! You're uncompromising about the right things! Yet I wonder . . . truth, love, beauty . . . have you never thought that these virtues belonged together?"

"So say the poets, but I've always preferred the prose of scientists."

"You're right that truth is the only valid reason for belief, but how do you know when you've found the truth?"

"Through observation and testing and–"

"Empirical knowledge isn't the only knowledge," interjected Ransom. "How do you know when you've found the other kind? How do you know whether to kill yourself or have a cup of coffee?"

Corwin's heart knew the answer, yet his mind drew a blank. He didn't doubt that truth was bigger than science, not anymore. Ransom had been right when he'd said that Corwin didn't have it in him to choose the razor blade apple. Some decisions *were* better than others. But what was the measure? Did goodness truly point to something real, to a meaning woven into the fabric of the universe?

"Happiness is no reason to believe a lie," said Ransom. "But when you find life's highest truths, you'll know it, because truth isn't just true. It's beautiful. To discover it is to know happiness, and I mean not some 'fuzzy feeling.' I mean a deep and abiding joy. Your chest will tighten, your heart will sing, and your soul will finally be at ease, for no longer will you be a man divided. Your mind will grasp what your heart knew all along: that you were made to be loved by your Father."

"And if your Christ doesn't bring me happiness?" Corwin asked fearfully. "What then, if all he brings is guilt and false

275

hopes? My heart has scars enough already, and it's too late for me to take that wager."

"You hedged your bets. That's why you're here. But you still don't understand the nature of the gamble."

Ransom pushed open the swinging doors at the hallway's end and stepped inside. A medical lamp cast a tent of white light over the operating table. Upon it, a patient lay sedated, bare feet sticking out from beneath the bottom of his gown. Bent over him was a bald doctor in a surgical mask and lab coat. His back blocked their view of the operation, but the bloody instruments on the tray beside him were already more than Corwin wanted to see.

"Christianity is like open heart surgery," spoke the angel over the steady *beep, beep, beep* of the heart rate monitor. "It's a risky undertaking, one that you might not survive. There's a chance that your doctor will make a mistake. Maybe he's a hypocrite who doesn't take his own advice. Maybe he failed to interpret his texts properly while in medical school. *But you need the surgery.* You're dying inside, and to live without taking that risk wouldn't really be living at all."

The patient shook with a violent convulsion and his heart rate spiked. Dropping a scalpel in the tray, the doctor clasped a pair of forceps, working feverishly at the unseen cavity in the man's chest. Another gyration rattled his body, and then his heart flatlined. A bleak, high-pitched tone blared through the monitor. The doctor rose to his full height and switched it off with a somber shake of his head.

"What a shame!" he declared, his voice dry and callous. "It seems that the operation was a failure!"

Turning, he pulled off his mask, the front of his lab coat spattered crimson.

Ransom thrust an arm out in front of Corwin.

"Get behind me!"

"You won't be slipping away this time," said Isley as all warmth and color drained from the world, enfolding the hospital in a field of closed space. "And I hope you don't mind, Ransom, but I've brought along a friend. Maybe you remember him? I'm told the two of you are old acquaintances."

A hulking figure darkened the side doorway. He wore a black suit and tie, his broad chest threatening to burst his shirt at the seams, but while the cut of his clothes was modern, the thick braids that fell from his beard hadn't changed.

"Strega," Ransom hissed. "I see you've moved down in the world."

The arch demon flexed his hands eagerly at his sides. Seeing the angel, a tingling burn awoke in his old wound— the scar where Ransom's soulrender had blinded him eight hundred years ago.

"Centuries have I waited, longing for this day!"

As he took a stride towards them, Ransom moved instantly, kicking a rolling tray table into the demon's knees.

"Corwin, run!"

It took a moment for the words to register in Corwin's head. Strega buckled forward and snarled, smashing the tray table to pieces with a swipe of his hand.

"I said *run!*"

Ransom's shove nearly knocked Corwin off his feet. He caught himself and crashed through the swinging doors, and his legs didn't stop. The portraits in the shady hallway flew by. No time to look back. No time to worry. His boots pounded the checkered tiles and Isley's bitter laughter rang in his ears.

"Too easy," gloated Strega. His fingers stroked the groove of his scar. "I could end you here and now, stop this wound from burning."

On his hands and knees, Ransom coughed fiery blood, yet he gazed back at Strega with the same invincible grin.

"I really think two glass eyes is a good look for you. You're like the poster child for grizzled warriors . . . or for running with scissors. I haven't decided which."

His ribs cracked and the halogen lights shattered as Strega's kick launched him into the ceiling. He landed with a thud, flakes of plaster raining from the crater overhead.

"Patience, Strega," urged Isley. "His client will be joining us soon."

Surely, Ransom would be alright. Any moment now, he would reappear by his side and whisk them off to some safe, secluded corner of an alternate universe, far from the clutches of any demonic legal teams. Or so Corwin told himself, but the hallway was only growing darker, the shadows shifting with a will of their own.

"Corwin," they whispered, first from one side, then the other. "Corwin . . . Corwin . . . Corwin . . ."

Silhouettes barred the passage ahead and he didn't have to check his back to know that the view would be equally grim. But Corwin wasn't defenseless.

I still have that.

Summoning his courage, he stopped and spun.

"Come on, you bastards!" he hollered into the gloom. "No more games!"

A blaze lit the hallway as his hand closed around the golden cross, and in that brief flash, he saw them—dozens of hollow-eyed demons surrounding him on every side. Again the shadows fell, but the sword knew. He sprang and slashed. The direction didn't matter. Any would do. The blade just wanted to cut. He felt the sweet pressure of it cleaving flesh, heard their cries as he swung and swung again. Then he felt something hard strike the back of his head.

25

THE CISTERN AND THE SEAL

A searing pain in his side brought consciousness rushing back. Corwin snapped awake, craning his neck and howling into the lightless shaft above. Stripped to the waist, he hung from a pair of long, clinking chains, their manacles cutting into his wrists. He wasn't sure how long he'd been out, but as lucidity slowly returned, each moment revealed a new source of agony. The back of his skull ached, his sore shoulders felt halfway torn from their sockets, and raw skin throbbed where the burn had jolted him out of his slumber.

"Rise and shine," croaked Isley. "We wouldn't want to start the night's festivities without our guest of honor."

Corwin leveled his gaze and stared into glassy white eyes. Though he was suspended off the ground, Strega's height was still a match for his own. The demon leered and raised an iron poker, its tip glowing red-hot.

With a twist of his head, Corwin recoiled the little distance that he could. From what he gathered, this place was a cistern, perhaps part of some medieval sewer system. A pool of water darkly shimmered beneath the grated floor. The chamber was circular and he noted archways belonging to several adjoining passages, along with a hollow where a fire had been lit. Dampness glistened on the grimy brick walls. They sloped to form a dome, but not a complete one. An oculus gave way to a tall shaft through which rainwater dripped and his chains dangled. And his weren't the only chains.

"Not you too . . ."

Covered in fresh bruises, Ransom's scarred body hung across from him. He had evidently been enjoying the demons' hospitality for some time. Three-foot-long needles of iron pierced his arms, legs and torso, skewering him with surgical precision so as to cause intense pain without rupturing any vital organs.

"Listen, Corwin," he strained to whisper. "There's a seed of hope sewn deep within you. Whatever happens, don't let go of–"

A brutal backfist from Strega cut short his words, a spray of blood and sweat sparkling in the air.

"He's telling you to lie to yourself," said Isley. "That's what his kind always preaches. But you were never one for delusions."

Ransom's head was tossed to one side and then the other as Strega relentlessly rained blows. For every twitch, the needles punished him, sending pangs of torment pulsing all the way to his fingertips. But Ransom refused to cry out. Grabbing him by the hair, Strega lifted his face.

"I want his eyes," he growled.

"Not yet, you fool!" snapped Isley. "He'll need them to watch."

Strega rounded on the Prosecutor with a snarl, but Isley's imperious stare didn't waver. The standoff lasted only an instant. Huffing angrily, Strega backed down and consoled himself by laying another punch into the angel.

Isley calmly returned his gaze to Corwin.

"Humans have toyed with torture, and while we occasionally inspire them, they've mostly proven themselves to be bumbling amateurs. You'll find that my methods are more excruciating by far. That is, if that's what you desire."

"Let me guess," said Corwin. "You'll set me free if only I renounce god, as if I haven't already been doing that this whole time?"

"Do you think I care what you believe?" Isley's tone was colder than ice. "I see you for what you truly are: a fruit rotted from the core. Your skin you've painstakingly polished, waxed to a ripe sheen, but peel away the rind . . ." he dragged a clawed finger down Corwin's chest, "and a feast for maggots festers."

All of Corwin's arguments, all his clever words, they meant nothing, he realized. This creature that wore a man's face, it despised him with a hatred that surpassed logic or reason. Corwin thought he knew what it was to be hated. His antireligious tirades had earned him the vitriol of many a staunch believer. Insults, cold shoulders, even violent threats were nothing new. But never in his mortal life had he felt hatred like this. The humans that lashed out against him had done so because of their own insecurities. They feared what he had to say. Isley didn't. His malice was pure, his black gaze more terrifying than any firing squad.

"However, I am not without mercy," resumed the Prosecutor. "You have a choice, unlike your attorney. That one has been the cause of much misfortune for my associates, and for you as well. Were it not for him, you wouldn't have to endure this unpleasantness."

He raised a hand, indicating a weapons rack on the chamber wall. Serrated blades, spiked flails, hammers, pliers and other more eccentric tools of torture decorated its rusty hooks, bloodstains crusting their metallic edges.

"Take these instruments, carve your vengeance into him, and I will ease your suffering."

Corwin looked at the cruel collection of weapons, then at Ransom. The angel's face was downcast, disheveled hair concealing his eyes. He said nothing.

"I think," whispered Corwin, his voice barely audible.

"Yes?"

Isley tilted his head. He leaned closer, and as he did so Corwin brazenly spat in the demon's face.

"That's what I think of your offer!"

Hissing to a boil, the saliva steamed off Isley's wrinkled skin.

"Unwise."

He reached out and a hot poker flew from the flames into his grasp. Corwin gritted his teeth as Isley pressed the iron to his side, a few inches above the first burn. Molten fire lanced through his veins. Arching his spine, he hollered, his chains rattling against the brick shaft.

"I had thought you to be more pragmatic than this," remarked Isley as he withdrew the scalding rod. "Don't you want to see your beloved Mary again?"

"What?" asked Corwin between heaving breaths.

While the poker's touch had ceased, pain still radiated from the spot. Cool drops of rainwater tapped his sweat-slicked shoulders, each one a tiny blessing, but it wasn't enough to dowse the blaze that ignited in his chest upon hearing Mary's name on the demon's lips.

"Perhaps the angel hasn't told you?" Isley intoned. "She's one of us now."

"You're lying!"

"Don't listen to him!" shouted Ransom, who promptly received another pummeling in response.

Isley sighed and hung his head remorsefully.

"After your death, the poor girl was very depressed. She took her own life, Corwin."

"Mary wouldn't do that!"

"Is it so hard to accept? You nearly did the same once, and the two of you are more alike than you think; soul mates, one might say, if you believe in that sort of thing."

"No!" Corwin insisted. "That time—it was because of my weakness, but Mary is stronger than me. She was always stronger than me!"

"Such faith!" exclaimed Isley. "But as you say, you *are* prone to weakness. Your flesh is weak. Your will is weak. Do you really think that you're a hero, or even a good person?"

Corwin tried to speak, but the words wouldn't come. Isley's stare penetrated his soul, laid bare every dark secret, every sin he'd buried beneath life's numbing distractions. He didn't need a demon to tell him that he was no saint. A hero? Would he have valiantly jumped onto those tracks if he had known the true cost? Not likely.

"Oh, but you've been hurt! You're a victim, aren't you? Your father was taken away at such a tender age. And your mother! Where was she when you needed her? Drowning her sorrows at the bottom of a bottle, no doubt. Yes, you always cursed her for that. Why should little Corwin have to grow up, act like a man and comfort his mother? Didn't she know that she was supposed to be the one comforting you? You vowed to shut her out of your life, and you kept that vow.

"So what if she felt like she had no one? So what if your father loved her? Why should that matter to you? Even years later when she finally got her life together, did you make even the slightest effort to mend what was broken? All those times when she called, did you ever once call back? All she wanted was to hear your voice, to see you, to tell you that she was sorry."

Isley's voice sharpened to a scathing whisper.

"You wouldn't even give her that. You died without ever saying *I forgive you,* without ever telling her *I love you.*"

There was a knot in Corwin's throat that he couldn't swallow. It was all horribly true. His perfect memory recounted every harsh word; all the times when he could have softened his heart, but didn't. And now it was too late.

"And you think that you deserve paradise?" mocked Isley. "You're no tragic hero, just another selfish, sniveling coward who thinks himself entitled to the mercy that he never gave."

Corwin's mutinous mind echoed the demon's words, the memories tearing at him, dragging him down to the blackest depths of the sea of oblivion. Wasn't that where he belonged?

I just want to forget.

He glanced at the iron poker.

I don't want to think about anything anymore.

Soon its scorching gift would save him, wash over him like an acid tide. Then he wouldn't have to remember. He wouldn't be able to. A thousand suns would explode beneath his skin, drowning out every other thought in a vague, white roar of pain.

And when finally you beg for the torture, then your soul will be theirs.

Hadn't Ransom said that once? The words anchored him—a luminous beacon slicing through the fog—and in that moment he saw himself clearly. Isley had spoken true. He didn't deserve Heaven. But there was something else Ransom had told him. That's right, *no one* deserves Heaven. It was a prize too great to be earned, one that was bestowed mercifully upon weak, unworthy sinners.

Sinners like me.

"Maybe you're right," said Corwin. "Maybe I am just another asshole who ought to be cast into Hell, but you're not the one I have to answer to!"

A sneer disturbed Isley's calm mask of hatred.

"Strega," he called. "Teach this human his place."

Grabbing a bullwhip off the rack, the brutish demon smiled with a mouth full of misshapen teeth. He stepped behind Corwin and the whip's braided leather tail uncoiled.

"Leave him be!" Ransom yelled. "Or I swear that scar will look like a beauty mark compared to the one I'll give you when I get out of here!"

But this time the angel's shout went unheeded. Strega swung back his arm. The whip cracked and Corwin felt the livid sting of his skin bursting. He locked his jaw, holding back the screams as the lashes fell.

Ransom's chains snapped taut. Furiously, he struggled against them. An ethereal shadow darkened his figure, but again the brand blazed. Caging his power, the divine seal burned bright on the back of his hand.

With a shudder, he fell limp, and Isley cackled.

"It's useless to struggle. The chains that bind you were forged in the First Age. Wrought of smoke and shadow, even I would have a difficult time breaking them."

Not for the first time, Ransom's gaze fastened on a spot beside the fire, where an unsheathed katana leaned against the wall.

"You desire this?" asked Isley.

Approaching the soulrender, he casually lifted it, unconcerned by the flames that immediately enveloped his hand.

"Your sword doesn't seem to like me very much."

"It's a smart sword," replied Ransom.

"I can feel its thirst for blood." Isley rested the blade near Ransom's throat. "Perhaps I should let it drink?"

"Go ahead."

"No," the demon decided, "for that would be to release you, and your punishment has only just begun."

Corwin reeled as another stripe was added to his blood-streaked back. Noise filled his mind, but from Isley and Ransom's short exchange, one word stood out.

"Hey, you good-for-nothing angel!" he shouted. "Speaking of punishments, there's something I've been thinking about for a while. The penalty that god slapped you with, it doesn't make any sense!"

"This really isn't the time," groaned Ransom.

Isley erupted into laughter.

"Even now he persists in your insipid debate!"

"So you killed a band of murderous thugs," continued Corwin. "So what? I'm sorry, but the punishment doesn't fit the crime."

"To take human lives is forbidden. I broke a sacred trust!"

Breathing through clenched teeth, Corwin endured a lash low across his legs. He molded the pain into fury and the fury into speech.

"I thought Christians were supposed to love their enemies!"

"Have you gone delirious? What are you talking about now?"

"I'm talking about what was in your heart! You think that your crime was spilling blood? That what you really did wrong was break a rule? That's bullshit! The truth is that you didn't want those men to repent!"

Ransom's eyes widened with understanding.

"No, I didn't . . ."

"You wanted them to burn!"

"I, you're right!" The angel's voice quavered. "All this time, have I been atoning for the wrong sin? Have I truly been so blind?"

He raised his head and the centuries-old weight that he'd carried with him began to crumble. Hands of mercy held him, taking him and the burden of his sin—taking it all and lifting it as though it were nothing. The darkness that had felt so heavy . . . Why had he worried? There was no sin too heavy for those hands to lift. He had only to ask.

"Father, forgive me!"

A stillness descended, a silence so complete that Corwin couldn't even hear himself breathe, and then, howling forth from nowhere, a mighty wind swept through the chamber. The fire flailed and the demons fought to stay on their feet. Ransom's seal seared, ringed in white flames, but the flames weren't long for his hand. Peeling free like flakes of ash, the seal's markings drifted, spiraling into the cistern shaft. As the last blot left him, the raging wind calmed.

"Thank you, Corwin." Ransom smiled with eyes ablaze, glowing tears running down his face. *"Now let's shine a light in this unholy abyss."*

A tremor ran through the needles piercing him, and all at once they were cast from his body, fired across the room with lethal force. Missing Corwin, a pair of darts buried themselves in the burly demon behind him. Isley batted one away, but lost his grip on the soulrender. It spun through the air and into Ransom's hand, severing one of the chains as it flew. A wave of the sword burst the cuffs from his other wrist and ankles.

"Restrain him!" Isley bellowed.

Scores of black-suited fiends poured into the cistern as Ransom freed Corwin from his fetters.

"Just wait here," he said.

Corwin scarcely had the strength to stand, not that he was planning to. *Now would be a good time to stay low.* If his instincts were correct, this place was about to turn into a battleground straight out of the Book of Revelation.

"Ransom!" roared Strega.

Ignoring the needles in his chest and thigh, the arch demon grabbed a battleaxe and charged. The grating rattled beneath his pounding boots. He raised the axe high with speed that defied his massive size—speed that meant nothing to Ransom. Like a razor wind, the soulrender sliced invisibly. Strega never got the chance to bring down his axe. His two halves slid gruesomely apart, his soul banished before he hit the ground.

The lesser demons hesitated, paralyzed by fear, and Ransom took a determined step towards Isley.

"The human!" Isley cried. "Slay the human!"

Hell was no escape from their master's wrath, and so his underlings abandoned all thought of self-preservation and hurled themselves at Corwin. Dozens of ebony swords darted towards him, but first they had to get past Ransom. The angel was death incarnate, a flickering shadow and a flashing blade. Corwin knelt in the eye of the storm as his attorney painted the walls black with demon blood.

There seemed no end to them. Torn limbs and corpses littered the cistern, and still another wave rushed on. But the Prosecutor made no move to join the fight. Amidst the commotion, he backed slowly away until only the pale disks of his inverted eyes were visible beneath the rear archway.

"Wherever you go, I'll find you," spoke Isley as the world dimmed, his eyes the lone source of luster. "You can't exist without me. I'll always be with you." To Corwin's horror, the voice twisted and blurred, and then it wasn't Isley's voice at all, but Mary's. *"I'll always be with you, Corwin."*

The demon's gaze vanished and so did the cistern. Corwin was alone, adrift in endless darkness. He couldn't see his body, wasn't sure that he even had one anymore. A crack of light split the gloom. He opened his eyes.

Corwin was lying on his back, the stiff cot of a hospital bed beneath him. A nurse was checking his IV fluids and Mary was clasping his hand.

"Call a doctor!" she shouted. "Corwin's awake!"

26

RECOVERING FROM REALITY

This was his world—the real world—and yet it seemed more surreal than the one he'd left behind. *Of course,* he reasoned with himself, *that probably has something to do with the fact that I'm pumped full of enough morphine to tranquilize a horse.* Corwin's left arm was encased in a big white sausage of a cast and Mary clutched his right. His body felt cumbersome and wrong, like an old suit that didn't fit quite so well as it used to. And he couldn't feel his right leg at all.

Teary-eyed, Mary buried her face in his chest.

"Oh my God!" she sobbed. "I thought I'd lost you!"

"If you think I look bad, you should see the train."

Behind Mary, a woman sat quietly against the wall, her folded hands trembling.

"Mom?"

Her almond hair had grayed and crow's feet creased the corners of her eyes, but as she rose and walked timidly towards him, all Corwin could think about was how much she looked like home.

Mary straightened up and he took his mother's outstretched hand.

"Corwin, I know that I don't have any right to see you," she said, "but I was so afraid."

"I'm sorry for making you worry, Mom." He squeezed her hand in his. "I missed you."

"You've got a handful of hairline fractures in your skull," reported Doctor Renner in his customary, no-nonsense tone. "We were able to reattach your left arm, but it will be a while before you can put any pressure on it. The good news is that in time, you should regain close to full motion. As for the bad news . . ."

"Is this the part where you show me the bill?" inquired Corwin.

The doctor chuckled. "You're going to have some loss of feeling. And then there's your right leg. I'm afraid that the damage was too severe. Frankly, it's a damn miracle you're alive at all."

"A damn miracle? Is that your professional opinion?"

"Not many people take a head-on collision from a train and live to crack jokes about it. If the clearance had been any lower, they'd be spraying you off of those tracks with a fire hose."

"Yet here I am," said Corwin. "Thanks for saving my life, Doc."

"You're welcome, but it wasn't just me."

"I guess I've got a whole lot of thanking to do."

"If you're planning to bake cookies, my wife likes double-chocolate chunk," Renner slyly informed him as he strolled out the door.

I feel like a wreck, thought Corwin. *So why can't I stop smiling?*

The gratitude that welled up inside was too big to contain. He had been dead, and now he was alive! All the things he wished he'd done and the people he wished he'd spent more time with—now he had a second chance, and there was no way a little thing like the loss of a leg was going to stop him.

He was thankful for the doctors and nurses whose talents had saved him, for the paramedics that had gotten him to the hospital in time, for Mary who never left his side. He was thankful for all of them, but his gratitude didn't end there. It overflowed! As absurd as it seemed, he had an undeniable urge to bow his head and whisper a heartfelt "thank you!"

To whom? Corwin wondered. *To the universe? To God?*

Ransom had once mentioned just this sort of sensation, as Corwin clearly recalled. In fact, there wasn't a single word or moment of their adventure that he didn't recall. The entire experience was etched into his mind. And that wasn't all. Somehow, the crystalline memory he'd gained while in that elaborate dream world had stuck with him.

I'd make a fine research project for an enterprising neurologist.

He would have to tell Mary all about it, but that could wait. For now, Corwin just wanted to lie back and watch the clouds drift by outside his window. He wasn't sure what he would do tomorrow, or what he would be, but today, just being alive was enough.

"How does it feel?" asked Maya as she finished adjusting Corwin's prosthetic leg. His first day of physical therapy had arrived ahead of schedule.

"Like I should have a parrot on my shoulder."

He gripped the safety rail and stood, testing his balance.

"You'll have to take it slow at first," said the therapist, "but you'll get used to it."

The length of steel and carbon-fiber that extended below Corwin's right knee was a firm fit, sturdy yet awkward. *It's all mental,* he told himself. The trick wasn't relearning to walk, but learning to trust that the foot he couldn't feel would nonetheless support him.

"I heard you were a frequent jogger," mentioned Maya.

"Every morning," Corwin said. "No more of that, huh?"

"Actually, we have prosthetics that are specifically designed for runners. You can even play sports, though I wouldn't recommend soccer."

Letting go of the railing, Corwin ventured a few steps on his new leg. *This isn't so hard.* Walking in a straight line almost came naturally. However, as he turned, he pivoted just a tad too fast.

"Careful!" cautioned Maya.

His top half teetered, but he managed to hold his feet steady.

"I got it," he said, raising one hand in assurance.

"You can't afford to take any spills with that left arm of yours, so don't push yourself, Mr. Invincible. This is going to take some time."

Corwin's former cast had been swapped for a smaller one with a neon-green sling supporting his arm. He could wiggle his fingers, which, all things considered, everyone agreed was a happy fact, but for the time being his left arm wouldn't be good for much more. The thought of falling on it certainly wasn't appealing, and so he graciously accepted Maya's assistance in making his way to the treadmill.

She instructed him to climb on.

"Now let's start with the basics."

With Corwin's right hand securely grasping the handle, Maya dialed the treadmill to its lowest setting. The black track slid towards him and Corwin kept pace, shambling with all the swiftness and grace of a peg-legged zombie. After only fifteen minutes his first session was over, but he returned to the fitness center the next day, and the day after that. The prosthetic became a part of him. Soon he was marching up inclines and down stairs. The sling went away, his cast shrank, and one morning in March it finally came time to hit the pavement.

The last gasps of winter were in the air, filling his lungs with frosty electricity. Corwin felt as though he could run forever.

He had jogged these streets hundreds of times, never really seeing them. The city wasn't, by ordinary standards, a beautiful place. Drab bricks and scarred concrete covered one block after the next. But to Corwin's reborn eyes, each one of those scars told a story. Dreams were born and crushed here, feeding the fires of this vampiric machine, but the machine remembered. Every life it devoured was enshrined in some little way. A stain on a windowsill, a skid mark on the road; if he could see things as Ransom did, would he be able to glimpse the stories behind the scars?

His prosthetic leg flexed, its carbon-fiber curving to absorb his weight as he leapt over a line of ants that processed in single file between a garbage can and a crack in the adjacent building's foundation. He imagined shrinking down and exploring the world beyond that fissure, uncovering a whole other city, a subterranean land uncharted by man. And perhaps the towers of that land would have cracks in their foundations as well.

Lights enlivened store windows as he passed between the park and the market. Half of the shops were already open, though it would be another hour before the crowds arrived. One shopkeeper recognized Corwin and waved. Like a lover, the city showed an intimate side of itself to those who woke with it, and every early riser shared a bond. They were all unofficial members of the same sleepless club.

The scent of coffee, bold and earthy, wafted through the doors of a corner café. Corwin could almost taste it, the beans mingling with the aroma of doughy, steaming bagels as the baker next door pulled hot racks from his oven. Young leaves garnished the oaks and sycamores in the park. The trees were coming back to life, just as Corwin had. Dewy branches sprouted new shoots on the dogwoods, their flower buds anxious for spring.

Each bend in the road arrested him with another view, hues vibrant and subtle, all blending and brimming with effusive detail beyond the skill of any painter's brush to capture. Corwin found himself pausing, not from exhaustion, but simply to take it all in. How many times in his life had he stopped, turned off the music and actually appreciated a sunrise? The eastern sky was a gold flood spilling between the high-rises. He propped his hands on his knees and stared.

Sliding glass doors parted for a woman and her daughter as they emerged from the grocer's.

"Mommy, that man's leg is *weird!*" declared the girl.

"Honey, that's not polite," said her mother, embarrassment flushing her cheeks.

The child's blunt assessment gave Corwin a laugh.

Reaching into one of the shopping bags, she withdrew a cherry-red apple and innocently approached him.

"Here, Mister," she said, holding it forth.

Corwin accepted the gift with a smile.

"Thanks."

As his gaze met hers, the gears in his head ground to a halt. Her eyes were arctic sapphires, coldly burning with the wonder of undiscovered stars. They were eyes that he had seen before. Corwin took a stunned step back. She looked younger, but those eyes, that mousy brown hair, that voice like a bell . . .

She's not Blue, his inner self said. *There is no Blue. She doesn't really exist.*

His phone rang, breaking the trance.

"Good morning, Sunshine."

"I knew you'd be awake," said Mary.

"Life is too short for sleep."

Corwin waved gratefully to the girl and her mother as the sidewalk's invisible current pulled them away.

"It feels nice to tackle the great outdoors again, but I just had the strangest sensation."

"Are you okay?" Mary's voice was concerned.

"Yeah, it's probably nothing, just a spell of déjà vu. Either that, or a rogue memory from one of my past lives."

"Maybe your karma is catching up to you."

"I hope not! Somebody once told me that karma is a dangerous thing."

"Since you're done doing time at the hospital, I was thinking that we should go out somewhere to celebrate," suggested Mary.

"You read my mind," said Corwin. "And there's this place that I've been dying to try. When you get home from work, why don't you slip into that green dress? I'll make reservations and pick you up at a quarter to seven."

27

The Last Great Adventure

Miles of spruce and fir trees rolled by. Sweeping down from the Appalachians, the forest spread its needles over rocky hills and valleys, treetops poking at the burnt orange sky. Mary sat absorbing the view while Corwin looked over the wine list. They shared the old-timey dining car with only a few fellow patrons. Another couple and a pair of business-men spoke in reserved tones over the thrumming of steel wheels against the tracks.

"Well this is romantic," remarked Mary, ". . . *and* un-expected. I didn't think I'd see you near a train any time soon."

"Near-death experiences aren't so bad once you get used to them," said Corwin. "I may even take up sky diving!"

"That sounds thrilling, but I'd prefer it if you didn't lose any more appendages."

"Must you always be so superficial?"

Mary giggled and Corwin found his eyes straying to the plunging neckline of her dress. She looked as lovely as ever, yet something was missing. The silver cross that she had worn almost every day since they first met no longer hung from her neck. Mary wasn't devoutly religious, not like her mother, but whether for the sake of tradition or fashion, she was seldom without the necklace. Searching his memory, it struck Corwin that not once had he seen her wearing it after his accident.

"You really *have* changed," Mary said. "And so have I." She reached across the white table cloth to hold his hand. "I've been thinking a lot these past few weeks. Remember how you used to tease me about not being an atheist? You were always polite and playful about it, never pressuring me too hard. I'd laugh it off and push your arguments out of my mind. Without faith, I didn't think there would be any meaning in my life. Maybe I was just afraid."

Corwin gulped, his conscience laden with an unexpected sense of guilt.

"But not anymore?"

"It took you getting hit by that train for me to see it. There was no meaning in that accident, just senseless, random violence. Why would God allow such a thing to happen to someone who was only trying to do a good deed?"

"At least I lived through it," offered Corwin.

"Just barely, and no thanks to God."

Breathing unsteadily, Corwin struggled to put his thoughts in order. He wasn't sure what was stranger, the change in Mary's convictions or his own conflicted feelings about it.

"I noticed that you're not wearing your cross."

"I'll never wear it again, Corwin."

"You're serious about this? You're honestly becoming an atheist?"

"Aren't you happy? I thought that this was what you always wanted."

"I, uh . . . It's just that this is a big decision. You've been a Christian all your life."

"I'm ready to start a new life. All I need is you."

As she stared passionately into his eyes, Corwin's heart melted. The person that he loved more than anyone else in the world was saying goodbye to God. Would she be happier? More cynical? She would definitely be changed. Mary was saying goodbye to a part of herself, and Corwin feared that it was a part he would miss.

Two sizzling slabs of beef, delicately seasoned, journeyed from the kitchen to where the other couple sat at a nearby booth. Once their sharply-dressed waiter had finished attending to them, he moved on to Corwin and Mary's table.

"Good evening," he said. "My name's James and I'll be serving you tonight. Would you care for some drinks to start off?"

"I'd say tonight calls for champagne," purred Mary.

Corwin gave the wine list one more look.

"We'll take a bottle of the Charles Heidsieck."

"An excellent choice," said James. "If I could just see your IDs, please?"

It had been a while since Corwin was last carded. *One year, eight months,* his memory told him. As he fumbled with his wallet, a small, laminated card slipped out and fell to the floor. He bent to retrieve it and felt a sudden chill. On the card was the artful scene of a dove in descent. It was the same holy card that the taxi driver had given him in his dream.

But that's impossible!

He tried to rationalize. Someone must have slipped him the card at some point in the past. He had glimpsed it and forgotten about it, only to have his unconscious mind dredge the memory back up while he was knocked out and medicated into the Twilight Zone.

That has to be it.

The only problem was that he had no recollection of ever receiving any holy cards, and Corwin's brain was even better at remembering than it was at rationalizing.

He snatched it up and handed his driver's license to the waiter. After taking a brief scan, James returned it.

"I'll be right back with that bubbly."

Corwin flipped over the curious card in his lap, finding "A Prayer to the Holy Spirit for Discernment" printed in gothic type.

"I'm surprised that you're not more excited," said Mary, studying his face.

"You do know that your mother is going to kill me?"

"The choice is mine, not hers."

"But have you thought it through? I mean, a decision like this . . ." Corwin chewed his lower lip. *Am I really about to say what I think I'm about to say?* "Maybe you should pray about it."

"What?" Mary's expression couldn't have been any more dumbfounded if Corwin had pulled off his skin to reveal that he was an alien impostor.

"There's no harm, right? If the Big Man doesn't exist, then you've wasted a minute or two, but if he does, maybe he'll send you a sign."

"Are you feeling alright?"

"You know what? I'll even say a prayer with you!"

"Corwin, I'd rather not."

He revealed the card, extending it towards her.

"I know this sounds weird coming from me, but somebody gave me this holy card, and—"

Her arm lashed out like a rattlesnake, striking the card from his grasp. It pinwheeled across the aisle, and just then the windows fell dark, the air humming as the speeding train plunged into a tunnel.

"I don't pray."

The voice that issued from Mary's lips belonged to nothing human.

Corwin sprang out of his seat.

"You're not Mary!" He yanked up his right pant leg, revealing not steel and carbon-fiber, but flesh and bone. "I never really woke up!"

"Imbecile!" The demon's features warped as she stood erect. "Did you think you'd get a second chance?"

Gone were the dining car's other patrons. They hadn't fled, but simply vanished, as if they'd never existed at all.

"Ransom!" Corwin called.

No one answered.

"The angel cannot help you here," spoke his date, her hands transforming into claws.

Corwin would have given anything for a soulrender. That this accursed monster had dared use Mary's face set his anger aflame, but armed only with his fists, he knew that he was sorely outmatched. And the demon knew it as well.

Vicious claws raked towards him. Corwin grabbed the nearest thing at hand—a table cloth—and swept it between them. Tableware flew and the fabric tore, but it also billowed, concealing him for a split-second. He sidestepped and kicked. The blinded demon crashed into a booth, more annoyed than harmed.

"The more you resist, the sweeter your pain will be."

She lunged again, faster than before.

So this is it.

The door to the kitchen swung open and a chef in white hurled a meat cleaver. Corwin leaned to the side as the shrieking demon toppled forward, the cleaver embedded in her back.

"My compliments to the chef!"

Glad for a weapon, he pulled the chef's blade free, and while doing so noticed two black-suited men hurriedly making their way through the rear car—more agents of the Collection Branch. His first instinct was to run, and already his feet were backpedaling.

As they breached the rear door, Corwin half-turned and the chef brushed past him, sprinting to meet the demons with another cleaver held high. Shots were fired and just as fast deflected, a window shattering in their path. Torn between fleeing and joining the fight, Corwin's choice was made for him when a third agent burst from the kitchen door. Obsidian steel rang against his cleaver.

The weapon might have lacked the elegance of Ransom's katana, but it was a soulrender nonetheless. Corwin could feel it guiding his motions, hungry for a chance to draw blood.

The demon bore down with a heavy slash and he leapt out of range. Landing, his shoulders bumped the man behind him. He and the chef stood back-to-back. They exchanged a quick glance. The chef was a robust man with a bushy black beard. And there was something else about him . . .

Haven't I seen that face before?

A sword thrust grazed Corwin's neck. He swatted the blade aside and slapped the demon with the blunt rear edge of his cleaver. At his back, the chef ducked. He sensed it and did the same, just as a dark katana skimmed both of their heads. An unspoken understanding passed between them and simultaneously they traded opponents. Corwin dealt a crippling blow to one of the agents while the chef parried the other and rammed a fist into his jaw.

"Thanks for the hand," said Corwin. He glanced at his ally again and his memory finally placed him. "Wait a second! Aren't you that bum? What the heck happened to you?"

"I sobered up," the chef gruffly replied.

He moved like a black-haired whirlwind with a cleaver, spinning and hacking the life from his foes.

"Must have been one hell of a twelve-step program," mumbled Corwin.

"When I finally got things straightened out, I figured I owed you one," said his ally as the last demon crumpled in the aisle. "The name's Rodney."

Several more agents were already charging their way from the adjacent train cars, and even with help, Corwin knew that he couldn't fight them off forever.

"Don't suppose you've got a plan?"

"Through the window!" Rodney shouted. "Head for the engine car! I'll hold them off."

Corwin kicked out the glass shards that clung along the rim of the window broken earlier by gunfire. With one foot on the frame, he angled his head through.

"What about you?" he yelled back to Rodney.

"My time here is limited. Hurry!"

A wall of hot, ash-flecked wind assailed him and Corwin hugged the side of the train as he climbed. Pistols blared and blades clashed in the dining car. Hooking one hand over the roof's edge, he began to climb, and was almost to safety when his left foot slipped. His other hand shot to the rooftop, saving him from a fall, but at the cost of his only weapon. The shining cleaver tumbled out of sight.

Cursing his luck, Corwin swung a leg onto the roof and rolled atop it. Though the wind blew fierce, he found that he could stand without crouching. The mountain passage was more spacious than any ordinary railroad tunnel. Sulfur tinged the air, and what he had taken for electric lamps set in the walls revealed themselves to be torches. Up ahead, their twin trails diverged with the broadening cavern. The floor fell away and a column of stone arches suspended the rails like a Roman aqueduct. A reddish glow crept up from the chasm. The heat was growing stronger.

Loud, metallic raps sounded at his feet as bullets pierced the roof. Corwin hastily scrambled forward, stopping short of jumping to the next car.

They always make this look so easy in the movies . . .

He made the mistake of looking down. Far, far below burned a magma river, its bubbles belching flames as they burst.

Why was I ever afraid of heights? Now lava, that's scary!

Corwin stepped back from the edge to give himself a short runway. Any trepidation was promptly erased when an onyx blade speared upwards between his legs. He bolted and leapt, flying clear over the gap, but was nearly tossed from the next car by a torrid blast of air and the sloping roof. Hands appeared along its edges.

The first demon to lift his head got a taste of Corwin's boot. So intense was the heat that his body ignited a dozen yards above the molten flow.

Corwin vaulted onto the car ahead, finding a dagger-wielding agent already on his feet. He couldn't afford to slow down. The knife tore a hole in his coat, but he twisted, throwing his shoulder into the man and sending him to join his comrade. The engine car was in sight.

In his haste, Corwin didn't even notice the air vent. He tripped in full stride and his skull bounced off the unforgiving floor. The world swam as he looked up, dim shapes resolving into a pair of polished leather shoes. Wasting no words, the demon savagely raised his blade.

He jolted, a sword's tip blossoming from his chest.

The sword turned and the demon with it. Corwin's savior kicked the lifeless fiend loose and then reached down to lend him a hand. It was a woman's hand, small but strong.

"Mary!" With a rush of joy, he opened his arms. "It's really you!"

Her slap stuck his cheek so hard that Corwin went horizontal.

"That's for mistaking a demon for me!"

"Sorry," he squeaked. "But she was one good-looking demon!"

Mary pulled him to her and they locked in an embrace.

"But why are you here?" questioned Corwin. "I thought I'd be waiting decades to see you."

"Where I am, there is no waiting."

So much had happened so quickly, leaving Corwin with more questions than he knew how to ask, but one thing that he didn't have was doubt. Death wasn't the end, and he sure as hell wasn't going to spend his afterlife begrudging God his victory.

"The way I died . . . I don't regret it, but I regret not being there for you."

"There's nothing to regret," said Mary. "Because you jumped onto those tracks, I didn't. Because you died that day, I didn't. If I had been hit by that train, your soul would have darkened. You would never had made it this far. But you did! Do you understand, Corwin? He brings goodness even out of evil! When you saved that man—when you saved me—you also saved yourself!"

Atop the rear cars, a mob of agents was fast approaching. Mary laid a hand on his shoulder.

"Now you had better get going."

"As if I would leave you!" protested Corwin.

"You need to keep . . ." her hand closed, firmly gripping his coat, "moving forward!"

Swept off his feet, Corwin sailed almost an entire car-length before hitting the roof. He might have rolled right off it if his fingers hadn't found another air vent.

"Mary!" he shouted as his gaze darted back.

She dropped, disappearing between the cars, and Corwin heard the sharp *swish-clang* of her katana rending steel. Losing speed, the train's severed tail began drifting away. Mary hung in the retreating doorway.

"This isn't goodbye!" she called. "Forever is just beginning!"

Corwin stared wistfully. He knew what he had to do. He knew also that there was no need to fear. The demons couldn't hurt Mary. No one could. It was time that he put his own soul in order. He turned and faced into the wind.

One of the bridge's supports broke away as he hopped onto the engine car. Like a huge cedar felled by a lumberjack, it collapsed into the seething lava. The bridge held, but the splash that erupted illuminated the entire cavern in fiery hues of red and gold. And Corwin saw him. At the head of the car he waited, a silhouette untouched by the light.

"You disappoint me," said Isley. "With your tenacity, you could have gone far at the firm. Those beneath you would have cowered at the sound of your name, but in the Father's Kingdom you will have no glory. You will be the very least of his groveling servants. Is that really what you want? In your earthly life, you boldly questioned that which lesser men took for granted. Godless and unafraid, you bent the knee to no one. Why betray all that you are?"

"Because I'm not godless!" declared Corwin. "What I really am is a prodigal son, and I'm going home! I may not know much about His ways, I may not know much about anything, but now I know that I don't know anything! I believe in truth and love and goodness and something higher than all the physical matter in all the universe! And that goes for any other universes out there as well! I will never be like you!"

"No, you won't," agreed the Prosecutor.

Behind him, a glow pricked the distant shadows.

"I am Isley Drakensun, Archlord of the Eighth Circle. You are no one. Your name won't even be remembered."

The train was racing closer, the light swelling in size and radiance.

"I am Corwin Holiday, least of the Father's children, and all your power will not gain you my soul!"

"You have no holy blade, no angel to protect you." Isley spread his arms and wings of darkness unfurled. "How can you hope to defeat me?"

"I don't have to," said Corwin. "He already has."

The glow's reflection flashed in his eyes.

"What?" Isley spun. "No!"

Pure white light rushed over them as the train rocketed out of the cavern.

"No!"

He guarded himself beneath folded wings, but to no avail. The light incinerated all that rejected it. Wreathed in silvery flames, Isley's charred skin cracked and burst. A terrible scream pealed, as if his very spirit were crying out, the sound lingering in the wake of his windswept ashes. And then Isley was no more.

Corwin released a shuddering breath.

It's done.

Glancing down, he saw with a start that he, too, was on fire. Strips of blackened crust marred his body, each one ablaze, but though the flames stung, Corwin felt no despair. The light wasn't destroying him. It was purifying him, burning away the sin that clung to his soul.

Despite the pain, his spirit soared. Corwin hoped bigger than he had ever dared to hope in his mortal life. With a penitent heart, he lifted his gaze. At first there was only the light. Sheer and infinite, it birthed a parade of soft silver shadows. Slowly his vision sharpened.

"The ride was a little bumpy, but you can't beat the view."

A landscape that transcended the senses unfolded, plunging in long, magnificent valleys and soaring in impossibly steep, cloud-ringed peaks. A crystal city reared from the center of a lake and a daylight aurora gilded the sky. And the colors! He had no words for them. Shades beyond the spectrum of the human eye painted the world in a dazzling array. Every tree and every flower and every blade of grass shone with a crisp glow, more vivid than even the fields of Eden, as if all things in this place were living light sources, prisms that magnified each other's splendor. If he stared at any one spot for long, the colors changed, and sometimes the land itself became something new. Overwhelming his mind, the kaleidoscopic sight blurred again into a silver-white haze, slashes of the rainbow vista flitting past, slipping from sight when he tried to look upon them directly.

It was clear that the train was still speeding onward, yet the belligerent headwind had relented. A breezy tailwind whistled, warm against his back.

"Stare too hard and you'll hurt yourself," spoke a voice from above.

Corwin turned to see his angelic attorney descending on wings of light.

"I didn't think you had wings."

Alighting on the roof, Ransom cracked his roguish grin.

"Wings like razors."

"You missed all the excitement," said Corwin.

"Sorry about that. The prosecution is allowed one test in which I can't interfere. I'll admit that I had my doubts, but apparently it was nothing you couldn't handle."

"Yeah, well, I had some help."

Ransom's hand vanished into his coat, reappearing with a familiar flask.

"Care for a drink?"

"I'll pass."

"Suit yourself."

As Ransom staved off the perils of dehydration, Corwin blithely shook his head.

"So about how many years of Purgatory am I looking at?"

"Can't say, but I wouldn't let it get you down. A sentence to Purgatory means that you're going to Heaven." Ransom poked at a blotch of burning crust on Corwin's arm. "You just need a bath first."

"And what's next for the illustrious Ransom J. Garrett?" inquired Corwin. "Does this mean that you'll be getting your old job back?"

"After I've tied up a few loose ends. This profession isn't the sort of thing that one just walks away from, at least not without training a replacement. It would have to be someone extremely stubborn, preferably with a debt to pay." The angel cocked an eyebrow. "Come to think of it, you haven't seen my legal fees yet . . ."

Corwin fixed his attorney with a humorless stare.

"I think I'll take that drink now."

ACKNOWLEDGMENTS

In so far as the arguments presented in Dead & Godless are sound and insightful, it's thanks to them being thought up by wiser men than myself. C.S. Lewis and Blaise Pascal laid the foundation, and Peter Kreeft and Scott Hahn reinforced the walls.

A steady diet of fantasy and science fiction novels (along with plenty of comics, manga and 80's cartoons) fed the fires of my imagination, with J.R.R. Tolkien, George Lucas, Gene Wolfe and many others playing prominent roles.

For their encouragement, inspiration and constructive criticism, I owe a debt of gratitude to my parents, my sister Christine and my friends and fellow Write Night compatriots, including Joshua Searles, Jen Klassen and The Three Steves: Steve Jiencke, Steve Skojec and Steve Kospender.

Penny Fletcher's editing services were invaluable in toning down my literary offenses (though she will no doubt bemoan my stubborn reluctance to follow every rule!), and Renu Sharma's artistic talents are to thank for bringing my vision for the cover wonderfully to life.

If you enjoyed this book, please recommend it to others. A great many young adults leave the Church when they leave home, and while fine books of Christian theology and apologetics are not in short supply, they are often either too dry (straight theological works) to hold the attention of those who aren't frequent readers, or too full of vague platitudes (many religious novels) to offer concrete answers to the challenges of atheism. It is my hope that Dead & Godless can help bridge that gap. Something needs to.

To learn more about this novel or to reach me, visit: DeadAndGodless.com

Made in the USA
Charleston, SC
17 February 2014